Submarines a Deep Dive into Self Discovery

By: Mustafa Nejem

CONTENTS

Chapter 1

Design Philosophy

Much like the streamlined and robust design of a submarine needed to withstand oceanic pressures, an individual must build mental resilience and adaptability to navigate life's challenges.

Within the complicated voyage of life, regularly compared to the endless and erratic profundities of the sea, people experience a heap of challenges that require a significant level of mental strength and flexibility. Comparable to the streamlined and strong plan of a submarine, which empowers it to resist the gigantic weights of the sea, people must develop a mental grit that engages them to explore the riotous waters of life. This prepare of building versatility and flexibility gets to be a significant angle of individual advancement, preparing people with the apparatuses required to not as it were persevere difficulty but too to flourish in the midst of the ever-changing landscapes of their presence

- **Understanding Resilience and Adaptability:**

Versatility, at its center, is the faithful capacity to bounce back from misfortunes, mishaps, or challenges. It typifies the mental and enthusiastic quality that permits an person to resist and recoup from life's unavoidable blows.

In substance, strong people have a tirelessness that propels them forward, indeed within the confront of seemingly insurmountable obstacles. On the other hand, versatility could be a energetic quality that includes not fair persevering alter but flourishing within the middle of it. It is the capacity to alter, advance, and reorient oneself when stood up to with modern circumstances, situations, or unforeseen shifts. Versatility is the aptitude that engages people to explore the perplexing labyrinth of life's instabilities, illustrating a adaptability of intellect and approach. The relationship between flexibility and versatility is advantageous. Strength shapes the bedrock upon which adaptability prospers. When misfortunes happen, flexible people draw upon their internal quality to assimilate the stun and start the method of recuperation. This prepare, in turn, cultivates versatility, as the person learns to not as it were recover but to recalibrate techniques, points of view, and behaviors to superior confront the another challenge. The interlaced nature of these qualities gets to be especially essential within the complicated embroidered artwork of life. Life is intrinsically unusual, displaying a mosaic of encounters that can extend from triumphs to tribulations.

Strength and flexibility act as directing lights, empowering people to explore this complexity with a sense of purpose and an capacity to successfully react to the recede and stream of circumstances. Together, strength and versatility serve as the building squares of individual development and improvement.

Versatility gives the stability needed to climate storms, and versatility guarantees that development isn't hindered but or maybe moved by the winds of alter. As people endeavor to get it and saddle these qualities, they set out on a transformative travel, developing a mentality that not as it were survives challenges but changes them into openings for learning and progression. Within the fast-paced and energetic scene of the modern world, where alter is consistent and challenges are assorted, the capacity to get it and exemplify flexibility and flexibility gets to be a principal survival skill. Professionals exploring unstable career ways, understudies confronting scholastic obstacles, and people standing up to personal upheavals all discover comfort and quality within the couple of strength and versatility. It is in these real-world scenarios that the genuine significance of these qualities shows, directing individuals through the complexities of life with a sense of strength within the confront of misfortunes and flexibility within the grasp of alter .

- **The Importance of Mental Resilience:**

Versatility, at its center, is the faithful capacity to bounce back from misfortunes, mishaps, or challenges.

It typifies the mental and enthusiastic quality that permits an person to resist and recoup from life's unavoidable blows. In substance, strong people have a tirelessness that propels them forward, indeed within the confront of seemingly insurmountable obstacles.

On the other hand, versatility could be a energetic quality that includes not fair persevering alter but flourishing within the middle of it. It is the capacity to alter, advance, and reorient oneself when stood up to with modern circumstances, situations, or unforeseen shifts. Versatility is the aptitude that engages people to explore the perplexing labyrinth of life's instabilities, illustrating a adaptability of intellect and approach. The relationship between flexibility and versatility is advantageous. Strength shapes the bedrock upon which adaptability prospers. When misfortunes happen, flexible people draw upon their internal quality to assimilate the stun and start the method of recuperation. This prepare, in turn, cultivates versatility, as the person learns to not as it were recover but to recalibrate techniques, points of view, and behaviors to superior confront the another challenge. The interlaced nature of these qualities gets to be especially essential within the complicated embroidered artwork of life. Life is intrinsically unusual, displaying a mosaic of encounters that can extend from triumphs to tribulations. Strength and flexibility act as directing lights, empowering people to explore this complexity with a sense of purpose and an capacity to successfully react to the recede and stream of circumstances. Together, strength and versatility serve as the building squares of individual development and improvement.

Versatility gives the stability needed to climate storms, and versatility guarantees that development isn't hindered but or maybe moved by the winds of alter.

As people endeavor to get it and saddle these qualities, they set out on a transformative travel, developing a mentality that not as it were survives challenges but changes them into openings for learning and progression. Within the fast-paced and energetic scene of the modern world, where alter is consistent and challenges are assorted, the capacity to get it and exemplify flexibility and flexibility gets to be a principal survival skill. Professionals exploring unstable career ways, understudies confronting scholastic obstacles, and people standing up to personal upheavals all discover comfort and quality within the couple of strength and versatility. It is in these real-world scenarios that the genuine significance of these qualities shows, directing individuals through the complexities of life with a sense of strength within the confront of misfortunes and flexibility within the grasp of alter.

- **Adaptability as a Key Life Skill:**

Within the perplexing move of life, where alter is the as it were consistent, versatility rises as a key life aptitude, directing people through the unusual turns and turns of their travel. At its center, flexibility engages people not fair to weather unexpected changes but to reply to them with flexibility, cleverness, and a capacity to thrive in the midst of instability.

Versatility, as a aptitude, is the energetic reaction instrument that permits individuals to alter their mentality, methodologies, and behaviors within the confront of unexpected circumstances.

It is the ability to rotate nimbly when gone up against with startling changes, empowering people to preserve a sense of control and composure indeed when the ground beneath them shows up to move. Rather than being paralyzed by the unanticipated, versatile people thrive within the middle of equivocalness, seeing alter as an characteristic viewpoint of life instead of an obstruction to advance. Within the modern scene, stamped by fast mechanical headways, worldwide interconnecting, and societal shifts, flexibility takes on increased importance. The world could be a energetic embroidered artwork where the as it were steady is alter, and versatility gets to be the linchpin for victory and well-being. Whether in proficient interests or individual connections, the capacity to adjust to advancing circumstances isn't fair beneficial; it is basic for remaining pertinent, versatile, and satisfied in an ever-shifting world. Flexibility ingrains a mentality that sees vulnerability not as a danger but as an opportunity for development. Rather than standing up to alter, versatile people welcome it as a catalyst for development, learning, and self-discovery. They recognize that within the ease of alter lies the potential for unused encounters, novel viewpoints, and strange accomplishments. This point of view changes the fear of the obscure into a canvas holding up to be painted with the dynamic colors of plausibility. A key facet of flexibility is its part in upgrading problem-solving capabilities.

Versatile people approach challenges with a flexible toolbox of methodologies, drawing from a supply of encounters and insights.

This flexibility permits them to explore complex issues with dexterity, imagination, and a willingness to explore unconventional arrangements. In essence, flexibility is not almost about responding to alter; it is around proactively locks in with challenges, transforming them from impediments into venturing stones for individual and proficient headway. Versatility is naturally connected to a development mindset—a conviction that insights, capacities, and abilities can be created through devotion and difficult work. Adaptable people see challenges as openings to grow their abilities and information, cultivating a persistent journey of self-improvement. This mentality not as it were improves flexibility but moreover powers a sense of reason and strength, contributing to an individual's capacity to flourish in different and ever-evolving situations. In the terrific embroidered artwork of human advance, flexibility acts as a catalyst for innovation and headway. Societal and mechanical evolution are impelled forward by people and communities competent of adjusting to rising patterns and challenges.

- **Facing Adversity with Resilience:**

Within the complex embroidered artwork of human encounter, flexibility stands as a impressive drive, giving people with the strengthening required to go up against and overcome difficulty.

It is the faithful inward quality that develops when confronted with challenges, impelling people to explore the storms of life with a immovable soul.

Flexibility goes past unimportant continuance; it is the catalyst that changes misfortune from a weakening drive into a cauldron for individual development and change. Misfortune, in its different shapes, regularly acts as a cauldron that tests the determination of people. Strength gets to be the inward grit that empowers people to persevere and overcome these deterrents. It is the capacity to bounce back from difficulties, difficulties that might something else disintegrate one's certainty, positive thinking, and sense of reason. In confronting misfortune head-on, strong people tap into a wellspring of internal quality, rising from challenges not lessened but braced by the involvement. Strength isn't only responsive; it effectively contributes to the improvement of a growth-oriented attitude. Rather than seeing challenges as inconceivably barricades, strong people develop a perspective that sees misfortune as an indispensably portion of the journey—one that provides openings for self-discovery and individual advancement. Challenges gotten to be not hindrances to advance, but or maybe venturing stones on the way to versatility, shrewdness, and a increased sense of self. A crucial viewpoint of flexibility is its transformative nature within the face of difficulty. Instead of surrendering to lose hope or getting to be paralyzed by misfortunes, versatile people tackle the vitality created by challenges to fuel their individual development.

It is within the cauldron of difficulty that modern abilities are sharpened, points of view are broadened, and the forms of one's character are refined.

Strength moves people to rise over their circumstances, turning challenges into openings for learning, adjustment, and ultimately, triumph. Versatility contributes to the creation of a positive account within the confront of difficulty. It shapes the story people tell themselves around their encounters. Versatile people recognize the troubles they experience but deny to be characterized by them. Instep, they cast their story in terms of overcoming, learning, and advancing. This positive surrounding not only influences their display but moreover becomes a source of motivation for others, outlining the transformative control inherent in a flexible attitude. Within the confront of misfortune, flexible people receive a solution-oriented approach. Instead of staying on the tremendousness of the challenges, they center on distinguishing significant steps and reasonable arrangements. Flexibility cultivates a attitude that seeks not as it were to persevere hardships but to effectively lock in with them, extricating important lessons and clearing the way for a more resilient and competent self. Resilience significantly contributes to enthusiastic well-being. It acts as a buffer against the negative enthusiastic toll of misfortune, making a difference people oversee stretch, uneasiness, and discouragement more effectively. By cultivating passionate insights, versatile people explore the turbulent enthusiastic waters of misfortune with more prominent ease, rising with a sense of passionate harmony and a more profound understanding of their claim enthusiastic scene.

Past overcoming quick challenges, strength energizes proactive adjustment.

Flexible people are not as it were capable at bouncing back from misfortunes but moreover at expecting and planning for future challenges. This forward-thinking approach upgrades an individual's capacity to explore the complexities of life with a sense of readiness and key prescience. Strong people regularly ended up guides of motivation for those around them.

Chapter 2

Exploration and Discovery

Submarines are used to explore unknown depths, much like introspection enables us to delve into the unexplored realms of our psyche. Both require courage and curiosity.
Within the baffling profundities of the sea, where light battles to enter and puzzles flourish, submarines explore the obscure, revealing insider facts covered up beneath the surface. Essentially, within the perplexing breaks of the human intellect, contemplation serves as a mental submarine, jumping into the unexplored domains of our mind. Fair as submarines require progressed innovation, boldness, and a thirst for revelation to explore the deep sea, contemplation requests a comparative mix of mental grit and interest to dig into the regularly unfamiliar domains of our inward selves. This relationship between submarines and contemplation divulges a significant parallelism, emphasizing the gallant travel into the depths—whether of the sea or the psyche— holds the potential for significant disclosure, understanding, and development.

- **The Depths of Exploration:**

In the silent embrace of the deep ocean, submarines descend into realms that remain unseen and untouched by the naked eye.

These vessels, marvels of engineering and technological prowess, carry with them the capacity to navigate the immense pressure and darkness of the abyss. Submarines plunge into the heart of the ocean, exploring landscapes that, until their arrival, existed in a state of perpetual mystery. The ocean's depths, with their unseen topographies, ancient secrets, and undiscovered life forms, become a canvas for exploration, pushing the boundaries of human knowledge and curiosity.

In a parallel narrative, introspection acts as the intrepid explorer of the inner world, venturing into the uncharted territories of human consciousness. Much like submarines unveil the mysteries concealed beneath the ocean's surface, introspection delves into the concealed corners of our thoughts, emotions, and memories. It is a psychological submarine equipped not with physical instruments but with the tools of mindfulness, self-awareness, and reflective inquiry. Through introspection, we navigate the intricate landscapes of our minds, peeling back the layers of our psyche to reveal hidden depths that may have eluded conscious awareness.

Submarines use advanced lighting systems to dispel the darkness of the ocean's depths, revealing the intricacies of the underwater landscapes. Similarly, introspection sheds light on the dark corners of our thoughts and emotions. It illuminates aspects of our inner selves that may be obscured by the shadows of daily life or buried beneath the weight of past experiences. In this mental exploration, the light of self-awareness becomes a beacon, uncovering the contours of our motivations, fears, and aspirations.

As submarines journey through the abyss, they encounter unexpected terrains, geological formations, and life forms. Introspection, too, leads to revelations in the psychological abyss. By plumbing the depths of our emotions and memories, we may stumble upon long-forgotten experiences, unresolved emotions, or aspects of our identity that have yet to surface. These revelations, like the discoveries made in the ocean's depths, contribute to a richer understanding of ourselves and the intricacies of the human mind.

They move through the ocean depths in near silence, isolated from the sounds of the surface world. Introspection, too, often unfolds in a quiet and contemplative space. It necessitates moments of solitude, allowing individuals to detach from external influences and immerse themselves in the quiet recesses of their own thoughts. This silent introspection becomes a medium for deep self-discovery, fostering a profound connection with one's innermost self.

Also contribute to mapping the unseen territories of the ocean floor, charting courses through landscapes previously unknown. Similarly, introspection involves mapping the unseen territories of our minds. It is a process of creating a mental map that outlines the terrain of our beliefs, values, and emotional landscapes. Through introspection, we become cartographers of our own consciousness, navigating and understanding the contours of our inner world.

Subs contend with immense pressure in the deep ocean, requiring robust structures to withstand the force. Introspection, too, encounters its own pressures—those of self-reflection, facing uncomfortable truths, and addressing unresolved emotions. The psychological pressure of introspection necessitates resilience, as individuals navigate through the sometimes challenging and confronting aspects of their inner selves.

Submarines unveil hidden wonders in the ocean depths—unique ecosystems, underwater formations, and creatures adapted to a life in darkness. Introspection similarly reveals the wonders hidden within our minds—

the complexities of our emotions, the resilience of our spirit, and the adaptive strategies we employ in the face of life's challenges. Each introspective journey unveils the richness and diversity of the human psyche.

- **Technology and Tools in Exploration:**

At the forefront of underwater exploration, submarines stand as marvels of engineering, equipped with state-of-the-art technology designed for the intricate dance of underwater navigation. Submerged in the depths where traditional tools fail, submarines rely on a sophisticated array of sonar systems, navigation equipment, and propulsion mechanisms. These technological marvels not only enable precise maneuvering through the ocean's expanse but also contribute to the meticulous mapping of submerged landscapes, unlocking the secrets hidden beneath the surface.

In the realm of inner exploration, introspection serves as the navigator of the human psyche, armed not with physical instruments but with mental tools honed through self-awareness and mindfulness. Much like subs rely on technology, introspection utilizes the power of conscious thought and mental acuity to navigate the complexities of the mind. Mindfulness, a key mental tool, acts as a compass, directing attention to the present moment and fostering an awareness of thoughts and emotions. Self-reflection, another crucial tool, becomes a guiding light, allowing individuals to delve into the recesses of their thoughts and feelings, unraveling the intricacies of the inner landscape.

Submarines embody precision in their technological prowess. Advanced sonar systems detect the subtlest underwater nuances, allowing submarines to navigate with accuracy even in the absence of natural light. Similarly, introspection demands a high level of precision in mental tools. Mindfulness, with its focus on the present, brings a heightened sensitivity to the fluctuations of emotions and thoughts. This precision allows individuals to navigate the inner currents with a level of awareness that goes beyond the surface, uncovering subtleties that might escape casual observation.

The complexities of the human mind rival the intricate ecosystems of the ocean floor. In this mental labyrinth, introspection becomes the compass, steering individuals through the convoluted terrains of thoughts, memories, and emotions.

Unlike submarines, which use sonar to detect physical structures, introspection employs mental tools to discern the underlying patterns and motivations that shape human behavior. The ability to navigate this complexity is reliant on the refined tools of self-awareness and reflective insight.

In they, various systems work in harmony to ensure seamless navigation. From navigation computers to propulsion systems, each component contributes to the overall functionality. Similarly, introspection involves a symbiosis of mental tools working in concert. Mindfulness, self-reflection, and emotional intelligence synergize to create a comprehensive approach to self-understanding. The integration of these mental tools allows for a holistic exploration of the mind's vast territories.

Just as submarines use sonar to enhance their perception in the dark depths, introspection enhances cognitive sonar within the mind. Mindfulness acts as a mental sonar, allowing individuals to scan their internal landscape, detect emotional undercurrents, and navigate through the murkier waters of subconscious thoughts. The clarity achieved through introspective mental tools illuminates the shadows within, providing insight and understanding.

Subs are designed to adapt to the unique challenges of underwater navigation, from pressure changes to the absence of natural light. Introspection, too, requires adaptability.

The mental tools of mindfulness and self-reflection become adaptive strategies, helping individuals navigate the challenges presented by their thoughts and emotions. This adaptability is key in maintaining mental equilibrium in the face of internal fluctuations.

The precise calibration of submarine technology is an ongoing process to ensure accuracy and efficiency. Similarly, introspection demands continuous calibration of mental tools. Regular self-reflection, mindfulness practices, and an openness to learning about oneself contribute to the ongoing refinement of these tools. This continual calibration ensures that introspection remains a dynamic and effective means of inner exploration.

Submarines navigate through varying oceanic conditions with precision, adapting to changes in temperature, pressure, and currents. Introspection, in navigating the sea of emotions, demands a similar precision. Emotional intelligence, a mental tool within the introspective toolkit, allows individuals to navigate the often turbulent waters of feelings, fostering an understanding of emotional cues and responses.

Just as submarines detect subtle echoes in the depths through sonar, introspection discerns the subtle echoes of thoughts within the mind. Mindfulness, as a mental sonar, picks up on the reverberations of thoughts and emotions, bringing attention to the nuanced aspects of one's inner experience. This heightened awareness allows for a more profound exploration of the subtle nuances that shape the contours of the mind.

- **Courage to Face the Unknown:**

Embarking on a submarine journey into the unknown depths of the ocean is an endeavor that demands unparalleled courage and resilience. Submariners plunge into an environment where darkness reigns, pressure mounts, and the uncharted territories stretch into an abyss. The prospect of the unknown is daunting, as submariners navigate through the silent expanse, guided by instruments and sheer determination. The courage required to face the mysteries concealed beneath the ocean's surface is a testament to the indomitable human spirit's quest for exploration and discovery.

In a parallel realm, introspection beckons individuals to summon a similar kind of courage—an internal fortitude required to confront the intricacies of the human psyche. This mental journey is not dissimilar to the submariners' odyssey into the depths. Introspection compels individuals to turn inward, navigating through the complexities of thoughts, emotions, and memories that may have long remained obscured. Much like submariners facing the unknown expanses of the ocean, introspection demands a courageous confrontation with buried emotions, fears, and uncertainties that linger within the recesses of our minds.

Just as submariners navigate through the physical depths, introspection delves into the emotional depths of the self. It requires the courage to confront suppressed emotions, unearth past traumas, and grapple with the complexities of one's own emotional landscape.

This emotional journey can be tumultuous, demanding resilience in the face of the unexpected currents of the human psyche.

The ocean's depths are veiled in darkness, challenging submariners to navigate without the aid of natural light. Similarly, the inner abyss of the mind, shrouded in the darkness of unexplored emotions and buried memories, necessitates courage during introspection. Facing the shadows within, individuals may encounter aspects of themselves that have long been ignored or obscured. It is a courageous confrontation with the unknown, seeking clarity and understanding in the midst of the mental darkness.

Subs endure intense pressure as they descend into the ocean's depths, adapting to the physiological challenges that come with the territory. Introspection, too, involves navigating psychological pressure. The process of confronting buried emotions and uncertainties may evoke internal pressures—cognitive dissonance, discomfort, or a sense of vulnerability. The courage to withstand this psychological pressure and continue the introspective journey showcases a remarkable resilience of the human mind.

The unknown depths harbor unseen creatures and mysteries that evoke primal fears. Submariners confront these fears head-on. Similarly, introspection brings individuals face-to-face with their own unseen fears—be they rooted in past experiences, anxieties about the future, or uncertainties about the self. The courage required to confront these fears within the internal landscape is a bold step towards self-discovery and personal growth. Submariners exhibit adaptability as they navigate through varying underwater terrains. In introspection, courage is intertwined with adaptability to navigate the mental terrain. It involves adjusting one's mental course as new revelations surface, acknowledging and adapting to the ever-changing landscape of thoughts and emotions. The courage to be flexible and open-minded in the face of internal discoveries is an essential aspect of the introspective journey.

Subs, isolated in the silent depths, confront the unknown in solitude. Introspection, too, demands a silent confrontation in the solitude of self-reflection. The courage to delve into the inner realms often involves a solitary journey, where individuals confront their innermost fears and uncertainties with only their thoughts as companions. It is a silent dialogue with the self, requiring a unique kind of internal bravery.

Just as submariners view the unknown ocean depths as a realm for potential discoveries, introspection regards the unknown aspects of the psyche as opportunities for growth. The courage to face the unknown within ourselves is not merely an act of confrontation; it is an acknowledgment that within the unexplored territories lie the seeds of personal development, resilience, and self-awareness.

They navigate through shadows beneath the ocean's surface, and in a metaphorical sense, introspection invites individuals to confront their personal shadows. These shadows may be composed of repressed memories, unacknowledged emotions, or aspects of the self that linger in the periphery.

Chapter **3**

Isolation

Submarine crews operate in seclusion, drawing parallels to the solitude often needed for deep personal reflection and growth.

Within the noiseless profundities of the sea, where daylight battles to enter and the endless region remains untouched by the exterior world, submarine groups explore through the strange chasm. Working in disconnection, these teams set out on a travel that mirrors the reflective visits of the human mind. The segregation inside the submerged vessel draws striking parallels to the isolation regularly required for significant individual reflection and development. Submarines, with their closed limits and self-sufficiency, ended up allegories for the mental vessels in which people set out on inside investigations. This similarity welcomes us to dig into the complex associations between the confined domain of submarine teams and the isolation that catalyzes profound individual introspection—both encapsulating a interesting pot for self-discovery, versatility, and transformative development.

- **The Profound Silence of the Abyss:**

In the deep recesses of the ocean, where sunlight fades into obscurity and the expanse plunges into profound darkness, submarine crews navigate in a world where sound takes on a unique quality.

Subs operate beneath the ocean's surface in an environment characterized by an almost eerie stillness. The external sounds that permeate the world above are muted, creating a profound silence that envelops the vessel in a sonic tapestry of tranquility. This silence is not merely an absence of noise but a distinctive atmosphere that holds a profound resonance—a backdrop against which the intricate dance of submarine operations unfolds.

As submarines delve into the abyss, they leave behind the cacophony of the surface world. The symphony of crashing waves, the calls of seabirds, and the hum of human activity are gradually replaced by an orchestration of muffled sounds—subdued echoes of the ocean's depths. The profound silence within the submarine is punctuated by the subtle mechanical hums of the vessel, creating a unique auditory ambiance. This orchestrated hush serves as a metaphorical curtain, separating the submarine crew from the external world and immersing them in an environment that amplifies the significance of internal contemplation.

In this underwater realm of silence, a canvas is unfurled—an expansive space where external distractions are hushed, allowing for an intimate connection with one's thoughts and emotions. The silence becomes a canvas on which the crew can paint their reflections, musings, and inner dialogues. It is within this unique auditory cocoon that the crew finds themselves immersed, not only in the ocean's depths but also in the depths of their own consciousness.

The canvas of silence becomes a catalyst for a contemplative journey—one that mirrors the introspective sojourns sought by individuals for deep personal reflection and growth.

The silence within the submarine finds a profound resonance with the quietude necessary for deep personal reflection. Just as the external sounds of the ocean are muted, the external noise of the world is intentionally dimmed during moments of introspection. In both instances, the quietude is not an absence but a deliberate choice—a conscious withdrawal from the external stimuli that often drown the subtler nuances of one's inner world. The stillness, whether in the submarine or in moments of personal reflection, creates a space for contemplation, allowing thoughts to echo with clarity and emotions to surface in the absence of external interference.

As submarines navigate through the silent oceanic expanse, the crew, in parallel, finds themselves submerged in an internal dialogue. The absence of external sounds amplifies the echoes of their own thoughts, creating an intimate environment for introspection. It's a space where the crew can engage in a dialogue with themselves, exploring the recesses of their minds without the external noise of the world diluting the clarity of their contemplations.

Within the submarine, the echoes of internal contemplation reverberate against the steel walls, creating a symbiotic relationship between the physical environment and the crew's mental state.

Similarly, the quietude sought for personal reflection allows the echoes of contemplation to reverberate within the mind, bouncing off the walls of consciousness and creating a resonance that fosters a deeper connection with one's inner self.

In the profound silence of the abyss, submarine crews find a serene sanctuary amidst the operational complexities of their mission. This tranquility is not a void but a calm center within the whirlwind of tasks and responsibilities. Similarly, in moments of personal reflection, the intentional embrace of silence offers a tranquil respite—a mental oasis where individuals can find solace and clarity amidst the complexities of daily life.

The silence within the submarine extends beyond the physical absence of external sounds. It permeates the mental and emotional landscape of the crew, creating an atmosphere conducive to introspection. Similarly, the quietude sought for personal reflection transcends the external environment, seeping into the depths of one's consciousness, fostering an internal silence that allows for a more profound connection with one's thoughts and feelings.

In the silence of the submarine, the crew consciously unplugs from the external world, immersing themselves in the self-contained environment of the vessel. This intentional withdrawal echoes the deliberate choice individuals make when seeking moments of personal reflection—a conscious unplugging from the external noise, creating a space for internal exploration.

The silence of the abyss serves as a sanctuary of solitude for submarine crews, offering a retreat from the bustling surface world. In a parallel manner, solitude becomes a sanctuary for personal reflection—an intentional withdrawal from external influences, providing individuals with the solitude necessary for a deep dive into their inner selves.

As submarine crews navigate through the silent depths, the intertwining of silence and self-discovery becomes evident. The absence of external sounds becomes a facilitator for internal revelations. This intertwining mirrors the symbiotic relationship between silence and self-discovery sought by individuals in moments of introspection, where the external quietude becomes the canvas upon which the intricacies of the inner self are unveiled.

The silence of the abyss transforms the submarine journey into a contemplative oceanic voyage. It becomes more than a medium of travel; it evolves into a vessel for introspective exploration. This parallels the individual's contemplative journey, where intentional moments of silence become the vessel for navigating the depths of personal thoughts and emotions.

Silence within the submarine is not only a canvas for introspection but also a testament to the crew's resilience. It echoes with the adaptability and mental fortitude required to operate in seclusion. Similarly, the silence sought for personal reflection becomes a canvas that echoes with the resilience of the individual—a resilience that enables them to confront and navigate the internal complexities of their own psyche.

- **Isolation as a Crucible for Self-Exploration:**

As submarine crews embark on their submerged odyssey, they traverse not only the physical depths of the ocean but also the profound realms of isolation. This isolation, akin to the solitude sought for introspection, becomes a crucible—a transformative vessel wherein individuals confront the uncharted territories of their thoughts and emotions without the interference of external distractions. The parallels between the seclusion of submarine crews and the isolation conducive to introspection reveal an intricate dance between external detachment and internal exploration.

The seclusion experienced by submarine crews emerges as a parallel realm to the isolation essential for introspective endeavors. Removed from the bustling surface world, the submarine becomes a microcosm—a self-contained environment that mirrors the self-imposed mental seclusion sought by individuals in moments of deep reflection. This intentional withdrawal from external influences creates a psychological vacuum, allowing the individual's inner world to come to the forefront.

Just as submarines confront the uncharted depths of the ocean, individuals in isolation face the uncharted depths of their own consciousness. The crucible of isolation becomes the testing ground where thoughts, emotions, and reflections surface, free from the external noise that often obscures their nuances.

It is a confrontation with the self—an opportunity to navigate the intricate landscapes of one's inner world.

Isolation, whether within the confines of a submarine or in personal introspection, serves as a sanctuary from external distractions. In the submerged vessel, crew members are shielded from the cacophony of the surface world, allowing them to focus on the tasks at hand. Similarly, individuals in isolation find a mental sanctuary—a space where the noise of daily life is muted, creating an environment conducive to deep self-reflection.

Isolation within the submarine functions as a mental crucible, much like the crucible of introspection. In this crucible, external influences are stripped away, leaving behind a concentrated space where thoughts and emotions are subjected to the heat of conscious awareness. The mental crucible of introspection, similarly, involves the intentional isolation of one's thoughts, providing an environment for profound self-exploration and understanding.

Submarine crews, isolated within their vessel, navigate not only the physical sea but also the sea of internal dialogue. The isolation becomes a vessel for the crew's conversations with themselves, fostering introspective moments amidst the operational tasks. Similarly, individuals in isolation engage in an internal dialogue—a journey through their thoughts and emotions, navigating the depths of their psyche without external disruptions.

Serves as a retreat, allowing submarine crews to distance themselves from the external influences that permeate the surface world. This intentional retreat mirrors the purpose of isolation in personal introspection—a deliberate stepping back from the demands of the external world to focus on the internal landscape.

Within the submarine's isolation, crew members experience the weight of solitude—a solitude that is both a challenge and an opportunity. This weight mirrors the gravity of solitude in introspection, where the intentional isolation may feel heavy with the responsibility of self-confrontation. However, it is within this weight that the transformative potential of solitude unfolds.

Isolation within the submarine functions as a protective shield for the crew's inner sanctum. The vessel becomes a fortress, guarding the mental and emotional space of its inhabitants from the external onslaught. Similarly, isolation in personal introspection acts as a shield, preserving the sanctity of the individual's inner world from the demands and influences of the external environment.

The seclusion of submarine crews creates a space where authentic reflection can unfold. Stripped of external pressures and distractions, crew members can authentically confront their thoughts and emotions. In a parallel manner, isolation for introspection creates a mental space for authentic reflection—an opportunity to engage with one's true self without the masks imposed by external expectations.

Isolation, whether in a submarine or in introspective solitude, becomes a vessel for a profound journey into the depths of self. Within the crucible of isolation, individuals navigate the currents of their own thoughts, diving into the uncharted territories of their emotions. It is a journey that goes beyond the surface, delving into the intricacies of identity and self-discovery.

In both the seclusion of submarine operations and the isolation sought for introspection, individuals confront the echoes of their minds. The silence amplifies these echoes, creating a space where the subtle nuances of thoughts and emotions reverberate. It is a confrontation with the echoes of the mind—an opportunity to decipher and understand the internal dialogues that often go unheard in the clamor of external life.

Isolation, whether within a submarine or in the pursuit of introspection, becomes a forge for resilience. The challenges posed by seclusion, much like the challenges of introspective isolation, contribute to the forging of mental fortitude. It is a resilience that emerges from confronting the self without the crutch of external distractions—a resilience that becomes a hallmark of the transformative power of isolation.

Isolation, as a crucible, engages in the alchemy of self-discovery. The process of being isolated, whether in the vastness of the ocean or in the quiet corners of one's mind, transmutes the raw materials of thoughts and emotions into the gold of self-awareness.

It is an alchemical process that, while demanding, holds the promise of personal transformation and growth.

As submarine crews emerge from their seclusion, having navigated the ocean's depths, they carry the transformations wrought by the crucible of isolation. Similarly, individuals emerging from periods of deep introspection bear the marks of a transformative journey—an evolution shaped by the crucible of confronting the self in isolation. The parallels between the two experiences highlight the profound impact of intentional solitude on personal growth and self-discovery.

Chapter **4**

Navigation Systems

Just as submarines use sonar for navigation in the murky depths, individuals use insight and awareness to navigate complex inner landscapes.

Within the tremendous field of the ocean's profundities, where obscurity reigns and perceivability decreases to approach lack of definition, submarines depend on sonar—a modern innovation that punctures through the dimness to explore strange territories. This navigational ability finds a striking parallel within the internal scenes of the human mind. Much like submarines utilize sonar to navigate the cryptic profundities, people utilize knowledge and mindfulness as their navigational instruments to travel through the complex maze of considerations, feelings, and self-discovery. The similarity between sonar-equipped submarines and the contemplative capabilities of people divulges a significant connection—the utilize of increased recognition to chart a course through the dinky and frequently puzzling domains of the self.

- **Navigating the Murky Depths:**

Submarines plunge into the abyss where darkness reigns, exploring the hidden recesses of the ocean. In a parallel narrative, individuals delve into the depths of their minds, confronting the darkness of unresolved emotions and undiscovered facets of the self.

The inner landscapes of the human mind, as complex as the underwater terrain, weave intricate patterns of memories, desires, fears, and aspirations. Submarines navigate through the physical complexities of the ocean, mirroring the psychological intricacies traversed by individuals in their internal exploration.

Subs deploy sonar, a sophisticated tool utilizing sound waves to navigate and understand the underwater topography. Similarly, individuals employ insight and self-awareness as tools, penetrating the murkiness of their emotions and thoughts to gain clarity and understanding.

Sonar unravels hidden contours of the ocean floor, exposing the unseen topography. In a parallel fashion, insight and awareness unveil the concealed contours of the human psyche, revealing layers of thought patterns and emotional complexities that may remain obscured.

They navigate through the complexity of underwater terrains, adjusting course to adapt to changing conditions. Individuals, in their introspective journey, similarly navigate the complexities of their minds, adapting to the ebb and flow of emotions and thoughts.

Sonar sends out sound waves that echo back, providing crucial information about the surroundings. Likewise, individuals experience echoes of their thoughts and emotions in the murkiness within, allowing for a deeper understanding of their internal landscape.

Subs encounter potential obstacles beneath the surface, ranging from hidden currents to undersea formations. Individuals, in their introspective navigation, face potential obstacles such as suppressed emotions or limiting beliefs that may impede their journey.

Submarines plunge to great depths in the ocean, and individuals engage in profound self-reflection, delving into the layers of their identity, values, and beliefs. The depth of introspection becomes a parallel descent into the profound abyss of the mind.

In the ocean's darkness, sonar becomes a catalyst for awareness, enabling submarines to operate in conditions where visibility is limited. Similarly, navigating the murkiness within prompts individuals to develop heightened self-awareness, using insight as a guiding light in conditions of emotional obscurity.

The symbiosis between submarine navigation and individual awareness lies in the shared understanding that effective maneuvering through physical or psychological depths necessitates a keen awareness of the surroundings and the ability to adapt to changing circumstances.

Sonar aids submarines in mapping uncharted territories of the ocean floor. Similarly, insight helps individuals map the uncharted territories of their minds, discovering facets of themselves that may have remained unexplored.

Also operates with precision, discerning underwater features with accuracy. Insight operates with a similar clarity, allowing individuals to discern nuances within their emotions and thoughts with a high level of precision.

In addition, sonar operates silently, communicating through echoes in the ocean's murkiness. Similarly, self-awareness often involves silent communication with one's inner self, where the echoes of thoughts and emotions convey valuable information.

Submarines dynamically adapt to underwater currents to maintain course. Individuals, in their inner journeys, dynamically adapt to the currents of emotions and thoughts, ensuring a balanced and steady course through the complexities within.

Moreover sonar provides clarity amidst the turbulence of underwater currents. In a parallel manner, insight offers clarity amidst the turbulence of complex emotions and conflicting thoughts, guiding individuals through the sometimes tumultuous inner waters.

Subs continuously monitor their surroundings with sonar. Similarly, individuals engage in continuous self-reflection and monitoring, using insights to navigate the ever-changing landscape of their inner worlds.

Sonar creates a feedback loop of understanding in submarine navigation. Likewise, the insights gained through self-awareness create a feedback loop, deepening one's understanding of oneself and fostering personal growth.

Sonar's precision in detecting underwater features finds resonance in the nuanced discernment of insight, where individuals navigate the subtle nuances of their thoughts and emotions with a level of precision that goes beyond surface-level understanding.

Submarines balance external navigation with internal systems, and individuals balance external engagements with internal self-awareness. Both endeavors require a delicate equilibrium to ensure effective navigation through external challenges and internal complexities.

Subs integrate various navigation systems for holistic guidance. Similarly, individuals integrate insight, self-awareness, and emotional intelligence for holistic navigation through the intricate landscapes of their minds, fostering a harmonious relationship with their inner selves.

- **Sonar as a Precision Instrument:**

Sonar operates as a symphony conductor in the underwater world, orchestrating precise movements through sound waves. It mirrors the meticulous precision required for navigating the vast and intricate oceanic expanse.

In the deep silence of the ocean's depths, sonar sends out sound waves that traverse the darkness, returning with valuable information.

These sound waves, like messengers in the quiet abyss, illuminate the path ahead, showcasing the precision with which submarines navigate through the unseen.

Sonar's precision extends to mapping the unseen terrain beneath the surface, revealing the topography of the ocean floor. This mirrors the mental mapping individuals undertake, navigating through the hidden recesses of their minds, uncovering the nuanced landscape of thoughts and emotions.

The echoes produced by sonar carry a clarity that allows submarines to discern underwater features. Similarly, the echoes of insight in the mind bring clarity to individuals, helping them discern the subtleties of their emotions and thoughts with precision.

Also becomes a guiding light through the murkiness of the ocean's depths. Likewise, insight and awareness serve as mental tools, cutting through the murkiness within the mind, providing clarity and guidance in navigating the intricate complexities of one's inner landscape.

Submarines, guided by sonar, adjust their course with pinpoint accuracy. Individuals, in their introspective journeys, adjust their mental course with similar accuracy, adapting to the ever-changing currents of thoughts and emotions.

Moreover, sonar navigates submarines through subtle underwater features, avoiding obstacles with finesse.

In a parallel manner, insight and awareness guide individuals through the subtle nuances of their inner world, helping them navigate through emotional intricacies and psychological obstacles.

Insight and awareness orchestrate a symphony of mental tools within individuals' minds. Each tool is finely tuned, playing a crucial role in the navigation through the diverse landscapes of thoughts, feelings, and self-awareness.

Sonar's precision is mirrored in the fine-tuning of emotional intelligence within individuals. The ability to navigate emotional currents with accuracy and sensitivity reflects the nuanced approach required in both submarine operations and the exploration of one's emotional landscape.

Also sonar senses subtle disturbances in the underwater environment. Similarly, insight allows individuals to sense subtle disturbances within themselves—small ripples of emotion or changes in thought patterns that might go unnoticed without heightened self-awareness.

Sonar penetrates the ocean's murkiness, revealing what lies beneath. Insight, as a mental tool, penetrates the emotional murkiness within, allowing individuals to delve into the depths of their feelings and thoughts with clarity.

As well, sonar waves dance through the water, creating a dynamic dance of navigation.

In a parallel manner, the waves of insight and awareness dynamically dance through the inner landscapes, guiding individuals in an ever-changing choreography of thoughts and emotions.

Sonar operates in harmony with other navigation systems in submarines. Similarly, insight operates in harmony with other cognitive processes, emotions, and self-awareness mechanisms, creating a holistic approach to mental navigation.

Sonar's precision stands out amidst the complex underwater environment. Similarly, insight shines with precision amidst the complexity of the human psyche, offering individuals a clear understanding of their internal complexities.

Navigating the intricate terrain of thoughts and emotions becomes an art—a mental navigation where each stroke of insight, like a masterful brushstroke, contributes to the creation of an ever-evolving internal masterpiece.

Just as sonar systems require continuous calibration, individuals engage in continuous calibration of their mental tools—refining insight, enhancing self-awareness, and adapting to the changing currents of their internal worlds.

Also, nurtures the resilience of submarines in navigating challenging underwater conditions. Similarly, insight fosters cognitive resilience in individuals, enabling them to navigate the challenges within their minds with adaptability and mental fortitude.

Sonar becomes a beacon guiding submarines through the depths. In a parallel metaphor, insight becomes a mental beacon, illuminating the path through the inner depths and offering guidance in the intricate exploration of one's thoughts and emotions.

Submarines pioneer the unexplored frontiers of the ocean, guided by sonar. Likewise, individuals pioneer the unexplored territories of their minds, forging ahead with insight and awareness as their guiding companions in the journey of self-discovery.

Furthermore, sonar stands as a precision instrument of underwater navigation. Similarly, insight and awareness become precision instruments of self-discovery, allowing individuals to navigate their inner landscapes with clarity, purpose, and a profound understanding of themselves.

- **Penetrating the Layers of the Mind:**

Sonar unveils the layers of oceanic depth, reaching into the darkness beneath the surface. Likewise, insight becomes a guiding light, reaching into the layers of the mind to illuminate the concealed aspects of one's thoughts and emotions.

Also, sonar navigates through underwater currents to reveal the hidden features of the ocean floor. In a similar fashion, insight navigates through cognitive currents, helping individuals uncover the underlying currents of their thoughts and emotions.

Sonar dives into the unconscious depths of the ocean, exposing the secrets hidden in the dark. Insight, as a mental diver, delves into the unconscious layers of the mind, bringing to light the hidden motivations, fears, and desires that shape behavior.

Sonar's echoes unveil the unexplored territories below the surface.

Echoes of insight reveal the unexplored realms of the mind, bringing to consciousness aspects that may have been submerged in the depths of the subconscious.

As well, sonar resonates with the subconscious realms of the ocean. Similarly, insight resonates with the subconscious layers of the mind, creating a resonance that allows individuals to connect with deeper aspects of themselves.

Sonar reveals undercurrents in the ocean, guiding submarines through emotional waters. Insight reveals emotional undercurrents within the mind, aiding individuals in navigating the emotional landscapes that shape their responses and behaviors.

Moreover, sonar maps the topography of the ocean floor. Insight maps the mental topography, providing individuals with a detailed understanding of the terrain within their minds, including the highs and lows of emotions and the peaks and valleys of thought patterns.

Sonar uncovers submerged features beneath the ocean's surface. Insight uncovers submerged memories within the layers of the mind, allowing individuals to revisit and make sense of experiences that may have been buried in the recesses of memory.

Chapter **5**

Pressure Management

Submarines must manage external pressures to avoid implosion; similarly, people must learn to cope with stress and emotional turmoil.

Within the fathomless profundities of the sea, where obscurity rules and the weight is colossal, submarines explore a world that requests versatility against outside powers. Much like these underwater vessels, people within the complicated embroidered artwork of human presence must hook with outside weights, though of a psychological nature. The similarity between submarines maintaining a strategic distance from implosion within the deep profundities and people overseeing stretch and enthusiastic turmoil underscores a significant parallelism. Both scenarios require a fragile adjust, versatility, and a vigorous inner structure to resist the outside weights that threaten implosion.

- **The Uncharted Terrain:**

Submarines venture into uncharted territories, facing the unknown of the ocean's depths. Similarly, individuals navigate through the uncharted terrain of life's abyss, encountering external pressures that may be unfamiliar and unpredictable.

The abyss represents personal and professional challenges for submarines. Individuals traverse through the depths of their own challenges, ranging from career aspirations to personal relationships, where external pressures can become overwhelming.

Subs grapple with the weight of oceanic pressure. Likewise, individuals contend with the weight of societal expectations, familial aspirations, and personal goals, creating an external force that can press heavily on their emotional resilience.

Beneath the ocean's surface, silent forces come into play. Similarly, in the complexities of life, silent forces—such as societal norms, cultural expectations, and internal struggles—shape the external pressures individuals face.

Also, submarines adapt to the changing dynamics of oceanic pressure. Individuals, too, must adapt to the dynamic nature of external pressures, adjusting their emotional sails to navigate through the unpredictable currents of life.

The ocean squeezes submarines with unrelenting pressure. Individuals cultivate resilience to withstand the squeeze of external pressures, developing emotional fortitude to resist being crushed under the weight of expectations.

Subs navigate through darkness in the ocean's abyss. Similarly, individuals navigate the darkness of life's abyss, where external pressures may cast shadows on their path, requiring them to navigate with resilience and purpose.

The ocean's abyss holds layers of complexity that submarines must traverse. Life's abyss, too, presents layers of complexity, with external pressures manifesting in intricate ways that individuals must navigate with a nuanced understanding.

Moreover, submarines grapple with the immensity of external demands. Likewise, individuals confront the vastness of external demands, be it in the professional realm with deadlines and responsibilities or in personal relationships with expectations and commitments.

Below the ocean's surface, submarines face emotional turbulence. Individuals, beneath the surface of their composed exteriors, contend with emotional turbulence induced by external pressures, requiring them to maintain equilibrium.

Submarines may endure sacrifices for their mission's success. Individuals, too, may navigate the abyss of life by making personal sacrifices to meet external expectations, whether in terms of time, personal pursuits, or aspirations.

Unseen forces influence submarines in the ocean's depths. Similarly, unseen societal, cultural, and interpersonal forces influence individuals, shaping the nature of external pressures they encounter in the intricate dance of life.

Furthermore, submarines encounter echoes of external challenges in the abyss. Individuals experience echoes of external challenges in their lives, with past pressures reverberating in their memories, influencing their present responses and decisions.

The ocean's abyss tests the fragility of submarine structures. Life's abyss tests the fragility of individuals' emotional equilibrium, challenging their mental resilience in the face of external pressures that threaten to disrupt their inner balance.

In addition submarines navigate the symbiosis of external oceanic forces and internal structural strength. Individuals navigate the symbiosis of external pressures and their internal emotional fortitude, seeking harmony between the demands of the external world and their inner resilience.

Subs persevere through storms in the ocean's depths. Individuals, too, must persevere through the storms of external challenges, maintaining their emotional compass even when faced with adversity.

The ocean's abyss holds mysteries influenced by external factors. Life's abyss holds mysteries shaped by external influences, and individuals must unravel these mysteries while navigating through external pressures that contribute to their personal narratives.

Submarines delve into the depths for reflection. Similarly, individuals delve into the depths of personal reflection, contemplating their responses to external pressures and seeking insights that foster emotional growth.

Moreover, submarines engage in a subtle dance with external oceanic forces. Individuals engage in a subtle dance with external forces, adapting their steps to the rhythm of life's pressures, finding a balance that allows them to navigate with grace.

Besides, submarines rely on inner strength to withstand external pressures. Similarly, individuals embrace their inner strength, honing resilience and emotional well-being as they confront and navigate the external pressures embedded within the abyss of life.

- **Structural Integrity and Mental Resilience:**

In the intricate dance between submarines navigating the crushing depths of the ocean and individuals traversing the complexities of life.

The concept of structural integrity finds a parallel resonance with the cultivation of mental resilience. Submarines, in their perilous journeys beneath the surface, reinforce their structures to resist the looming threat of implosion—a cataclysmic consequence of succumbing to the external pressures exerted by the ocean's immense weight. Similarly, individuals embark on a journey of fortification, nurturing their mental resilience as an indispensable shield against the implosive effects of stress, societal expectations, and the relentless pressures that characterize the human experience.

Submarines meticulously engineer their foundations to withstand oceanic pressure. In a parallel endeavor, individuals lay the foundation of mental resilience through self-awareness, emotional intelligence, and adaptive coping mechanisms.

Subs adapt their structures to external forces. Individuals, too, adapt their mental structures, allowing for flexibility and adaptability in the face of ever-changing external pressures.

Just as submarines reinforce their physical structures, individuals reinforce their emotional framework through self-reflection, learning, and the cultivation of coping mechanisms that bolster their psychological well-being.

Furthermore, submarines identify stress points and reinforce accordingly. Individuals identify stressors in their lives and proactively reinforce their mental resilience, creating a robust defense against the impact of external pressures.

Also, submarines balance internal pressure with external forces. Individuals strive for a harmonious equilibrium, balancing their internal mental states with the external forces that exert pressure on their emotional well-being.

Moreover, submarines implement structural measures to prevent implosion. Likewise, individuals implement mental health strategies—such as mindfulness, self-care, and seeking support—to prevent emotional implosion when faced with overwhelming stress.

Subs strengthen their cognitive architecture against external forces. Individuals engage in cognitive fortification, enhancing their mental architecture to withstand the cognitive pressures induced by external stressors.

Submarines rely on foundational structures to resist collapse. Similarly, individuals rely on their emotional foundations, cultivating resilience to resist collapsing under the weight of emotional turmoil and external pressures.

As well, submarines cultivate a crisis-resistant design. Individuals cultivate a crisis-resistant mindset, fortifying themselves mentally to navigate through crises and adversities without succumbing to the implosive effects of stress.

Subs strategically adapt to external pressure variations. Individuals strategically adapt their mental resilience to navigate through the variations in external pressures, adjusting their coping strategies as circumstances evolve.

Moreover, submarines guard against weaknesses in their structure. Individuals guard against vulnerabilities in their mental resilience, actively addressing and strengthening weak points to ensure a robust defense against external pressures.

In addition, submarines integrate stress-tested strategies into their design. Individuals integrate stress-tested mental health strategies, drawing from experiences and learning to refine their resilience against external pressures.

Submarines continuously reinforce their structures for ongoing protection.

Similarly, individuals engage in continuous mental reinforcement, recognizing that the journey through life's challenges requires an ongoing commitment to mental well-being.

Also, submarines view resilience as a dynamic, evolving process. Individuals embrace resilience as a dynamic aspect of their mental landscape, recognizing its evolution over time and adapting to the changing nature of external pressures.

Moreover, submarines employ adaptive mechanisms for structural integrity. Individuals employ adaptive coping mechanisms, developing a repertoire of strategies to maintain mental integrity in the face of diverse external pressures.

Besides, submarines boast pressure-resistant foundations. Individuals, too, cultivate pressure-resistant emotional foundations, nurturing their emotional core to withstand the external pressures that threaten to compromise mental well-being.

Furthermore, submarines engage in preemptive maintenance to avoid structural deterioration. Likewise, individuals practice preemptive mental maintenance, engaging in self-care, mindfulness, and healthy habits to avoid the deterioration of their mental resilience.

- **Balancing Internal and External Forces:**

Submarines face internal pressures such as maintaining optimal buoyancy and managing system functions.

Individuals, too, contend with internal pressures—emotional well-being, personal goals, and self-regulation.

External forces like water currents and underwater terrain impact submarines' navigation.

Life presents external forces, such as societal expectations, work dynamics, and relationships, influencing individual experiences.

Submarines adjust ballast to balance buoyancy, preventing tilting or uncontrolled ascent.

Individuals strive for emotional equilibrium, adjusting their internal "ballast" to maintain balance amid life's challenges.

They navigate through underwater currents, adjusting their course to withstand external pressures.

Also, individuals navigate emotional tides, adapting to external pressures while staying true to their internal compass of values and well-being.

Submarines use navigational tools to maintain course alignment despite external forces.

Individuals employ personal values and goals as navigational tools, ensuring alignment with their life path amidst external influences.

Continuous monitoring of systems ensures submarines respond effectively to external pressures.

Regular self-assessment and reflection enable individuals to respond thoughtfully to external pressures, fostering adaptability.

Submarines exhibit flexibility to navigate diverse underwater terrains.

Flexibility is key in life; individuals adapt to diverse circumstances, showcasing resilience in the face of changing external forces.

Submarines optimize resource use for energy and propulsion.

Individuals optimize personal resources, managing time, energy, and skills efficiently to navigate the demands of external forces.

Chapter **6**

Life Support Systems

Inside a submarine, systems must support life in an inhospitable environment. In personal development, support mechanisms like relationships and self-care practices are vital for well-being.

Setting out on a travel into the profundities of the sea, submarines serve as innovative wonders, outlined to resist the unforgiving and aloof conditions that win underneath the surface. These vessels dive into an environment where weight is monstrous, and obscurity covers the profundities. In a striking parallel, the complexities of personal advancement unfurl within the different scene of human encounter. Inside the profundities of our claim lives, we explore challenges and vulnerabilities associated to the submarine's investigation of the ocean's pit. The relationship takes root, drawing attention to the basic part of back mechanisms—much just like the complicated frameworks interior a submarine—in maintaining life and cultivating well-being within the confront of life's unwelcoming minutes.

- **Life-Supporting Systems:**

Just as submarines rely on an oxygen supply for survival, individuals depend on relationships as the life-sustaining oxygen that enriches their personal development journey.

Emotional connections with family, friends, and partners infuse vitality into the human experience, offering a supportive atmosphere for growth.

Submarines endure intense environmental pressure. Similarly, individuals face emotional pressure in the crucible of personal development. Relationships act as a buffer, alleviating emotional stress and providing a supportive environment to withstand the challenges.

The circulatory systems in submarines ensure the distribution of essential resources. In personal development, relationships act as circulatory systems, facilitating the exchange of emotional support, encouragement, and shared experiences crucial for individual growth.

Also, submarines regulate temperature to withstand extreme conditions. Relationships contribute to emotional temperature control in personal development, offering warmth, empathy, and understanding that help individuals navigate through the highs and lows of life.

Subs require nutritional support for the crew. Similarly, relationships provide the nutritional support of emotional well-being, nurturing individuals with a sense of belonging, love, and shared experiences that contribute to their psychological health.

Moreover, submarines create a holistic environment for survival. Relationships offer holistic environmental support in personal development, creating a space where individuals feel emotionally secure, fostering mental well-being and resilience.

Just as submarines have internal life-support systems, individuals cultivate self-care practices as internal mechanisms vital for sustaining life in personal development. Practices like mindfulness, self-reflection, and healthy habits nourish mental and emotional well-being.

In addition, Submarines adapt to diverse ecosystems. Individuals, too, adapt to emotional ecosystems within relationships, recognizing that each connection brings unique challenges and opportunities for growth in their personal development journey.

Subs filter the air for a breathable atmosphere. Relationships act as emotional filters, contributing to a breathable atmosphere in personal development by offering understanding, empathy, and constructive feedback that fosters growth.

Furthermore, Submarines store emergency supplies. Relationships serve as emotional reservoirs, providing individuals with a wellspring of support during challenging times in personal development, enhancing their capacity for resilience.

Also, Submarines monitor critical gauges for operation. In personal development, individuals monitor emotional gauges within relationships, staying attuned to the dynamics and adjusting their responses to maintain a healthy and supportive connection.

Subs navigate through deep oceanic depths. Relationships become navigational tools, guiding individuals through the emotional depths of personal development, helping them navigate complex feelings and experiences.

They have control panels for responsiveness. Relationships act as emotional control panels, allowing individuals to respond effectively to the challenges of personal development by offering a platform for open communication and understanding.

Submarines have interconnected systems for symbiotic functioning. Relationships and self-care practices create a symbiotic system in personal development, with each element influencing and supporting the other for the holistic well-being of the individual.

Also, submarines conduct life-support drills. Individuals engage in life-support drills through self-care practices and active engagement in relationships, honing the skills necessary for maintaining mental and emotional well-being.

Moreover, Submarines aim for harmony in operation. Relationships contribute to the harmony of emotional frequencies in personal development, fostering an environment where individuals experience emotional resonance and balance.

Subs navigate dynamically. Relationships facilitate responsive emotional navigation in personal development, adapting to changing circumstances and contributing to the adaptive capacity of individuals facing life's challenges.

They have survival kits. Relationships serve as emotional survival kits, offering the essential tools of love, support, and understanding that individuals require for emotional survival and growth.

Subs have sustainable infrastructure. Relationships and self-care practices contribute to the sustainable emotional infrastructure of personal development, creating a foundation for long-term well-being and growth.

Also, submarines require ongoing maintenance. Similarly, relationships and self-care practices demand ongoing emotional maintenance, as individuals continuously invest in nurturing and sustaining the life-supporting systems crucial for their personal development journey.

- **Oxygenating Relationships:**

Submarines require oxygen for survival, and individuals seek emotional breath within relationships. These connections serve as the essence of emotional respiration, infusing life into personal development by providing the necessary support and understanding.

Just as submarines inhale oxygen for sustenance, individuals inhale empathy and understanding from relationships. These connections become a source of emotional oxygen, allowing individuals to breathe in an atmosphere of mutual understanding and shared experiences.

They exhale carbon dioxide to maintain balance. Individuals exhale emotional burdens within relationships, using these connections as a medium to release stress, share concerns, and find relief in a supportive environment.

Subs utilize oxygen as a catalyst for various processes. Relationships act as oxygen catalysts for personal development, fostering growth, self-discovery, and resilience by providing the emotional nourishment required for flourishing.

Also, submarines circulate oxygen for the entire crew. Similarly, relationships circulate shared breaths of affection and support, creating an emotional atmosphere that benefits not just individuals but the collective well-being of those involved.

Moreover, submarines engage in respiratory exchange. In relationships, individuals partake in an emotional respiratory exchange, inhaling the positivity and exhaling the challenges, creating a harmonious and balanced atmosphere for personal development.

They navigate challenges in the ocean's depths. Relationships become the medium through which individuals breathe through life's challenges, finding solace, advice, and encouragement to navigate the complex currents of personal development.

Submarines need oxygen for endurance. Relationships provide emotional endurance, oxygenating individuals in personal development, enabling them to persist through difficulties and emerge stronger on the other side.

Moreover, submarines seek oxygen for revitalization. Individuals seek revitalization through the oxygen of meaningful connections, finding energy and enthusiasm within relationships that fuel their personal development journey.

They have a pulse of oxygen. Relationships become the pulse of emotional oxygen, pulsating with encouragement, love, and support that sustains individuals in their personal development pursuits.

Submarines aid in the discovery of the unknown. Relationships aid in the self-discovery journey, oxygenating individuals with perspectives, feedback, and shared experiences that contribute to a deeper understanding of themselves.

Also, submarines carry oxygen tanks for emergencies. Relationships act as emotional oxygen tanks, providing a reserve of support during challenging moments in personal development, ensuring individuals have the resources needed to navigate rough waters.

They navigate vulnerable situations. Relationships offer a space for breathing through vulnerability, allowing individuals to express their authentic selves and find acceptance, understanding, and encouragement in the process.

Subs continuously inhale oxygen. Relationships provide a continuous stream of emotional inhalation, creating an environment where individuals can consistently draw inspiration, motivation, and support for ongoing personal development.

As well, submarines require oxygen for mental clarity. Relationships contribute to mental well-being by providing the necessary emotional oxygen, aiding individuals in maintaining clarity, focus, and resilience in their personal development journey.

Furthermore, submarines breathe life into exploration. Relationships breathe life into individuals' dreams and aspirations, providing the emotional oxygen required to explore and pursue personal and professional goals.

Submarines engage in a symbiotic exchange of oxygen. Relationships foster a symbiotic exchange of emotional oxygen, where individuals and their connections mutually benefit, creating an atmosphere conducive to flourishing personal development.

They utilize oxygen for propulsion. Relationships serve as a source of emotional propulsion, fueling individuals with motivation, encouragement, and inspiration to propel them forward in their personal development endeavors.

Also, submarines filter and breathe-in fresh air. Relationships act as filters, allowing individuals to breathe-in positivity, optimism, and constructive energy that contribute to a buoyant and thriving personal development atmosphere.

Subs oxygenate the depths of the ocean. Relationships oxygenate the depths of the heart and soul, providing the emotional sustenance necessary for a profound and meaningful personal development journey.

- **Pressure-Resistant Relationships:**

Submarines require structural integrity for survival. Similarly, individuals seek structural integrity in relationships, where the foundation is built on trust, open communication, and mutual respect, forming a resilient structure for personal development.

Also, submarines bear the weight of external oceanic pressure. Individuals face the weight of external challenges in personal development. Pressure-resistant relationships become a metaphorical exoskeleton, offering support to withstand and navigate through the external pressures.

They reinforce structures for turbulent waters. Likewise, individuals reinforce their relationships during turbulent times, finding strength and stability within these connections to weather the storms of personal development.

Moreover, submarines navigate emotional depths beneath the surface. In personal development, pressure-resistant relationships help individuals navigate their emotional depths, providing a secure and stable environment for introspection and growth.

They counteract external oceanic forces. Pressure-resistant relationships act as a counterforce, helping individuals counteract external pressures and maintain their emotional and mental equilibrium during the challenges of personal development.

Furthermore, submarines distribute pressure across their structures. Similarly, individuals in pressure-resistant relationships share the load-bearing responsibilities, distributing the challenges and supporting each other in the collective journey of personal growth.

Also, submarines use ballast for stability. Pressure-resistant relationships serve as emotional ballast, providing stability during times of personal development where uncertainties and challenges may otherwise threaten to disrupt the equilibrium.

They display flexibility within their resilience. Likewise, pressure-resistant relationships exhibit flexibility within their resilience, allowing individuals to adapt and grow together through the dynamic phases of personal development.

Subs drop anchors to stabilize. In personal development, pressure-resistant relationships become anchors in the storm, offering stability and grounding amid the tumultuous seas of challenges and changes.

As well subs maintain cohesiveness under pressure. Individuals in pressure-resistant relationships maintain cohesiveness during challenges, fostering a sense of unity and solidarity that becomes a source of strength in personal development.

Chapter **7**

Tight Quarters and Social Dynamics

The close quarters of a submarine can teach us about the importance of interpersonal dynamics and communication, essential skills for self-awareness and relationship management.
Within the baffling world underneath the ocean's surface, where light scatters, and weight gets to be discernable, submarines explore through the profundities with exactness and coordination. The near limits of these vessels, planned for investigation and defense, reflect the complexities of interpersonal flow and communication—an relationship that draws a significant association between the life inside a submarine and the crucial abilities required for self-awareness and relationship administration. As the submarine digs into the obscure with a team depending on consistent collaboration, the lessons learned inside its near quarters reverberate with the centrality of cultivating effective communication and understanding within the complicated move of human connections.

- **Seamless Coordination in Confined Spaces:**

In the depths of the ocean, submariners navigate through a confined space where every movement must be deliberate.
Similarly, in the complex landscape of human relationships, individuals must navigate through the intricacies of emotions, personalities, and varying perspectives. The confined spaces of a submarine become a metaphor for the human depths where understanding and coordination are paramount.
Submarines are microcosms of teamwork, relying on the synchronized efforts of the crew. Interpersonal dynamics within the vessel become a critical aspect of its functioning. Likewise, in our personal and professional lives, the quality of our relationships and how we navigate the dynamics between individuals significantly influences our collective success and well-being.
Within the submarine's tight confines, clear communication is a lifeline. Misunderstandings can have profound consequences. This mirrors the importance of effective communication in relationships. The ability to articulate thoughts, express emotions, and actively listen becomes the lifeline that ensures mutual understanding and prevents the escalation of conflicts.
The close quarters of a submarine demand mutual understanding among its crew members. Likewise, in the close quarters of personal and professional interactions, individuals need to cultivate a deep level of understanding.
This involves recognizing differences, appreciating diverse perspectives, and fostering an environment where everyone feels heard and valued.
Conflicts within a submarine demand swift and effective resolution. The confined space doesn't allow room for prolonged discord. In interpersonal relationships, the ability to address conflicts promptly and constructively is crucial for maintaining harmony. Learning from the confined environment of a submarine, individuals can develop skills in conflict resolution that contribute to healthier relationships.

- **Communication as the Lifeblood:**

Within the high-stakes environment of a submarine, communication is not a mere formality but a mission-critical necessity. The success of the mission depends on the crew's ability to convey information accurately and promptly. This echoes the importance of communication in personal and professional realms, where effective communication is the linchpin for success, understanding, and collaboration.
Submariners trust their lives to the information shared with them. Similarly, in relationships, trust and transparency are interwoven with effective communication. Open and honest communication builds trust, creating a foundation upon which strong, resilient connections can thrive.
The confined space within a submarine amplifies the impact of shared challenges.
To navigate these challenges, clear and open communication is indispensable.
In relationships, whether personal or professional, the ability to communicate effectively becomes the compass that guides individuals through the complexities of life, ensuring they can weather storms together.
Communication within a submarine amplifies shared understanding. In relationships, the clarity and precision of communication amplify shared understanding, reducing the likelihood of misinterpretations and fostering a harmonious environment where individuals are attuned to each other's needs and aspirations.

Subs operate as a collaborative unit, with communication being the conduit for coordinated efforts. Likewise, in personal and professional collaborations, effective communication serves as the conduit that enables individuals to work together seamlessly. It allows for the sharing of ideas, the alignment of goals, and the collective pursuit of shared objectives.

They adapt to changing underwater conditions through constant communication. Similarly, in the dynamic landscape of relationships, the ability to adapt to changing circumstances relies on continuous and adaptive communication. It allows individuals to stay informed, make informed decisions, and adjust their course as needed.

Also, submarines mitigate risks through thorough information sharing. In relationships, sharing information through communication becomes a risk mitigation strategy.

Openly discussing concerns, expectations, and aspirations reduces the potential for misunderstandings and prevents the escalation of conflicts.

Submarines bridge the gap between missions and headquarters through communication. In relationships, communication serves as a bridge connecting individuals emotionally and intellectually. It allows for the transmission of thoughts, emotions, and intentions, fostering a sense of connection and understanding.

They respond swiftly to navigational challenges through effective communication. Similarly, in relationships, the ability to respond promptly to challenges relies on clear communication. It enables individuals to address issues before they escalate, maintaining the health and stability of the connection.

Moreover, submarines create a unified vision through communication channels. In relationships, articulating shared goals, values, and aspirations creates a unified vision. Effective communication ensures that individuals are on the same page, working together towards a common purpose.

- **Navigating Depths of Self-Awareness:**

Submariners dive into the ocean's depths, a metaphorical submersible journey akin to the introspective exploration individuals undertake in their quest for self-awareness. The vessel becomes a cocoon for self-discovery, mirroring the introspective spaces individuals create for understanding their inner selves.

In the close quarters of a submarine, submariners experience the proximity of the vessel's inner workings. Similarly, individuals in their introspective journey come face to face with their inner turbulence—emotions, thoughts, and memories that may have been concealed in the vast expanse of the mind.

The limited space within a submarine challenges submariners, prompting them to adapt and innovate. Likewise, the constraints of introspection—facing one's emotions and vulnerabilities—present challenges that push individuals to adapt their perspectives and innovate in their approach to self-awareness.

Steel walls surround submariners in their voyage. In a parallel manner, the introspective journey involves reflection amidst the mental 'steel walls'—the protective barriers individuals erect around their inner selves. These walls require contemplation and understanding to navigate.

Submarines use technology to illuminate the dark ocean depths. Similarly, introspection serves as a mental flashlight, illuminating the dark corners of the psyche. It enables individuals to shed light on their thoughts, emotions, and experiences that may be hidden in the depths of their consciousness.

Subs encounter pressure in the ocean's depths. Likewise, individuals in their journey of self-awareness encounter emotional pressures. These may surface as they delve deeper into their feelings, facing the weight of past experiences, expectations, and societal influences.

Submariners navigate through ocean currents. In a parallel manner, individuals navigate through emotional currents within themselves. Understanding these emotional flows becomes a crucial aspect of self-awareness, allowing individuals to steer through their inner landscape.

In the close quarters of a submarine, submariners evaluate the vessel's structural strengths. Similarly, introspection prompts individuals to evaluate their personal strengths—the resilient aspects of their character that support them in the face of challenges.

They acknowledge the vulnerabilities of their vessel. Likewise, individuals in self-awareness recognize their emotional weaknesses. This acknowledgment is a pivotal step, as it opens avenues for growth and development in the introspective journey.

Subs need mental fortitude to endure the pressures. In the introspective journey, individuals cultivate mental fortitude to withstand the pressures of self-discovery. This involves facing uncomfortable truths, challenging assumptions, and fostering resilience in the face of internal challenges.

Also, submarines use depth soundings to navigate. Similarly, individuals use introspection as a tool for depth soundings of their inner terrain. It involves probing beneath the surface, understanding the layers of thoughts, emotions, and experiences that shape their identity.

Moreover, Submarines use sonar for navigation. In the introspective journey, individuals utilize the sonar of emotional intelligence.

This heightened awareness allows them to navigate the complex emotional landscape, fostering empathy, self-regulation, and interpersonal understanding.

Furthermore, submarines operate in an environment of silence beneath the ocean's surface. Similarly, self-reflection requires moments of silence and solitude, creating an internal environment where individuals can hear the whispers of their own thoughts and feelings.

They balance internal pressure with external forces. Likewise, individuals strive for equilibrium, balancing internal pressures such as self-expectations, fears, and aspirations with the external forces of societal norms and expectations.

Subs navigate through the ocean's depths to fulfill their mission. In a parallel journey, individuals navigate through the depths of their personal identity, seeking to understand who they are, what they value, and what drives their actions and decisions.

Submarines are equipped with tools for navigation. Similarly, individuals leverage introspective tools—such as mindfulness, journaling, and self-analysis—to navigate their internal landscape. These tools facilitate the examination of thoughts and emotions with greater clarity.

They explore uncharted territories in the ocean. Likewise, individuals in their journey of self-awareness embrace the exploration of uncharted territories within themselves. This involves confronting aspects of the self that may be unknown or overlooked.

Besides submarines operate in the realm of submerged emotions. In the introspective journey, individuals grapple with submerged emotions—feelings that may have been buried or unexplored. Bringing these emotions to the surface is a courageous step in self-awareness.

Moreover, submarines navigate through the darkness of the ocean's depths. Similarly, individuals navigate through the darkness of their inner selves. The introspective journey involves developing internal navigation skills to traverse the complex and sometimes challenging terrain of one's psyche.

They have a captain overseeing the journey. In the introspective journey, individuals play the role of the captain, cultivating insight into their own motivations, aspirations, and desires. This self-guidance becomes a compass in the exploration of self-awareness.

- **Mutual Reliance for Mission Success:**

Much like a submarine's success hinges on the interdependence of its crew, successful relationships find a cornerstone in interdependence. The acknowledgment that each partner's contributions are vital for collective flourishing becomes the foundation for a resilient and thriving connection.

The symphony of collaboration within a submarine's tight confines resonates with the harmonious collaboration essential in successful relationships. Each individual becomes a unique instrument, contributing distinct notes that, when played together, create a beautiful and functional composition.

Submariners share responsibilities for the overall success of the mission. Similarly, in relationships, shared responsibilities translate into shared triumphs. The understanding that individual roles contribute to collective achievements fosters a sense of shared accomplishment.

The complementary contributions of crew members in a submarine echo the harmonious balance required in relationships. Recognizing and embracing each other's strengths and weaknesses, individuals create a symphony of complementary contributions that lead to the overall harmony and success of the connection.

The mutual reliance of submariners catalyzes the mission's success. Likewise, mutual reliance in relationships acts as a catalyst for growth. It nurtures an environment where individuals support each other's aspirations, celebrate achievements, and collectively progress towards shared goals.

Chapter **8**

Technical Mastery

Operating a submarine requires specialized knowledge and skills, analogous to the need for self-discipline and continuous learning in personal development.

The operation of a submarine, with its furtive ventures into the significant profundities of the sea, stands as an complex move between innovation, skill, and the unflinching commitment of its team. The submariners, prepared with specialized information and sharpened aptitudes, explore through the challenges of the submerged world. In a captivating parallel, the operation of a submarine serves as a compelling representation for the travel of individual improvement. Much like submariners require specialized information to explore the ocean's profundities, people within the domain of individual improvement require self-discipline and a commitment to ceaseless learning. This comparison reveals the significant cooperative energy between the technical ability required to function a submarine and the natural qualities fundamental for individual development.

- **Specialized Knowledge as the Helm:**

Operating a submarine involves a deep dive into the understanding of intricate systems that sustain life beneath the ocean's surface. In personal development, individuals must delve into the complexities of their own mental and emotional systems.

This involves unraveling the layers of thought patterns, belief systems, and ingrained habits that shape behavior, allowing for a comprehensive understanding of the self.

A submariner's proficiency in navigation parallels the importance of emotional intelligence in personal development. Specialized knowledge in personal development extends beyond intellectual capacities to include a heightened emotional intelligence. Navigating the seas of emotions, understanding their undercurrents, and effectively managing them become vital skills at the helm of personal growth.

They are trained to adapt to the unique challenges posed by the underwater environment. Similarly, individuals in personal development must navigate through the challenges unique to their own journey—be it overcoming past traumas, facing fears, or addressing self-limiting beliefs. Specialized knowledge equips individuals with the tools needed to adapt and thrive in the face of these challenges.

In submarine operations, precise navigation is guided by instruments, and in personal development, self-awareness becomes the compass.

Specialized knowledge allows individuals to cultivate a deep understanding of their values, motivations, and aspirations, providing the necessary guidance to navigate the vast and sometimes turbulent waters of personal growth.

The helm of a submarine is in constant motion, steering toward optimal performance and safety.

Similarly, the helm of personal development is always in action, steering individuals toward continuous improvement. Specialized knowledge acts as the rudder, facilitating intentional course corrections, learning from experiences, and propelling the individual toward their desired destination of self-actualization.

- **Skills Precision in Execution:**

Submarine crews meticulously navigate through the vast expanses of the ocean, relying on their navigational skills for safe passage. Similarly, in personal development, individuals must develop the skill of navigation— charting the course of their lives with purpose and direction. The precision lies in setting goals, creating a roadmap, and making intentional choices that align with their aspirations.

The ability of a submarine crew to handle crises with precision is a defining aspect of their skill set. Likewise, personal development demands proficiency in crisis management—navigating through life's turbulent waters with resilience and adaptability. The precision here lies in the ability to stay composed, make informed decisions, and emerge stronger from challenging situations.

Communication within a submarine is a finely tuned skill, often relying on clear signals in the murky depths. In personal development, effective communication is equally crucial. The precision in expressing thoughts, feelings, and intentions becomes a skill that fosters meaningful connections, resolves conflicts, and ensures clarity in the sometimes unclear waters of personal relationships.

Also, submariners exemplify resilience, weathering storms and challenges beneath the ocean's surface. Similarly, personal development requires the skill of resilience—the ability to bounce back from setbacks, adapt to changes, and navigate through the storms of life with fortitude. The precision in cultivating resilience lies in the intentional practice of maintaining a positive outlook amidst adversity.

Submarine crews must adapt swiftly to dynamic underwater environments. In personal development, the skill of adaptability becomes indispensable. The precision in adapting to changing circumstances, embracing new opportunities, and learning from experiences ensures that individuals can navigate the ever-evolving landscapes of their personal and professional lives.

- **Adapting to Unseen Depths:**

Submariners confront limited visibility beneath the ocean's surface, akin to the murkiness that life sometimes presents. In personal development, individuals encounter situations where clarity is obscured, and decisions must be made in the midst of uncertainty.

The adaptability to navigate through life's murkiness becomes a crucial skill for making informed choices and steering the course with resilience.

The underwater environment is rife with unforeseen circumstances, demanding submariners to swiftly adjust their course.

Similarly, personal development throws unexpected plot twists—analogous to the unseen ocean floor—requiring individuals to adapt to the ebb and flow of life's dynamic circumstances. The ability to recalibrate in response to unexpected events becomes an invaluable skill.

Besides, Submariners face changing tides and currents that impact their navigation. Likewise, personal development involves adapting to life's ebb and flow—navigating through periods of challenges and opportunities. The skill of adaptability allows individuals to ride the waves of change, embracing challenges as opportunities for growth and transformation.

They execute precise course corrections to navigate through the ocean currents. In personal development, the skill lies in making calculated adjustments to one's trajectory when faced with unforeseen challenges. The ability to maneuver through life's currents with precision ensures that individuals stay on course towards their goals despite the changing dynamics.

The unseen depths often bring unpredictable storms in the underwater world. Similarly, personal development involves weathering the storms of uncertainty and adversity.

Adaptability here becomes synonymous with resilience—the ability to flexibly endure and overcome challenges, emerging stronger on the other side of life's tempests.

Also, submariners embrace the unknown with a curious mindset, exploring uncharted territories. In personal development, individuals are encouraged to cultivate a similar curiosity towards the unknown aspects of their own potential and possibilities. The adaptability to explore, learn, and grow in uncharted territories becomes a transformative force in the journey of self-discovery.

In addition, submariners navigate through ambiguous underwater landscapes. In personal development, individuals often find themselves in situations marked by ambiguity and uncertainty. The skill of adaptability fosters a sense of comfort in the unknown, allowing individuals to navigate through ambiguity with a level-headed approach and a willingness to explore new possibilities.

They learn from the depths they explore. Similarly, personal development involves extracting wisdom from life's experiences, especially those encountered in the unseen depths of challenges. The adaptability to glean insights, learn from setbacks, and integrate newfound wisdom becomes a continual process in the journey of personal growth.

- **Self-Discipline: The Engine Room of Growth:**

The engine room of a submarine demands meticulous attention to every cog and gear, ensuring seamless operations.

Similarly, in personal development, self-discipline revolves around meticulous attention to daily habits.

It entails the conscious cultivation of habits that contribute to growth, well-being, and the alignment of actions with long-term goals.

The engine room signifies the commitment to a submarine's continuous operation and improvement. Likewise, self-discipline in personal development manifests as an unwavering commitment to consistent self-improvement. It involves an intentional and ongoing effort to enhance skills, broaden knowledge, and refine various aspects of the self.

Also, the engine room requires a constant supply of fuel for the submarine's journey. In personal development, daily habits become the fuel for progress. Self-discipline is reflected in the commitment to cultivate positive and constructive habits that contribute to personal and professional growth, providing the necessary energy for the journey towards self-actualization.

Turbulence in the ocean demands resilience from the submarine's systems. Similarly, self-discipline equips individuals with the resilience needed to navigate through life's challenges. It instills the mental toughness to stay the course even when faced with adversity, setbacks, or unforeseen circumstances.

The engine room operates with a consistent and rhythmic precision. In personal development, self-discipline establishes a rhythm of consistency.

It involves showing up daily, adhering to goals, and maintaining a steady pace toward growth. This rhythmic consistency becomes the driving force that propels the individual forward.

Just as the engine room ensures the optimal functioning of a submarine's mechanical systems, self-discipline ensures the optimal functioning of an individual's mental and emotional systems. It involves maintaining a balance, cultivating a positive mindset, and addressing challenges with a focused and resilient approach.

Distractions can disrupt the smooth operation of a submarine. Similarly, in personal development, self-discipline is the compass that navigates through distractions. It involves the ability to prioritize tasks, stay focused on goals, and resist the allure of immediate gratification in favor of long-term success.

Moreover, the engine room of self-discipline cultivates mental toughness—the ability to endure and persevere in the face of difficulties. This mental resilience becomes a valuable asset, allowing individuals to withstand the pressures, challenges, and uncertainties that often accompany the pursuit of personal growth.

The engine room builds and sustains the habits of excellence in submarine operations. Similarly, self-discipline in personal development involves building habits of excellence—habits that contribute to the pursuit of excellence in various aspects of life, whether personal or professional.

- **Continuous Learning: Charting New Courses:**

Submariners recognize the dynamic nature of the underwater environment, prompting continuous learning. Similarly, in personal development, individuals embrace the dynamic nature of their own growth. They understand that the landscape of life is ever-changing, requiring a commitment to ongoing learning to adapt to new challenges and opportunities.

They diversify their knowledge to enhance their understanding of the ocean's intricacies. Likewise, in personal development, continuous learning involves acquiring fresh perspectives. This may involve seeking new experiences, engaging with diverse perspectives, and broadening one's worldview to enrich the understanding of self and the world.

Subs adapt to evolving technologies to enhance their operational capabilities. Similarly, individuals in personal development adapt to technological advances and changing societal landscapes. Continuous learning involves acquiring digital literacy, understanding emerging technologies, and navigating the digital era to stay relevant in a rapidly changing world.

Furthermore, submariners remain open to new ideas that can improve their strategies and operations. In personal development, a commitment to continuous learning involves remaining open to new ideas, challenging existing beliefs, and being receptive to innovative approaches that can elevate one's personal and professional life.

They incorporate lessons learned from past operations into their future strategies. Likewise, personal development entails incorporating lessons learned from experiences and challenges into one's life. This reflective process allows individuals to refine their approaches, make informed decisions, and continually progress on their journey.

Submariners maintain a sense of curiosity and inquisitiveness to explore the unknown. In personal development, staying curious and inquisitive fuels continuous learning. It involves a proactive approach to seeking knowledge, asking questions, and exploring new avenues that contribute to intellectual, emotional, and spiritual growth.

Also, submariners exhibit flexibility in their approach based on the evolving underwater conditions. Continuous learning in personal development requires a similar flexibility. Individuals must adapt their approaches, strategies, and goals based on evolving circumstances, embracing change as an integral part of the growth process.

Moreover, submariners navigate through the depths of the ocean for discovery. Similarly, continuous learning in personal development involves navigating through personal discovery. Individuals explore new facets of themselves, uncover hidden talents, and deepen their self-awareness through a commitment to ongoing learning.

Chapter **9**

Stealth and Strategy

Submarines often operate stealthily; this can be likened to the strategic and sometimes private nature of personal goals and aspirations.

Within the puzzling profundities of the sea, where quiet rules and privileged insights lie covered up, submarines float stealthily, their nearness concealed underneath the waves. This covert maneuvering draws an captivating parallel to the key and, at times, private nature of individual objectives and goals. Submarines, with their clandestine operations and the capacity to explore undetected, offer a compelling allegory for the regularly concealed, strategic pursuits people harbor within the profundities of their claim aspirations. Much like submarines work underneath the surface, hidden from the examination of the outside world, individual objectives and goals regularly unfurl within the calm hallways of an individual's intellect, absent from the open look.

- **Concealed Ambitions:**

Much like submarines meticulously design covert operations beneath the ocean's surface, individuals craft their aspirations in the silence of their minds.

The early stages of goal formation are akin to the delicate construction of a submarine's mission, undertaken with precision and care.

This private crafting allows for the incubation of ideas, the exploration of possibilities, and the refinement of objectives away from external influences.

Submarines, shielded by the ocean's depths, remain impervious to external forces. Similarly, individuals shield their ambitions from the vulnerabilities that external exposure may bring. The sensitivity of certain objectives or the nascent stage of development prompts individuals to keep their aspirations concealed, fostering an environment where vulnerability can be shielded until the goals are robust enough to withstand external pressures.

They move stealthily, and personal goals unfurl like delicate petals in the privacy of an individual's consciousness. The decision to keep aspirations concealed may arise from a desire to allow personal growth to take root and blossom away from the spotlight. This private unfurling ensures that the goals are nurtured in an environment where authenticity and personal investment can flourish unencumbered.

The strategic concealment of submarines shields them from premature detection. Similarly, individuals shield their ambitions from premature judgments that external scrutiny might bring. The early stages of goal pursuit are fragile, and premature judgments can stifle growth. Concealing ambitions until they reach a level of maturity allows for a more robust and self-assured presentation when the time is right.

Subs surface strategically, revealing their presence with calculated precision. Likewise, individuals strategically unveil their aspirations, choosing the opportune moment for maximum impact. The strategic unveiling is not just about showcasing success; it's about aligning the revelation with a broader narrative, ensuring that the unveiling contributes to the overall trajectory of personal growth.

In the concealed chambers of submarines, authenticity is preserved from external influences. Similarly, when personal goals are kept private, individuals preserve the authenticity of their aspirations. This preservation allows for the development of goals that are true to one's values and passions without the risk of external influences diluting the authenticity of the pursuit.

They operate in seclusion beneath the waves, focusing on their mission away from external distractions. In a similar vein, the strategic concealment of personal goals allows for focused development in seclusion. Away from external pressures and distractions, individuals can dedicate their energy to nurturing their aspirations, ensuring a more meaningful and intentional journey towards realization.

The concealed ambitions of submarines mirror a dance of intention and secrecy. Similarly, personal aspirations involve a delicate dance between intention and secrecy. This dance is orchestrated to protect the purity of goals, allowing them to evolve organically before being exposed to the external world. It is a choreography of personal growth, where each step is taken with thoughtful consideration and purpose.

- **Strategic Maneuvering:**

Submarines chart their course through the ocean's vastness with meticulous precision, avoiding obstacles and potential threats. Similarly, individuals engaged in personal development strategically chart their course toward their goals. This involves a detailed plan that considers the nuances of the journey, potential challenges, and the optimal route to success. Precision in planning ensures a clear path through the complexities that may arise.

They anticipate obstacles in the form of underwater terrain and potential adversaries. In personal development, strategic maneuvering involves anticipating obstacles and challenges on the path to achieving one's goals. Individuals engage in thorough foresight, identifying potential hurdles and devising contingency plans to navigate through adversity without losing sight of the ultimate objective.

Also, submarines operate in stealth to minimize external interference. Similarly, individuals strategically minimize external interference in their pursuit of personal goals. This might involve keeping certain aspects of their aspirations private to shield them from external pressures or distractions. The strategic approach ensures that the individual's focus remains on the internal compass guiding their journey.

They adapt to changing underwater conditions to maintain their stealth. Strategic maneuvering in personal development requires individuals to adapt to changing circumstances.

Whether it's shifting priorities, unexpected challenges, or evolving aspirations, the ability to adapt with agility ensures that the pursuit of goals remains resilient and effective in the face of uncertainties.

Subs surface strategically to leverage opportunities and fulfill their mission. Similarly, individuals strategically time their actions to leverage opportunities in personal development. This involves a keen awareness of the right moments to take significant steps, unveil achievements, or collaborate with others. The strategic leveraging of opportunities enhances the effectiveness of the pursuit.

In addition, submarines carefully balance the risks and rewards associated with their maneuvers. In personal development, strategic maneuvering involves a similar balancing act. Individuals assess the risks associated with their goals, taking calculated steps that offer the potential for significant rewards. This balanced approach minimizes unnecessary risks while maximizing the potential for success.

They develop covertly beneath the ocean's surface. Similarly, personal development often involves covert growth, where individuals strategically work on themselves away from external scrutiny. This covert development allows for a genuine and unfiltered evolution, ensuring that personal growth is driven by internal motivations rather than external expectations.

In addition, submarines maintain a focus on their mission objectives during maneuvers.

Strategic maneuvering in personal development requires individuals to maintain unwavering focus on their goals. Amidst the twists and turns of the journey, the strategic approach ensures that the ultimate objective remains the guiding North Star, providing direction and purpose throughout the pursuit.

They adhere to ethical considerations in their maneuvers. In personal development, strategic maneuvering involves an ethical compass, ensuring that the pursuit of goals aligns with one's values and principles. This commitment to ethical conduct adds a layer of integrity to the strategic approach, fostering a sense of authenticity and moral responsibility.

Submarines engage in iterative learning from maneuvers to enhance future operations. Similarly, in personal development, strategic maneuvering involves continuous learning and adjustment. Individuals reflect on past experiences, learn from successes and setbacks, and adjust their strategies accordingly. This iterative process ensures that the approach to personal goals becomes increasingly refined and effective over time.

- **Shielding from External Pressures:**

Subs operate as sanctuaries beneath the ocean's surface, shielded from the external elements. Similarly, individuals carve out a sanctuary for their authentic aspirations, shielded from external pressures.

This sanctuary becomes a space where personal goals can develop organically, uninfluenced by external expectations, providing a fertile ground for the germination of authentic ambitions.

Also, beneath the waves, experience uninhibited movement away from external scrutiny. In personal development, individuals seek a similar uninhibited growth, shielded from external pressures that may inhibit their progress. This shielding allows for an exploration of personal growth without the constant gaze of external judgment, fostering an environment where individuals can genuinely discover and refine their aspirations.

Moreover, submarines, shielded beneath the ocean's surface, operate with intrinsic motivation. Similarly, shielding personal goals from external pressures preserves intrinsic motivation. When external expectations and opinions are kept at bay, individuals are free to pursue their goals driven by internal passion, values, and a genuine desire for personal fulfillment rather than conforming to external benchmarks.

Submarines operate in the serenity beneath the waves, shielded from external turbulence. Shielding personal aspirations creates a similar serene environment for focused development. Away from external turbulence, individuals can dedicate their energy to the intricate development of their goals, ensuring that the pursuit is guided by an inner compass rather than being swayed by the chaotic currents of external influences.

They shield themselves from external distractions in their submerged state. Similarly, individuals, by shielding their aspirations, mitigate external distractions that may divert them from their path. This intentional shielding ensures that the pursuit of personal goals remains undeterred by external noise, allowing for a more immersive and concentrated journey towards the realization of authentic aspirations.

Submarines, shielded from external forces, explore the depths without hindrance. Shielding personal aspirations enables individuals to explore the depths of their potential without external hindrance. This unhindered exploration fosters a deeper understanding of one's capabilities, passions, and unique strengths, paving the way for a more authentic and fulfilling personal development journey.

Furthermore, submarines shield themselves from the ocean's external forces. In personal development, individuals shield their aspirations against societal expectations. This protection becomes a shield against the often rigid norms and expectations of society, allowing individuals to forge their own path without succumbing to external pressures that might dictate their goals based on societal norms rather than personal authenticity.

Also, submarines, shielded from external forces, maintain their individual identity. Shielding personal goals cultivates a similar individual identity for individuals.

It allows them to define success and fulfillment based on their unique values, beliefs, and aspirations rather than conforming to external definitions of achievement that may not align with their true sense of self.

- **Unveiling Success at the Right Time:**

Submarines master the art of timing, surfacing strategically to achieve their mission objectives. Similarly, individuals navigating personal development master the art of unveiling success at the right time. Timing becomes a crucial element in the orchestration of their journey, ensuring that achievements are shared when they carry the most impact and align with the overarching narrative of their personal growth.

Also, submarines surface to accomplish specific milestones. In personal development, individuals align the unveiling of success with their personal milestones. Whether it's completing a significant project, achieving a career milestone, or reaching a personal goal, the strategic unveiling becomes a celebration of these achievements, marking pivotal moments in their journey.

They foster a sense of anticipation with their strategic surfacing. Similarly, individuals unveil their successes in a way that cultivates anticipation. This deliberate approach creates a buzz around their accomplishments, allowing for a more impactful and memorable sharing of success that resonates with those who have been following their journey.

Moreover, submarines maintain control over their operations. In personal development, individuals maintain control over the narrative surrounding their aspirations.

Choosing when to unveil success allows them to shape the story in a way that aligns with their values, vision, and personal growth trajectory. It ensures that external perspectives do not overshadow the authentic narrative they wish to convey.

Subs avoid premature revelations to safeguard their missions. Similarly, individuals avoid premature revelations of their successes. This cautious approach prevents premature judgments, allowing accomplishments to unfold fully and ensuring that they are shared with the world when they have reached a level of maturity and completeness.

They emphasize the importance of the journey alongside mission success. In personal development, individuals emphasize their journey by strategically unveiling success. It's not just about the destination; it's about showcasing the milestones, lessons learned, and personal growth achieved along the way. The intentional revelation becomes a narrative that goes beyond mere achievement.

.

Chapter **10**

Deep-Sea Missions

Submarines undertake specific missions, serving as a metaphor for setting and pursuing deep, meaningful personal objectives.

Within the tremendous field of the ocean's covered up domains, submarines set out on particular missions, wandering into the deep profundities with a exact reason. These missions are a confirmation to human resourcefulness, as these vessels explore the obscure, equipped with a significant sense of course and the assurance to fulfill characterized goals. This significant travel into the submerged world gives a compelling representation for people setting and seeking after deep, meaningful individual goals within the complex scene of personal advancement. Much like submarines charting courses within the ocean's profundities, people explore the complexities of their claim lives, moved by a vision of reason and guided by the interest of significant individual missions.

- **Defining the Destination:**

Submarines, before setting sail, undergo meticulous inspections, ensuring every component aligns with the mission ahead. Similarly, individuals engage in visionary introspection, delving deep into the recesses of their minds and hearts.

This introspective phase involves a profound exploration of personal aspirations, desires, and the underlying motivations that will shape the defined destination. It's about understanding the self at a fundamental level, uncovering the latent dreams that will guide the entire personal development journey.

They meticulously plan each detail of their missions, and in personal development, this meticulousness is mirrored in goal-setting precision. Individuals translate their introspective insights into tangible goals—clear, specific, and aligned with the envisioned destination. These goals act as navigational waypoints, guiding the journey with clarity and purpose. Whether they pertain to career achievements, personal relationships, or internal self-mastery, these goals become the milestones that mark progress toward the defined destination.

Also, submarines align their missions with strategic objectives, and individuals align their personal development journey with deeply held values. The defined destination is not just a superficial aspiration; it's a place that resonates with one's core beliefs, principles, and authentic self. Aligning with personal values ensures that the journey is not only about reaching a destination but also about fostering a sense of fulfillment and authenticity in the pursuit.

Subs follow blueprints that detail every aspect of their design, and similarly, individuals craft a blueprint for their personal growth.

This involves developing a strategic plan that outlines the steps, milestones, and resources needed to reach the defined destination. The blueprint becomes a dynamic guide, allowing for adaptability while maintaining the overarching vision. It considers potential challenges, alternative routes, and the continuous refinement of goals to ensure a resilient and evolving path forward.

They embark on missions with a clear sense of purpose, and individuals, in defining their destination, establish a profound sense of purpose. This purpose serves as the driving force behind every action, decision, and perseverance along the journey. It becomes the motivational core that fuels resilience during challenges and propels individuals forward. The clarity of purpose transforms the defined destination from a distant dream into a compelling reality that beckons the individual to strive for continual self-improvement.

- **Precision in Goal Formulation:**

Subs outline specific mission objectives, and in personal development, goals require the same level of specificity. Instead of vague aspirations, individuals articulate precisely what they aim to achieve. Specificity clarifies the direction, leaving no room for ambiguity. For example, a goal might evolve from a generic desire to "improve fitness" to the specific target of "running a half-marathon within the next six months."

Also, submarines have precise instruments to measure their progress, and similarly, personal development goals need measurable criteria.

Establishing clear metrics allows individuals to track their advancement objectively. Whether it's tracking daily word counts for a writing goal or monitoring incremental weight loss for a fitness objective, measurability provides tangible evidence of progress.

Moreover, submarines set achievable mission goals, avoiding unrealistic expectations. In personal development, goals must be attainable within the individual's capabilities and resources. While it's crucial to aim high, setting objectives that are too ambitious can lead to frustration and demotivation. Goals should be challenging yet within the realm of feasibility, encouraging a steady and sustainable pace of progress.

Submarines align their missions with overarching strategic objectives, and personal development goals must align with the broader vision. Each goal should contribute meaningfully to the individual's overall mission. Relevance ensures that efforts are directed toward outcomes that truly matter and resonate with the individual's values and aspirations.

They adhere to strict timelines for their missions, and personal development goals benefit from the same time-bound structure. Establishing deadlines creates a sense of urgency and fosters commitment. Individuals set specific timeframes for achieving their goals, whether short-term, medium-term, or long-term, providing a framework for progress assessment and ensuring a dynamic and evolving journey.

- **Navigating the Unknown:**

Submarines traverse uncharted waters, and individuals in personal development embrace unfamiliar realms. The pursuit of deep, meaningful objectives often leads individuals beyond their comfort zones into unexplored territories. This entails stepping into the unknown, whether it's a career change, a new relationship, or a personal challenge, requiring a readiness to explore uncharted aspects of oneself and the world.

They confront uncertainties beneath the ocean's surface, and similarly, personal development involves facing uncertainties head-on. The journey towards profound objectives is marked by unpredictability, ambiguity, and the absence of a predetermined path. Confronting uncertainties demands a resilient mindset—a willingness to navigate the ambiguity without succumbing to fear or hesitation.

Subs endure the pressure of the unknown depths, and in personal development, resilience becomes a cornerstone. Individuals encounter challenges, setbacks, and moments of doubt as they tread through unfamiliar territories. Resilience allows them to withstand the pressures, bounce back from setbacks, and view challenges not as roadblocks but as opportunities for growth and self-discovery.

Also, submarines adapt to the ever-changing underwater environment, and adaptability is equally crucial in personal development. The unknown territories may require shifts in strategies, perspectives, or even goals.

Individuals cultivate adaptability, embracing change with an open mind and adjusting their approach as the journey unfolds. This dynamic adaptability ensures a responsive navigation through the intricacies of personal growth.

They confront the unknown with courage, and in personal development, courage is the beacon that guides individuals through uncharted territories. Stepping into the unknown requires a boldness to face fears, uncertainties, and potential risks. Coupled with courage is curiosity—a genuine desire to explore, learn, and extract wisdom from the unknown. This combination propels individuals forward, transforming the unknown from a daunting challenge into an exciting adventure.

- **Strategic Course Corrections:**

Submarines encounter unexpected challenges in the depths, and individuals, in their personal development journey, face unforeseen challenges. These challenges can manifest as setbacks, obstacles, or unforeseen complexities that disrupt the original trajectory. The recognition of challenges as inherent to the journey prompts individuals to approach them not as roadblocks but as opportunities for recalibration and growth.

They adapt to shifting underwater circumstances, and personal development demands a similar adaptability. Circumstances in life are seldom static; they evolve, shift, and sometimes take unexpected turns.

Individuals must possess the flexibility to adapt their plans in response to these shifts without compromising the ultimate vision. This adaptability ensures that the pursuit of deep, meaningful objectives remains relevant and effective.

Subs maintain their ultimate mission objectives, and in personal development, preserving the ultimate destination is paramount. While strategic course corrections are necessary, individuals must ensure that these adjustments align with the overarching vision. The ultimate destination serves as the North Star, providing guidance even amidst adjustments. This requires a delicate balance—making changes without losing sight of the profound personal mission and the transformative destination.

Also, submarines execute skillful maneuvers to stay on course, and individuals in personal development engage in strategic adjustments without losing momentum. Skilled navigators understand that course corrections should be executed seamlessly to maintain the flow of progress. Likewise, individuals must make strategic adjustments with precision, ensuring that the momentum towards their profound personal missions remains strong.

They learn from course corrections to enhance future missions, and individuals in personal development extract valuable lessons from strategic adjustments.

Each correction becomes an opportunity for learning, growth, and refinement. Understanding the factors that led to the need for adjustment equips individuals with insights that can enhance their resilience, adaptability, and strategic decision-making for future endeavors.

- **Mission Fulfillment and Reflection:**

Submarines returning from missions understand the significance extends beyond reaching a destination. Similarly, individuals achieving profound objectives recognize that the essence of personal development lies not solely in the destination but in the entire journey. Mission fulfillment is the realization that the transformative experiences, challenges, and growth encountered along the way contribute profoundly to the overall narrative.

They engage in a reflective pause upon returning, and individuals in personal development similarly pause to reflect. This phase allows individuals to absorb the impact of their achievements, to appreciate the distance traveled, and to assimilate the wisdom gained. It's a moment of introspection that goes beyond celebration, delving into the deeper layers of personal evolution.

Subs extract lessons from their missions, and individuals extract valuable lessons from the achievement of profound objectives. Reflection involves a critical examination of the challenges faced, the strategies employed, and the moments of resilience.

These lessons become guiding principles for future endeavors, offering insights that contribute to enhanced self-awareness and continuous improvement.

Submarines returning acknowledge their growth, and individuals acknowledge personal growth in the reflective phase. The attainment of deep, meaningful objectives is a testament to the individual's evolution—mentally, emotionally, and sometimes spiritually. Recognizing this growth is essential for building confidence, fostering a positive self-image, and reinforcing the belief in one's ability to navigate future challenges.

They returning from missions deepen their understanding of the ocean's depths, and individuals deepen their understanding of themselves. The reflective process in personal development allows individuals to explore the layers of their thoughts, emotions, and reactions during the pursuit of profound goals. This deeper self-understanding becomes a cornerstone for continued self-discovery and refinement.

Also, submarines insights are integrated into future missions, and personal development insights are seamlessly woven into the ongoing evolution. The reflective phase is not a conclusion but a bridge to what lies ahead. Individuals integrate the lessons learned into their ongoing personal development journey, ensuring that each accomplishment becomes a stepping stone for future growth.

They utilize insights for strategic planning, and individuals employ the reflective phase for future endeavors. The lessons learned from the achievement of profound objectives become strategic markers. Individuals meticulously plan their next steps, leveraging newfound insights to navigate the evolving landscape of personal development with purpose and foresight.

Subs fortify themselves for future challenges, and individuals, through reflection, build resilience for what lies ahead. Recognizing the challenges overcome during the pursuit of profound goals, individuals reinforce their mental and emotional fortitude. This resilience becomes a valuable asset, empowering them to face future challenges with a sense of strength and optimism.

Chapter 11

Maintenance and Upkeep

Regular maintenance is crucial for a submarine's functionality, reminiscent of the need for consistent self-care and mental health upkeep.

Within the cryptic profundities of the sea, where light battles to enter and puzzles proliferate, submarines noiselessly explore, carrying out complicated missions and diving into the obscure. In the midst of the challenges of this submerged world, a basic viewpoint that guarantees the submarine's operational ability is regular maintenance. Much just like the fastidious care presented upon these vessels, the similarity between a submarine's normal upkeep and the basic of steady self-care and mental wellbeing upkeep in people uncovers a significant parallelism. This comparison rises above the mechanical and expands into the domains of individual well-being, underlining the importance of proactive consideration to guarantee ideal usefulness. Fair as submarines require precise checks and mediations to courageous the erratic maritime profundities, people as well must prioritize self-care and mental wellbeing support to explore the complexities of life viably.

- **Preventive Vigilance:**

Submarine crews conduct routine inspections and preventive measures, meticulously examining each component of the vessel.

This includes checking the integrity of hull structures, assessing propulsion systems, and ensuring that navigation instruments are finely tuned. The preventive approach aims to identify potential issues before they escalate, safeguarding the submarine from unexpected breakdowns, particularly during critical missions.

Parallelly, in the realm of personal well-being, individuals engage in proactive self-assessment and preventive measures. This involves regular introspection and self-awareness to identify emotional and psychological well-being indicators. Taking preventive measures may include stress management techniques, mindfulness practices, and the cultivation of healthy coping mechanisms. This proactive approach aims to maintain emotional resilience and prevent the escalation of mental health challenges.

The analogous principles between submarine maintenance and personal well-being reside in the acknowledgment that both systems, whether mechanical or human, are susceptible to wear and tear. The intention is not merely to react to problems as they arise but to anticipate and prevent them from occurring in the first place. Both contexts emphasize the value of being ahead of potential challenges, ensuring a state of optimal functionality.

Submarine crews comprehend that the prevention of malfunctions is not only cost-effective but also crucial for risk mitigation. Identifying vulnerabilities before they escalate minimizes the chances of critical failures, enhancing the safety and reliability of the vessel.

This preventive mindset is integral to the overall success and efficiency of submarine operations.

Similarly, in personal well-being, proactive mental health practices are recognized as cost-effective investments in one's overall quality of life. Regular self-assessment and the adoption of preventive measures, such as maintaining a balanced lifestyle, seeking social support, and addressing stressors promptly, contribute to emotional well-being. This proactive mindset aligns with the understanding that preventing mental health challenges is more manageable than addressing them after reaching a critical point.

The cultivation of a preventive mindset is a shared philosophy between submarines and personal well-being. In submarines, this is achieved through routine maintenance protocols, adherence to checklists, and the implementation of standardized preventive measures. Likewise, individuals cultivate a preventive mindset through self-awareness, mental health check-ins, and the adoption of healthy lifestyle habits.

The common goal in both submarine maintenance and personal well-being is optimal functionality. Whether it is the efficient operation of a submarine or the well-being of an individual, the objective is to function at the highest level possible. Preventive vigilance becomes the means to achieve this goal, acknowledging that early intervention and regular maintenance contribute to sustained performance and resilience.

- **Identifying Vulnerabilities:**

Within submarine maintenance, regular inspections are conducted to scrutinize every aspect of the vessel's structure and systems. This involves examining the hull for signs of wear, assessing the integrity of propulsion systems, and ensuring the functionality of critical instruments. The objective is to identify vulnerabilities, potential weak points, or areas requiring attention before they develop into critical issues that could compromise the submarine's operational integrity.

In the realm of personal well-being, individuals engage in consistent self-care practices that include emotional vulnerability assessments. This involves introspection and self-awareness to recognize emotional vulnerabilities and potential stressors. By actively identifying areas of emotional sensitivity or triggers, individuals can proactively address and manage these aspects before they escalate into more significant mental health challenges.

The submarine's approach to identifying vulnerabilities aligns with a proactive mindset. The focus is not solely on reacting to problems as they arise but on actively seeking out potential weaknesses through regular inspections. This proactive approach is essential for maintaining the submarine's operational readiness and preventing unexpected failures during critical missions.

Similarly, in personal well-being, a proactive approach involves regular self-assessment to recognize emotional vulnerabilities.

This may include monitoring stress levels, understanding triggers for anxiety or depression, and identifying patterns of behavior that could indicate potential challenges. By proactively addressing these vulnerabilities, individuals enhance their emotional resilience and well-being.

The identification of vulnerabilities in submarines facilitates timely intervention. When potential issues are recognized early through inspections, the necessary measures can be taken to address them before they escalate. This timely intervention is critical for preventing major malfunctions and ensuring the continued functionality of the submarine.

In personal well-being, recognizing emotional vulnerabilities allows for timely intervention. Whether through seeking support from friends and family, practicing stress management techniques, or accessing professional mental health resources, individuals can address challenges before they become overwhelming. This timely intervention contributes to maintaining emotional well-being and preventing the exacerbation of mental health issues.

- **Adaptability to Change:**

In the realm of submarine maintenance, adaptability is essential to keep pace with evolving technologies and changing environmental conditions. Submarines must undergo updates and modifications to integrate the latest advancements in navigation, communication, and safety systems.

Additionally, they must adapt to diverse underwater environments, adjusting their operational strategies based on factors such as water temperature, pressure, and potential threats.

Similarly, in personal well-being, adaptability involves tailoring self-care practices to changing life circumstances. Individuals encounter various life stages, career transitions, and personal challenges that necessitate adjustments in their well-being routines. Adapting self-care practices involves recognizing the evolving needs of one's mental and emotional health, modifying coping mechanisms, and embracing new strategies to navigate life's twists and turns.

Submarines proactively evolve by integrating the latest technologies and adapting to emerging threats. Regular updates ensure that the vessels remain technologically competitive and resilient in the face of changing geopolitical landscapes. This proactive approach allows submarines to maintain their effectiveness and adaptability to diverse mission requirements.

In personal well-being, a proactive approach to adaptation involves anticipating life changes and adjusting self-care practices accordingly. This might include modifying mindfulness techniques, exercise routines, or stress management strategies to align with shifting priorities, responsibilities, or personal goals. Proactively evolving self-care practices enhances an individual's ability to cope with new challenges and promotes a continuous state of well-being.

Submarines operate in environments characterized by uncertainties, requiring constant adaptation to unforeseen challenges. From underwater terrain variations to potential security threats, the ability to navigate uncertainties demands flexibility and quick decision-making. Submariners are trained to adapt protocols and strategies in response to unexpected situations.

Life is inherently uncertain, and individuals face a multitude of unpredictable events. Adapting self-care practices to life's uncertainties involves developing a mindset that embraces change and uncertainty. This adaptability allows individuals to navigate challenges with resilience, maintaining mental well-being even in the face of unforeseen circumstances.

Submarine protocols are designed with flexibility, allowing crews to adjust operational plans based on real-time information. This flexibility ensures that submarines can respond effectively to dynamic situations, making on-the-fly decisions to optimize their performance.

Similarly, personal well-being benefits from flexible self-care strategies. While foundational practices like regular exercise and healthy eating remain constant, the specific strategies may need adjustment. Flexibility in self-care acknowledges that what works during one phase of life may require modification to address changing needs, ensuring sustained mental and emotional well-being.

- **Holistic Approach:**

In the realm of submarine maintenance, a holistic approach is imperative to cover all facets of the submarine's functionality. This includes meticulous attention to mechanical components, navigation systems, communication infrastructure, and overall structural integrity. A comprehensive examination ensures that every aspect contributes synergistically to the submarine's operational excellence.

Parallelly, in personal well-being, adopting a holistic approach means addressing physical, emotional, and psychological dimensions. This comprehensive self-care strategy recognizes that well-being extends beyond mere physical health. Emotional and psychological aspects are equally vital, necessitating a well-rounded approach that considers mental resilience, emotional balance, and overall psychological well-being.

In submarines, a holistic approach involves not only routine checks but also in-depth examinations of mechanical and technical components. From propulsion systems to sonar capabilities, each element is scrutinized to ensure optimal functionality. This meticulous inspection extends to preventive maintenance and timely replacements to preempt potential breakdowns.

Similarly, in personal well-being, the physical dimension is a crucial component of the holistic approach. Engaging in regular exercise, maintaining a balanced diet, and ensuring adequate sleep are foundational aspects.

These practices contribute to physical health, energy levels, and overall vitality, forming the cornerstone of a comprehensive self-care routine.

Navigation systems in submarines play a pivotal role in guiding the vessel through underwater terrains. A holistic approach encompasses the inspection, calibration, and constant improvement of these systems to ensure precise navigation, especially in challenging conditions. This involves staying abreast of technological advancements to enhance navigational capabilities.

The holistic self-care approach recognizes the significance of emotional well-being. Managing stress, cultivating positive emotions, and fostering emotional resilience are integral components. Practices such as mindfulness, meditation, and emotional expression contribute to the cultivation of emotional well-being, creating a robust foundation for overall health.

Submarine communication infrastructure is critical for effective collaboration and response during missions. A holistic approach involves assessing and maintaining communication systems to ensure seamless connectivity. Protocols for clear communication are integral, promoting effective information exchange among crew members.

Psychological well-being is a key dimension in the holistic self-care approach. This involves self-reflection, managing thoughts and beliefs, and fostering a positive mindset. Practices like therapy, journaling, or engaging in activities that promote mental well-being contribute to the holistic nurturing of the psyche.

The structural integrity of a submarine is paramount for its safety and functionality. A holistic approach in maintenance includes regular inspections of the hull, pressure systems, and other structural elements. Strengthening and reinforcing these components prevent structural vulnerabilities and ensure the overall resilience of the vessel.

The holistic approach in personal well-being involves balancing physical, emotional, and psychological elements. Recognizing the interconnectedness of these dimensions, individuals engage in activities that promote balance and harmony. This might include hobbies, social connections, and practices that address both emotional and psychological needs.

Chapter 12

Emergency Procedures

Submarines are equipped with protocols for crisis situations, analogous to coping mechanisms in times of personal distress.

Within the puzzling profundities of the sea, where weight is tireless and the environment is eccentric, submarines explore with exactness and reason. Prepared with cutting-edge innovation and a group prepared for difficulty, these vessels are not as it were pioneers but guardians of steadiness within the confront of potential emergencies. So also, people explore the complexities of life, experiencing minutes of individual trouble that request versatility and vital reactions. The relationship between submarines' crisis protocols and adapting instruments in individual trials may be a significant investigation into the human experience—unveiling the techniques that empower not fair survival but a triumphant rise from the profundities of misfortune.

- **Structured Response to Turbulence:**

Subs possess blueprints for crisis response, outlining step-by-step procedures. Likewise, individuals can construct a blueprint for emotional resilience, developing a comprehensive plan to navigate and overcome personal challenges.

Submarines' crisis protocols include identifying stress triggers. Individuals can apply this by recognizing their stress triggers, allowing them to proactively address and mitigate the impact of potential emotional turbulence. Just as submarines activate crisis protocols swiftly, individuals can learn to initiate coping mechanisms promptly when faced with emotional turbulence. Timely responses enhance the effectiveness of coping strategies.

They maintain clear navigation amidst turbulent conditions. Individuals can adopt structured coping mechanisms as their navigational tools, providing clarity and direction when emotions become chaotic.

Also, submarines engage in predictive planning for potential storms. Individuals, too, can foresee challenging times and implement proactive coping mechanisms, preparing themselves emotionally for the storms that life may bring.

- **Rapid Decision-Making in Crisis:**

Submarines assess various signals during crises. Similarly, individuals, through coping mechanisms, learn to assess their emotional signals swiftly, recognizing the onset of distress and the need for immediate attention. They maintain clarity in crisis scenarios. Personal coping mechanisms aim to provide individuals with mental clarity amidst emotional turbulence, enabling them to make decisions with a focused and rational mindset.

Moreover, submarines prioritize immediate needs during crises. In personal coping, individuals learn to prioritize their immediate emotional needs, addressing pressing concerns to stabilize their mental well-being. Subs strategically implement crisis protocols. Similarly, individuals strategically apply coping tools, selecting the most relevant and effective methods to address specific emotional challenges promptly.

Submarines take decisive actions for regulation during crises. Personal coping mechanisms empower individuals to take decisive actions for emotional regulation, ensuring a swift return to a balanced and stable emotional state.

They integrate past learning into crisis responses. In personal coping, individuals draw upon past experiences and lessons learned, utilizing this knowledge to make informed decisions in the midst of emotional turmoil.

- **Communication as a Lifeline:**

Submarines recognize the importance of emotional connection in crisis communication. Similarly, individuals can develop coping mechanisms that involve establishing emotional connections—reaching out to those who provide a sense of understanding and empathy. They articulate their operational states during crises. Coping mechanisms can include the skill of articulating emotional states, allowing individuals to express their feelings with clarity, fostering a better understanding of their internal struggles.

They operate within a support network. Personal coping mechanisms encourage individuals to create and strengthen their support networks, acknowledging the significance of friends, family, and mental health professionals in navigating through crises. Also, submarines prioritize open dialogue for effective communication. Coping mechanisms involve encouraging open dialogue about emotions, enabling individuals to express their thoughts and concerns without judgment or inhibition.

Subs may seek professional guidance during crises. Similarly, coping mechanisms can include reaching out to mental health professionals, providing individuals with expert support and strategies for managing and overcoming personal distress. They value active listening in crisis communication. Personal coping mechanisms involve developing active listening skills, allowing individuals to better understand the perspectives and concerns of those offering support.

They engage in empathetic communication. Coping mechanisms focus on empathetic communication, where individuals express understanding and compassion towards themselves and others, fostering a positive and supportive environment. Submarines prioritize clarity in expressing needs during crises. Coping mechanisms teach individuals to articulate their needs clearly, helping them convey how others can provide effective support.

Moreover, submarines utilize diverse communication channels. Personal coping mechanisms involve recognizing and utilizing various communication channels, such as verbal expression, written communication, or creative outlets, based on individual preferences.

They develop crisis communication plans. Similarly, coping mechanisms may involve pre-established communication plans during challenging times, ensuring individuals have a strategy for reaching out to their support network.

Submarines prioritize timely communication in crises. Coping mechanisms stress the importance of timely communication, urging individuals not to delay seeking support when facing emotional challenges.

Also, submarines build resilient relationships through effective communication. Personal coping mechanisms aim to build resilient relationships, emphasizing communication as a foundation for strong, supportive connections.

Subs engage in shared decision-making during crises. Coping mechanisms involve sharing decision-making responsibilities with trusted individuals, fostering a collaborative approach to navigating through personal distress.

Furthermore, submarines create safe spaces for communication. Personal coping mechanisms include the creation of safe spaces—environments where individuals feel comfortable expressing their emotions without fear of judgment.

Submarines provide and receive feedback for continuous improvement. Coping mechanisms encourage individuals to provide and receive constructive feedback in communication, enhancing the effectiveness of support networks.

They express gratitude for effective communication. In personal coping, individuals can express gratitude for the support they receive, fostering a positive and appreciative atmosphere within their relationships.

Submarines navigate difficult conversations during crises. Coping mechanisms include skills for facilitating difficult conversations, enabling individuals to address challenging topics with sensitivity and clarity.

Also, submarines respect boundaries in communication. Personal coping mechanisms emphasize the importance of respecting personal boundaries, ensuring that individuals communicate in a manner that considers the comfort and preferences of those offering support.

Submarines use non-verbal cues in communication. Coping mechanisms recognize the significance of non-verbal communication—body language, gestures, and expressions—in conveying emotions when words may fall short.

They encourage reciprocal communication. Personal coping mechanisms involve fostering reciprocal communication, where individuals both share their struggles and actively listen to others, creating a balanced and supportive exchange.

- **Adaptable Coping Mechanisms:**

Submarines' crisis protocols emphasize the need to adapt to changing circumstances swiftly. Similarly, adaptable coping mechanisms involve cultivating a mindset that embraces change rather than resisting it. Being open to new approaches and strategies enhances an individual's ability to navigate evolving challenges.

Adaptable coping mechanisms are essential for developing a dynamic stress response. Instead of relying on fixed reactions, individuals can cultivate responses that adjust to the intensity and nature of the stressor. This adaptability allows for a more nuanced and effective approach to managing stress.

Subs tailor crisis protocols to specific situations, and individuals can do the same with their coping strategies. Adaptable mechanisms involve the ability to tailor responses based on the unique aspects of each challenge, recognizing that a one-size-fits-all approach may not be effective.

Practicing mindfulness fosters adaptability by anchoring individuals in the present moment. Adaptable coping mechanisms include cultivating awareness of current emotions and stressors, allowing for real-time adjustments to coping strategies based on the immediate context.

Adaptable coping involves learning from past experiences. Individuals can reflect on what coping strategies worked in similar situations and make informed adjustments for future challenges.

This iterative learning process enhances adaptability over time.

Setting flexible goals is a key aspect of adaptable coping. Instead of rigid objectives, individuals can establish goals that allow for adjustments based on evolving circumstances. This flexibility ensures that the pursuit of objectives remains realistic and achievable.

Resilience is a cornerstone of adaptable coping. Building resilience involves developing the capacity to bounce back from setbacks and adapt positively to adversity. Resilient individuals are better equipped to adjust their coping strategies in the face of unexpected challenges.

Submarines employ creative problem-solving during crises, and individuals can apply this concept to coping mechanisms. Adaptable coping involves thinking creatively about challenges, exploring innovative solutions, and being open to unconventional approaches for managing stress and distress.

Adaptable coping requires finding a balance between exerting control and accepting what cannot be changed. Individuals should discern when to take proactive steps to manage stressors and when to practice acceptance, adjusting their coping strategies accordingly.

Adaptable coping involves regular self-assessment. Individuals should assess their emotional well-being, stress levels, and the effectiveness of current coping mechanisms. This ongoing evaluation allows for timely adjustments based on changing internal and external factors.

Embracing new coping tools is crucial for adaptability. Individuals should be open to exploring and integrating new techniques and strategies that align with their evolving understanding of personal well-being and stress management.

Adaptable coping recognizes the intricate connection between the mind and body. Strategies that promote physical well-being, such as exercise or relaxation techniques, can be adjusted based on the individual's current physical and emotional state.

Individuals can create a coping plan that is adaptable. This involves outlining various strategies and regularly revisiting and modifying the plan based on changing circumstances, ensuring its relevance and effectiveness over time.

Adaptable coping extends to social support networks. Recognizing when to seek support, adjusting the level of communication, and diversifying sources of support contribute to a more flexible and effective coping approach.

Coping techniques should be personalized to fit individual preferences and needs. Adaptable coping involves experimenting with different approaches and customizing them to align with the individual's unique personality, preferences, and lifestyle.

Effectively managing time for coping activities is part of adaptability. Individuals should adjust their coping routines based on the demands of daily life, ensuring that these activities remain feasible and sustainable within evolving schedules.

Adaptable coping includes experimenting with stress-reduction methods. Trying out different techniques, assessing their impact, and adjusting the repertoire of stress-reduction tools contribute to a more adaptable and effective coping toolkit.

Coping flexibility is a skill that individuals can develop. This involves consciously cultivating the ability to switch between coping strategies based on the specific demands of different situations, enhancing overall adaptability.

Chapter **13**

The Silent Service

The "silent service" designation of submarines reflects the often-unrecognized inner work individuals do that goes unnoticed by others.
Within the tremendous scope of the world's seas, a special classification is given to submarines – the "quiet benefit." This title typifies the surreptitious nature of their operations, where these submerged vessels move stealthily underneath the surface, their activities regularly concealed from the prying eyes of the world over. Be that as it may, past the maritime domain, the representation of the "noiseless benefit" amplifies into the complexities of human involvement. It serves as a strong update of the often-unrecognized inward work that people constantly embrace, work that regularly goes unnoticed by those around them. This reflective travel mirrors the quiet and single nature of submarine operations, highlighting the significant profundity of individual growth and strength developed within the quietude of one's internal world.

- **Unseen Struggles and Triumphs:**

The clandestine movements of submarines beneath the ocean's surface draw a compelling parallel to the unseen struggles and triumphs that unfold within the human experience.

Much like submarines operate away from the gaze of the world, individuals navigate the complex waters of their personal journeys in a silent and introspective manner. The battles fought within the corridors of the mind, the victories achieved in moments of solitude, and the continuous quest for self-improvement all constitute a form of silent service to personal growth.

Within the private confines of their emotional and psychological depths, individuals grapple with challenges that often go unnoticed by external observers. These challenges may range from overcoming deep-seated fears and insecurities to navigating the intricate complexities of relationships and self-discovery. Just as submarines encounter obstacles beneath the surface, individuals confront and surmount their own internal barriers, often without public acknowledgment.

The victories achieved in these private struggles are akin to the successful execution of a submarine mission. Individuals celebrate small triumphs—moments of resilience, self-discovery, or personal growth—that contribute significantly to their overall development. These triumphs might include overcoming a long-standing fear, breaking through self-imposed limitations, or achieving personal milestones that hold profound meaning.

The silent service to personal growth involves more than just overcoming challenges; it encompasses the continuous commitment to self-improvement.

In the quiet recesses of introspection, individuals embark on a journey to conquer their inner demons, hone their strengths, and cultivate virtues that contribute to their overall well-being. The silent battles fought within become the crucible for personal transformation, forging individuals into more resilient, self-aware, and empathetic beings.

- **Quiet Resilience in Adversity:**

The term "silent service" not only characterizes the stealthy operations of submarines beneath the ocean's surface but also encapsulates the resilient spirit that defines these vessels. Similarly, individuals demonstrate a quiet resilience in the face of adversity, embodying an internal fortitude that becomes the driving force propelling them forward during challenging times. This silent perseverance, forged through self-reflection and inner strength, is a powerful yet often unnoticed aspect of their character, instrumental in navigating life's storms.

In the world of submarines, the quiet resilience is evident in their ability to operate stealthily and endure external pressures without drawing attention. Similarly, individuals exhibit a profound strength that enables them to weather the storms of life without necessarily broadcasting their struggles to the external world. This resilience is a product of internal fortitude, shaped through moments of introspection, self-discovery, and the silent battles fought within the recesses of the mind.

The quiet resilience of submarines is tested in the face of adversities such as challenging weather conditions, potential security threats, or technical malfunctions. Similarly, individuals face a myriad of challenges in their personal journeys—be it setbacks, disappointments, or unforeseen circumstances. The quiet resilience cultivated within them serves as a steadfast anchor, allowing them to navigate through the tumultuous seas of life with grace and determination.

Much like submarines operate with a sense of purpose despite the silent nature of their service, individuals draw on a quiet sense of purpose that propels them forward during adversity. The internal fortitude gained through self-reflection and inner strength becomes a guiding light, helping individuals persevere in the face of challenges. This quiet resilience, though unspoken, is a testament to their ability to endure, adapt, and emerge stronger from life's tribulations.

- **Invisible Acts of Kindness:**

In the realm of submarines, their missions unfold with a cloak of invisibility, operating in stealth beneath the ocean's surface. This parallels the often-unseen acts of kindness that individuals engage in daily. Whether it's a supportive gesture, a listening ear, or a small act of generosity, these silent services contribute significantly to the well-being of others. Individuals, through their often-unrecognized kindness, become architects of positivity, creating ripples that subtly but profoundly impact their communities.

Submarines execute their missions with an emphasis on remaining unseen, and in a similar vein, individuals perform acts of kindness without seeking recognition or praise. The quiet support they offer, whether in helping a neighbor, comforting a friend, or lending a helping hand, echoes the silent but impactful nature of submarine operations. These invisible acts of kindness are the threads that weave the fabric of compassionate communities.

Much like submarines navigate the depths of the ocean with a commitment to remaining unnoticed, individuals engage in unseen acts of kindness as a part of their daily lives. The humility embedded in these gestures is reminiscent of the quiet strength exhibited by submarines in fulfilling their missions without drawing attention. Individuals, through their invisible acts of kindness, become unsung heroes, fostering a culture of compassion that uplifts those around them.

Invisible acts of kindness have a cumulative effect, creating a positive atmosphere that extends far beyond the immediate recipients. Just as submarines operate quietly to fulfill their missions, individuals, through their subtle but impactful deeds, contribute to the creation of harmonious communities. The unseen support, understanding, and empathy they offer become integral elements that strengthen the social fabric and promote a culture of mutual care and respect.

The parallel between submarines executing missions in stealth and individuals performing invisible acts of kindness lies in the deliberate choice to operate without seeking the spotlight.

Both scenarios underscore the idea that impactful actions do not always need grand gestures or public recognition. The silent services, whether in the depths of the ocean or the corners of daily life, embody a commitment to making a positive difference without the need for external validation.

- **Personal Development Away from the Limelight:**

Submarines, with their "silent service" designation, meticulously fulfill their duties away from the limelight, operating beneath the surface and out of public view. This operational ethos draws a parallel to the personal development journey that individuals often undertake in solitude, away from external scrutiny. The process of self-improvement, encompassing learning, introspection, and skill-building, unfolds quietly, driven by an intrinsic commitment to continuous growth, even when the efforts go unnoticed by others.

In the world of personal development, the journey towards self-improvement is an intimate and often solitary endeavor. Individuals engage in learning, acquiring new skills, and reflecting on their experiences without seeking external validation or applause. This quiet dedication to personal growth is akin to the discreet operations of submarines, where every advancement contributes to the overall mission success, even if it occurs away from the watchful eyes of the world.

The commitment to personal development away from the limelight reflects a deep understanding that true growth is a personal and internal process. Submarines operate quietly beneath the ocean's surface, driven by a sense of duty and purpose, much like individuals who, in their pursuit of self-improvement, draw motivation from an inner calling rather than external recognition. This intentional choice to develop in solitude allows individuals to focus on their intrinsic goals, values, and aspirations.

The "silent service" nature of personal development highlights the humility embedded in the journey towards self-improvement. It emphasizes the idea that genuine growth is not fueled by the desire for external praise but rather by an internal commitment to becoming the best version of oneself. Submarines, in their covert operations, and individuals, in their private quests for personal development, share a common thread of humility and dedication to continuous improvement.

The quiet evolution that occurs in personal development away from the limelight is a testament to the sincerity of the individual's commitment to growth. Submarines fulfill their missions diligently without fanfare, and similarly, individuals engage in self-improvement with a sense of purpose that transcends external recognition.

This unassuming approach to personal development allows for a genuine and transformative journey, where the focus remains on the intrinsic value of the growth process rather than the visibility it may attract.

- **The Strength of Silent Leadership:**

The concept of silent leadership, exemplified by submarines in their covert operations, draws a fascinating parallel to a form of leadership prevalent in personal development. In the silent depths of submarines, individuals operate with implicit trust in each other's expertise, executing tasks efficiently and seamlessly. This unique leadership style mirrors the subtle but powerful influence individuals can have on others during their personal growth journeys.

In the submarine context, silent leadership involves a tacit understanding among crew members, where trust is built on competence, expertise, and a shared commitment to the mission. This form of leadership is not characterized by loud commands or explicit directives but relies on a deep sense of mutual respect and reliance. Similarly, in personal development, individuals often exhibit a form of silent leadership, leading by example rather than explicit instruction.

In the realm of personal growth, silent leadership manifests as an individual's ability to influence and inspire others through their actions, choices, and demeanor. It's about embodying the values, resilience, and commitment to growth that others can observe and draw inspiration from. This influence is often subtle, operating beneath the surface of overt leadership, yet its impact is profound, shaping not only the individual's destiny but also resonating with those who observe from afar.

In the submerged world of submarines, a unique form of leadership emerges, marked by quiet efficiency and a mutual trust in each other's expertise. This silent leadership, based on trust and the execution of tasks with precision, mirrors a parallel phenomenon in personal growth – a concept known as silent leadership in the realm of individual development.

Silent leadership in personal development is characterized by a commitment to authenticity and integrity. In this context, individuals lead by example, influencing others through their actions rather than vocal directives. The impact of this silent guidance is subtle yet profound, shaping not only personal destinies but also inspiring those who observe from afar.

In the "silent service" of personal development, leaders in their own right navigate the intricate waters of growth with a quiet determination. This silent leadership manifests as a commitment to authenticity, where individuals stay true to their values and principles. The consistency and resilience displayed in the face of challenges become a source of inspiration for others on similar journeys.

Authenticity is a cornerstone of silent leadership in personal development. Leaders in this context strive to be beacons of consistency, reflecting their values through purposeful actions. It's a demonstration that personal development is not about grand proclamations or ostentatious displays but about the daily, intentional choices that align with one's values.

In the quiet execution of personal growth, silent leaders inspire through authenticity. Their commitment to navigating challenges with resilience serves as a subtle yet powerful example for others undertaking their own journeys. The impact of silent leadership extends beyond individual growth, fostering a culture where authenticity, consistency, and resilience become shared values in the broader community of personal development.

Chapter **14**

Diving and Resurfacing

The process of submerging and emerging from the water mirrors the ebb and flow of diving into introspective states and returning to everyday consciousness.

The human involvement may be a consistent wavering between submersion within the profundities of self-reflection and rise into the outside world. Much like a submarine submerging underneath the ocean's surface and reemerging, people lock in within the interminable recede and stream of reflection and ordinary awareness. This allegorical travel mirrors the significant nature of exploring the inner realms of considerations, feelings, and recollections, as it were to reemerge with recently discovered bits of knowledge and self-awareness. The method of submerging and developing gets to be a captivating allegory for the cadence of individual investigation, typifying the excellence and challenges of digging into the significant profundities of one's possess mind.

- **The Descent into the Abyss:**

As submarines navigate through the murky depths, individuals, in their introspective descent, confront the initial ambiguity and uncertainty within their own minds. The metaphor captures the inherent challenge of traversing through the sometimes-clouded waters of introspection.

The profound darkness below mirrors the depth of unresolved thoughts and emotions that individuals may grapple with during introspective states. It's a descent into the emotional abyss, where the weight of unexplored aspects of the self becomes palpable.

Just as submarines contend with undercurrents beneath the ocean's surface, the introspective descent delves into the undercurrents of subconscious forces. This involves confronting hidden fears, desires, and memories that shape the individual's inner landscape.

Submarines face increasing pressures with depth, mirroring the internal pressures individuals may encounter during introspection. These internal pressures could manifest as the weight of unresolved conflicts, self-reflection, or the need to confront uncomfortable truths.

The journey into the intricate landscapes of the mind mirrors submarines uncovering the complexity of the ocean floor. Similarly, individuals unravel the complexity of their thoughts, emotions, and memories, gaining insights into the nuanced aspects of their own psyche.

Submerged submarines exist in a world of silence, echoing the internal silence sought during introspective states. This metaphorical silence becomes a space for introspection, where individuals can listen to the subtle whispers of their own thoughts, devoid of external distractions.

The descent into the abyss is not merely a venture into darkness; it is also a journey toward self-illumination. In introspection, individuals seek the inner light that shines through self-awareness, understanding, and the revelation of personal truths.

This metaphorical descent into the abyss is not a one-time journey but a continuous exploration, emphasizing the ongoing nature of personal introspection and the boundless depths of the human psyche that await discovery.

- **Navigating Unseen Terrains:**

The comparison to submarines traversing through unseen terrains reflects the initial murkiness encountered during introspection. Just as submarines navigate through the unclear waters, individuals confront the ambiguity and uncertainty inherent in the depths of their subconscious.

The unseen terrains symbolize the vastness of the subconscious mind, where individuals probe the abyss of their thoughts, emotions, and memories. This introspective journey involves delving into the hidden recesses, uncovering layers that may have remained concealed.

The intricate complexities of unseen terrains mirror the intricate nature of thoughts and emotions explored during introspection. Individuals grapple with the multifaceted aspects of their inner selves, unraveling layers of complexity that contribute to a deeper understanding.

Submarines navigate through various depths, analogous to the emotional depths individuals encounter during introspection. Exploring one's emotions involves descending into the layers of feelings, confronting both the surface-level sentiments and those buried in the profound recesses of the subconscious.

Just as submarines rely on navigation systems to traverse unseen terrains, individuals engaging in introspection depend on mental navigation—mindfulness, self-awareness, and introspective practices—to guide them through the uncharted territories of their inner selves.

Unseen terrains represent the challenges of ambiguity and uncertainty. During introspection, individuals grapple with the uncertainty of self-discovery, facing questions that may not have straightforward answers and navigating through the ambiguity that characterizes the inner journey.

The metaphor extends beyond surface-level impressions, emphasizing that the unseen terrains represent more than what meets the eye. Similarly, introspection involves going beyond superficial self-perceptions, seeking a deeper understanding that goes beneath the surface of one's conscious awareness.

Navigating unseen terrains is not a one-time event, just as introspection is an ongoing, continuous exploration. The comparison highlights the perpetual nature of the inner journey, encouraging individuals to delve into the complexities of their inner worlds with curiosity and self-compassion.

- **Pressures of Introspection:**

The analogy to submarines encountering intense pressures draws a parallel to the internal pressures individuals may experience during introspection. Just as submarines delve into the depths of the ocean, individuals plunge into the intricate layers of their minds, facing the weight of internal complexities.

Similar to submarines facing increasing pressure with depth, individuals may feel the intensification of emotional pressures during introspection. Unresolved emotions, buried beneath the surface, exert their force as individuals venture deeper into the recesses of their psyche.

Introspective states often involve confronting uncomfortable truths, akin to submarines navigating through the pressures of the ocean's depths. The internal pressures can manifest as the challenges of facing aspects of oneself that may be uncomfortable or difficult to acknowledge.

The pressures of introspection manifest as the weight of self-reflection. Individuals may feel the burden of evaluating their thoughts, actions, and life choices, creating an internal environment where the pressures of self-awareness become palpable.

As submarines descend into the ocean's depths, individuals unravel layers of complexity within themselves during introspection.

The pressures encountered are symbolic of the intricate nature of the human mind, where each layer holds the potential for self-discovery and understanding.

Analogous to the gradual increase in pressure as submarines descend, the internal pressures of introspection may escalate gradually. Individuals may find that the deeper they delve into their thoughts and emotions, the more pronounced the internal pressures become.

The pressures experienced during introspection reflect the personal depth individuals are willing to explore. It symbolizes a journey into the profound aspects of one's identity and experiences, where the pressures serve as indicators of the depth of self-exploration.

Much like the silent service of submarines, the pressures of introspection often go unnoticed by external observers. This silent struggle within reflects the inner battles individuals face as they navigate through the complexities of their minds.

Submarines are equipped to cope with external pressures, and similarly, individuals must develop coping mechanisms to navigate internal pressures during introspection. This involves building emotional resilience and developing a supportive mindset to withstand the challenges encountered in the depths of self-discovery.

The analogy emphasizes the importance of balancing internal pressures during introspection.

Like submarines maintaining equilibrium in the depths, individuals strive to find a psychological balance that allows for deep self-reflection without succumbing to overwhelming internal pressures.

- **The Silence Within:**

Submerged submarines navigate the ocean's depths in profound silence, a world where external sounds are muted. This mirrors the necessity for individuals to embrace inner stillness during introspective states, creating a mental space free from external disturbances.

The analogy underscores the importance of quieting external noise, much like submarines avoiding detection through silent operations. During introspection, individuals seek environments free from distractions, allowing them to turn inward and engage in meaningful self-reflection.

Submarines in silence rely on advanced sonar systems, and similarly, individuals in introspective states rely on attentive listening to internal whispers. This involves tuning into one's thoughts, emotions, and inner dialogues, fostering a deeper understanding of the self.

Submerged submarines plunge into a profound stillness beneath the waves. In introspection, individuals explore the depth of their own inner stillness, creating a mental sanctuary where clarity, self-awareness, and profound insights can emerge.

Submarines disconnect from the tumultuous surface world, finding solace in the silence below.

Similarly, individuals in introspective states disconnect from external turmoil, seeking solace in the quiet recesses of their minds to explore their thoughts without external interference.

The silence within allows for reflective contemplation, akin to submarines maneuvering silently beneath the ocean's surface. Introspective individuals engage in contemplative thought, unraveling the layers of their consciousness and gaining insights that might remain elusive in the noise of everyday life.

Internal silence serves as a canvas for self-discovery. Submarines navigate through silent depths as explorers of the ocean floor, and individuals navigate through the silent corridors of their minds, discovering facets of themselves that might go unnoticed in the hustle and bustle of external noise.

Submarines tune into specific frequencies to navigate, and similarly, individuals tune into their inner frequencies during moments of introspection. This involves attuning to emotions, thoughts, and subtle nuances within, enhancing the capacity for self-awareness.

The silence within encourages silent conversations with the self. Submarines, through sonar communication, engage in silent exchanges, and individuals, through introspection, converse with their inner selves, fostering a dialogue that leads to personal growth and understanding.

Submerged submarines navigate the depths of the ocean, and individuals navigate the depths of their emotions in internal silence.

Introspection allows individuals to explore and navigate through complex emotional landscapes, fostering a deeper connection with their feelings and reactions.

The silence within becomes a sanctuary for mindful presence. Just as submarines navigate silently to avoid detection, individuals navigate the realms of mindfulness during introspection, cultivating a heightened awareness of the present moment and their internal states.

The silence within resonates with inner peace. Submarines maneuver silently to maintain stealth, and individuals seek inner silence to cultivate a sense of peace within, creating a mental environment conducive to personal tranquility and well-being.

- **Emergence into Consciousness:**

Submarines resurface, breaking through the water's surface with a symbolic acknowledgment of the return to visibility. Likewise, individuals emerge from introspective states, breaking through the layers of deep self-reflection to re-enter the conscious realm of everyday awareness.

The act of resurfacing signifies a transition from internal contemplation to engagement with the external world. Individuals, having delved into their inner depths, return to the surface of consciousness, integrating the insights gained into their interactions and experiences.

Similar to submarines breaking the surface to expose their periscope, individuals bring insights gained during introspection to the light of consciousness.

These insights, often profound and transformative, become guiding beacons in navigating the challenges and opportunities of daily life.

Resurfacing marks the integration of self-knowledge into conscious thought. Individuals, having explored the depths of their psyche, resurface with a deeper understanding of themselves. This integrated self-knowledge becomes a powerful tool for personal growth and decision-making.

The emergence into consciousness brings renewed clarity and focus, much like submarines resurfacing for a fresh perspective. Individuals, having taken the time for introspection, return to their daily lives with a clearer understanding of their goals, values, and priorities.

Insights gained in introspective states are not left in the depths. Individuals apply these insights upon resurfacing, leveraging newfound self-awareness to navigate challenges, build meaningful connections, and make decisions aligned with their authentic selves.

Resurfacing signifies a reconnection with the external world. Submarines, having navigated silently below, re-engage with the surface environment. Similarly, individuals, having explored their inner worlds, re-enter the external realm with a fresh perspective and a reinvigorated sense of connection.

Chapter 15

Limited Visibility

Navigation through dark waters relates to venturing through uncertainty in one's personal journey, relying on intuition and inner guidance.

The representation of exploring dull waters typifies the significant relationship between the dangerous profundities investigated by submarines underneath the ocean's surface and the complex, regularly unusual, travel through vulnerabilities in an individual's life. Submarines, prepared with progressed innovation and guided by talented groups, navigate the dinky profundities with vital exactness, reflecting the way people explore the complexities of their individual ways. The similarity reverberates with the dependence on instinct and inward direction, emphasizing the transformative control of grasping vulnerability as an fundamentally portion of the human involvement.

- **Submerging into the Unknown:**

Submarines, as they dive into the abyss of the ocean, confront the mysteries and challenges hidden beneath the surface. Similarly, individuals plunge into the depths of their own lives, willingly facing challenges and uncertainties. This act of submerging becomes a metaphorical descent into the abyss of life's complexities, where resilience and fortitude are tested, and hidden strengths are discovered.

Just as submarines explore uncharted territories underwater, individuals navigate through unexplored facets of themselves. The personal journey involves delving into the depths of one's character, motivations, and emotions. This process of self-discovery, akin to submarines uncovering the unknown ocean floor, reveals hidden aspects waiting to be explored and understood.

Subs venture into uncharted territories beneath the ocean's surface, relying on sophisticated navigation systems. Similarly, individuals navigate through unexplored realms in their lives, seeking new experiences and opportunities. The metaphorical exploration becomes a testament to the adventurous spirit inherent in personal growth, embracing the unknown with curiosity and courage.

The act of submerging suggests a fluidity that is mirrored in personal growth. Life is dynamic, ever-changing, and full of uncertainties. Individuals willingly submerge into this fluidity, understanding that growth is not a linear path but a dynamic process of adaptation and evolution. The willingness to navigate this fluidity becomes integral to the personal journey.

They do not shy away from the uncertain depths, and similarly, individuals acknowledge the call of uncertainty in their personal journeys. The act of willingly stepping into the unknown becomes a conscious decision, fueled by a recognition that transformative moments and self-discovery often reside in the uncharted territories of life.

Submarines symbolize resilience in the face of the ocean's pressures. Likewise, individuals, by submerging into the unknown of their lives, undergo a metamorphosis of resilience. Confronting challenges head-on, adapting to unforeseen circumstances, and emerging stronger become integral aspects of the transformative journey beneath the surface.

Also, submarines use advanced lighting to illuminate the darkness of the ocean depths. Similarly, individuals bring their own light – courage, wisdom, and introspection – to illuminate the depths of their personal journeys. This internal illumination becomes a guiding force, allowing individuals to navigate through challenges and uncertainties with clarity and purpose.

Submerging into the unknown isn't merely about reaching a destination; it's about the journey. Individuals, by embracing the uncertainties of their personal odysseys, understand that the richness of life's experiences lies in the journey itself. The act of submerging becomes a metaphorical invitation to savor every moment, learn from challenges, and appreciate the ongoing process of self-discovery.

- **Darkness as a Canvas for Transformation:**

Submarines, adept at maneuvering in dark waters, symbolize the profound significance of navigating through the unknown. Similarly, individuals, in their personal odysseys, encounter periods of darkness – moments of ambiguity, uncertainty, and introspective shadow.

Recognizing darkness as a canvas for transformation is acknowledging the rich potential inherent in the challenges and complexities faced during personal growth.

They navigate through darkness with strategic precision, utilizing the shadows to execute crucial maneuvers. Likewise, individuals, when confronted with life's uncertainties, can view these challenges as opportunities for strategic personal maneuvers. The darkness becomes a backdrop for resilience, adaptability, and the honing of newfound strengths – essential elements in the transformative process.

The dark waters that submarines traverse represent ambiguity, mirroring the uncertainties in personal journeys. Acknowledging this ambiguity becomes a catalyst for personal growth. Like artists who embrace the blank canvas, individuals can view life's uncertainties as an opportunity to create something meaningful. The transformative brushstrokes on the canvas of uncertainty become integral to the evolution of the self.

Submarines navigate through periods of shadow, and individuals, during their personal journeys, encounter metaphorical shadows in the form of challenges, doubts, and fears. Just as the canvas of transformation requires the interplay of light and shadow, personal growth unfolds through the intricate dance between confronting shadows and discovering the light within.

Darkness, whether in the ocean depths or personal challenges, becomes a testing ground for resilience. Submarines emerge from the shadows, and individuals, too, emerge from the depths of personal struggles transformed. The canvas of darkness becomes a narrative of resilience, where each challenge met becomes a stroke on the canvas, contributing to the masterpiece of personal growth.

The journey through dark waters serves as a metaphor for inner exploration. Submarines delve into the unknown oceanic depths, and individuals embark on a parallel journey into the intricate landscapes of their minds and emotions. The canvas of darkness becomes a reflection of the inner landscapes explored during moments of introspection and self-discovery.

Just as submarines strategically navigate through darkness, individuals, when faced with life's uncertainties, unveil newfound strengths. The canvas of transformation captures the emergence of resilience, courage, and adaptability – qualities that might not have been fully realized without navigating through the shadows.

Submarines navigate dark waters with precision, turning challenges into opportunities for strategic movement. In the same vein, individuals can view the canvas of darkness as an opportunity for artistry in personal resilience. Each stroke of resilience becomes an integral part of the masterpiece, shaping the narrative of personal growth.

- **Intuition as a Guiding Light:**

Submarines communicate silently through advanced navigation systems, and individuals, in their personal journeys, engage in a silent dialogue with their intuition. This unspoken language becomes a guiding force, offering insights and directions that may not be immediately apparent in the conscious mind.

They rely on intuition to navigate through the uncertainties of dark waters. Similarly, individuals harness the power of intuition to navigate through the uncertainties of life. In moments of ambiguity and indecision, intuition acts as a beacon, providing a sense of direction and clarity that transcends rational analysis.

Just as submariners trust advanced navigation systems, individuals are encouraged to trust their inner compass—intuition. The act of trusting oneself in the face of uncertainty becomes a transformative practice. Intuition, when embraced, leads individuals toward decisions and paths that resonate with their authentic desires and aspirations.

Subs make informed decisions based on a combination of intuition and technological guidance. Similarly, individuals, when navigating the complexities of personal choices, benefit from a balanced approach. Intuition becomes a valuable tool, complementing logical reasoning and contributing to decisions that align with one's values and innermost aspirations.

Intuition serves as a conduit for deepening the connection with the authentic self.

In the silent depths of introspection, individuals can tap into their intuitive wisdom, gaining profound insights into their true desires, fears, and motivations. This enhanced self-awareness becomes a cornerstone of personal growth.

Submariners must listen to the subtle cues provided by navigation systems, and individuals, in their personal journeys, engage in the art of listening within. Tuning into intuitive nudges and gut feelings allows individuals to navigate through the shadows with a heightened awareness, attuned to the whispers of their inner guidance.

Intuition often operates in the realm of the unseen, guiding individuals through subtle impressions and feelings. Submarines, when submerged, rely on non-visible cues for navigation. Embracing the unseen aspects of intuition invites individuals to trust in the intangible, embracing a deeper understanding of themselves and the world around them.

Submariners value navigational precision, and individuals navigating personal journeys find precision in intuitive insights. Intuition, when cultivated and honed, contributes to a more precise understanding of one's path, allowing for course corrections and adjustments based on an intuitive understanding of the evolving circumstances.

- **Adaptability to Unseen Challenges:**

Submarines navigate through the murkiness of the unknown, and individuals encounter the uncertainty of life.

The journey involves facing challenges without a clear view of what lies ahead. Adaptability becomes the compass that allows individuals to navigate through the shadows, embracing the ambiguity with a flexible and resilient mindset.

Submarines, when encountering unexpected turns, adjust course to navigate effectively. Similarly, individuals must adjust their course in the face of life's unexpected twists and turns. The ability to pivot, reassess goals, and recalibrate one's path becomes essential for overcoming challenges and moving forward on the personal development journey.

Unforeseen challenges in the darkness of the ocean become lessons for submariners. Similarly, life's adversities provide profound learning opportunities for individuals. The journey of personal development involves extracting lessons from challenges, cultivating wisdom, and integrating these insights into the fabric of one's character for continued growth.

Submariners exhibit resilience in the face of unknown challenges, and individuals must cultivate a similar resilience in personal development. Resilience becomes the anchor that keeps individuals steady amid the uncertainties. It involves bouncing back from setbacks, maintaining composure during turbulent times, and staying committed to the journey despite the shadows.

They showcase flexibility to navigate through dynamic underwater environments.

In personal development, flexibility emerges as a strength. The ability to adapt plans, embrace change, and remain open to new possibilities allows individuals to navigate the unseen challenges with a mindset that fosters growth and innovation.

Also, submarines use various tools to illuminate the shadows underwater when faced with challenges. Similarly, individuals illuminate their personal shadows through adaptation. Adaptability becomes a tool to shed light on aspects of the self that may remain hidden during smooth sailing, fostering a deeper understanding and acceptance.

Submariners understand the evolution of their mission, adapting as needed. Similarly, personal development is an evolving journey. Embracing the evolution involves recognizing that challenges contribute to growth, and adaptation becomes a conscious choice to navigate the ever-changing landscape of life.

Submarines proactively adapt to avoid potential issues, and individuals can cultivate proactive adaptation in personal development. Anticipating challenges, staying vigilant to potential obstacles, and making adjustments before crises arise showcase a proactive approach that minimizes disruptions and enhances the overall journey.

- **Inner Guidance Amidst Murkiness:**

The murkiness of dark waters symbolizes the ambiguity individuals face in their personal journeys. Life's uncertainties often present situations where the path forward is unclear.

Inner guidance becomes the compass, allowing individuals to navigate through the ambiguity with a sense of purpose and direction.

Submariners trust advanced navigation systems, and individuals can trust their intuition as a sophisticated inner navigation tool. Inner guidance involves trusting the subtle cues and instincts that arise within, providing a deeper understanding of situations and aiding in decision-making. Intuition becomes a trustworthy companion in the journey through life's murkiness.

Inner guidance serves as a source of clarity amidst the shadows of uncertainty. Submarines use advanced systems to illuminate their surroundings, and individuals can illuminate the shadows within by relying on their inner wisdom. This clarity allows for a better understanding of challenges and opportunities, enabling informed and aligned choices.

Submariners align their actions with mission objectives, and individuals can align decisions with their core values. Inner guidance involves reflecting on one's values, aspirations, and authentic self. Decisions made in alignment with these internal principles contribute to a sense of purpose and fulfillment, even in the face of ambiguity.

Inner guidance contributes to the strengthening of resilience. Submarines navigate through challenging conditions with resilience, and individuals can draw upon inner wisdom to navigate through personal challenges.

Chapter **16**

Observing the Unknown

Just as submarines enable us to witness uncharted sea life, self-exploration allows us to uncover hidden talents and facets of our character.
The investigation of the tremendous and strange sea profundities through submarines has long captivated our collective creative ability, uncovering a world overflowing with unfamiliar ocean life. In a parallel account, the travel of self-exploration serves as the vessel for revealing the covered up abilities and perplexing features of our character. Much like submarines divulge the riddles of the sea, locks in in self-discovery empowers people to dig into the unexplored domains of their potential, bringing to light gifts and qualities which will have remained concealed.

- **The Submerged Potential:**

Submarines descend into the ocean's depths, and individuals embark on a similar descent into self-discovery. The journey inward involves peeling back layers, exploring thoughts, emotions, and experiences to uncover the hidden aspects of one's identity. It is a process of self-revelation and self-understanding.

Just as submarines navigate uncharted sea life, self-exploration delves into the uncharted depths of character. Individuals encounter aspects of themselves that may have been unexplored or overlooked. This revelation allows for a more comprehensive understanding of personal strengths, values, and potential.

They use advanced technology to illuminate hidden sea life, and self-exploration serves as the inner light that reveals hidden talents. Through introspection, individuals discover latent abilities, creative talents, and skills that may have remained dormant. The process brings to light the unique gifts waiting to be harnessed.

Also, submarines navigate through the subconscious world of the ocean, and individuals navigate through their own subconscious realms during self-exploration. Delving into the subconscious mind uncovers deeply rooted beliefs, motivations, and desires, providing valuable insights into the inner landscape.

Submarines unveil the complexity of marine ecosystems, and self-exploration unveils the layers of personal complexity. Each layer represents a dimension of one's identity—beliefs, experiences, values—that contributes to the multifaceted nature of an individual. Understanding these layers is integral to unlocking hidden potential.

Furthermore, submarines are vulnerable in the vast ocean, and individuals, too, embrace vulnerability during self-exploration. It is an acknowledgment of the imperfections, fears, and insecurities that may be concealed. Embracing vulnerability becomes a catalyst for authentic self-discovery and growth.

Submarines harness the power within the ocean's depths for exploration, and individuals harness their inner power through self-exploration. Uncovering hidden talents and facets of character empowers individuals to leverage their strengths, fostering a sense of self-efficacy and personal agency.

Just as submarines continually explore the ocean, self-exploration is a continuous journey. The uncovering of hidden talents is not a destination but an ongoing process of growth and self-discovery. Individuals navigate the currents of personal development, always ready to unveil new layers of potential.

- **Illuminating Hidden Realms:**

Submarines deploy advanced technology to pierce the darkness of the ocean's depths. This technological light serves as a guide, revealing the mysteries hidden beneath the surface. Similarly, in the journey of self-exploration, individuals leverage introspection as their guiding light, illuminating the uncharted territories within.

In the depths of self-exploration, individuals turn inward, using self-reflection as a source of inner illumination. This introspective light exposes the intricacies of thoughts, emotions, and experiences, allowing individuals to navigate through the hidden realms of their character and gain a clearer understanding of who they are.

Subs reveal the marine life that might be overlooked in the dark abyss.

Similarly, self-exploration casts a light on overlooked talents within individuals. It is a process of acknowledging and bringing forward skills and abilities that might have been neglected or underestimated, recognizing their value and potential contribution.

Just as submarines bring attention to unique sea life, self-exploration shines a spotlight on the unique attributes that define an individual. Whether it's creative talents, innate strengths, or distinctive personality traits, the light of self-awareness accentuates the qualities that set individuals apart.

Submarines uncover the depths of the ocean, and self-exploration unveils the depths of character. The light of introspection allows individuals to explore their beliefs, values, and motivations, uncovering layers that contribute to the richness of their identity.

They embark on journeys of discovery, and individuals, through self-exploration, embark on a personal journey of self-discovery. The light of awareness guides individuals through the complexities of their own psyche, revealing hidden aspects and fostering a deeper connection with the self.

Submarines' technology uncovers opportunities for scientific exploration. Similarly, self-exploration's light reveals personal growth opportunities. It is a process of identifying areas for improvement, learning, and development, creating a roadmap for individuals to evolve and maximize their potential.

Submarines navigate the shadows of the deep with clarity. In self-exploration, the light of awareness enables individuals to navigate through the shadows of their own uncertainties, fears, and unresolved aspects. The clarity gained fosters resilience and a sense of purpose in the face of personal challenges.

- **The Diversity of Sea Life and Personal Talents:**

The ocean's ecosystem thrives on diversity, with various species coexisting and contributing to the overall balance. Similarly, in the realm of self-exploration, individuals uncover the diverse attributes that make up their unique identity. This might include talents, skills, passions, and perspectives that contribute to the multifaceted nature of personal existence.

Uncharted sea life often reveals hidden marvels beneath the waves. In the process of self-exploration, individuals unveil their own hidden talents, those undiscovered facets of themselves that add depth and richness to their character. These talents, once brought to the surface, contribute to personal growth and fulfillment.

Just as the ocean harbors a myriad of unique species, each individual possesses a distinct set of skills and abilities. Self-exploration acts as a guide to identify and appreciate these personal skills, viewing them as unique species within the diverse ecosystem of one's capabilities.

The ocean's depths harbor passionate and often undiscovered species. Similarly, individuals, through self-exploration, unveil their passions that may have been submerged in the depths of daily life. Recognizing and nurturing these passions becomes a crucial aspect of embracing personal diversity.

Diverse marine species offer different perspectives within the underwater world. Likewise, self-exploration reveals the mosaic of perspectives that individuals bring to the table. It involves understanding one's worldview, beliefs, and values, acknowledging the richness that arises from the diversity of individual perspectives.

The underwater world is a testament to the beauty of uniqueness. Similarly, the journey of self-exploration encourages individuals to appreciate and celebrate their own uniqueness. It is an acknowledgment that personal diversity contributes to the intricate and beautiful mosaic of human existence.

Just as the ocean sustains a diverse ecosystem, self-exploration aids in cultivating a personal ecosystem. This involves recognizing the interplay between different aspects of oneself—talents, passions, skills—and fostering an environment where these elements can thrive and contribute harmoniously to personal well-being. Diversity in sea life fosters the health and balance of the ocean ecosystem. Similarly, personal diversity nurtures growth and balance in individual lives.

- **Adapting to the Unknown:**

Much like submarines navigating through unknown seas, individuals engage in self-exploration to uncover the depths of their character. The uncharted waters symbolize the aspects of oneself that are yet to be discovered, presenting an opportunity for personal growth and self-awareness.

Submarines are designed to adapt swiftly to surprises in the depths, and in self-exploration, individuals must likewise embrace the element of surprise within themselves. Unexpected talents, passions, or aspects of character may surface, necessitating adaptability to make the most of these revelations.

Self-exploration involves confronting uncertainties within one's character. Just as submarines face the unpredictable nature of the ocean, individuals navigate through uncertainties such as unresolved emotions, undiscovered talents, and unexplored potential. Adaptability becomes the compass guiding them through this intricate journey.

Subs venture into unfamiliar territories, and individuals, in the pursuit of self-discovery, must be willing to explore the uncharted aspects of their personality. This may involve delving into hidden passions, addressing neglected emotions, or acknowledging talents that have yet to be fully realized.

Adaptability is not just a response to the unknown; it is a catalyst for personal growth. Just as submarines adapt to the dynamic underwater environment, individuals, through adaptability, facilitate their own growth by remaining open to new possibilities, experiences, and dimensions of self.

Submarines navigate through emotional depths beneath the ocean's surface, and similarly, self-exploration requires navigating through the emotional intricacies within. Adaptability becomes a vital tool for understanding, processing, and learning from various emotions that may arise during the exploration of one's inner world.

They explore with curiosity, and individuals, in their journey of self-discovery, cultivate a similar curiosity about their own inner workings. Adaptability is closely tied to curiosity, as it encourages individuals to approach unknown aspects of themselves with an open mind, fostering a sense of wonder about the richness within.

Also, submarines uncover unseen landscapes, and in self-exploration, individuals unearth their unseen potential. The adaptability to embrace and develop this potential becomes transformative, as individuals tap into talents and capabilities they might not have realized existed within them.

Submarines adjust their course based on the underwater environment, and individuals, in self-exploration, must be willing to adjust their course along the journey.

Adaptability involves recognizing when to pivot, reassess, and navigate through evolving aspects of oneself for a more profound exploration.

The unknown waters of self-exploration are dynamic, ever-changing. Adaptability reflects an understanding of the dynamic nature of personal discovery, where each revelation and self-awareness moment necessitates a flexible and adaptive approach to fully appreciate and integrate newfound aspects of oneself.

- **Delving into Passionate Depths:**

Submarines navigate through the vastness of the ocean, seeking areas of interest and importance. In self-exploration, individuals navigate their internal seas, identifying and delving into areas that evoke genuine passion. This process involves introspection and a conscious effort to discover what truly ignites one's inner fire.

Just as submarines unveil the richness of the ocean's depths, individuals unveil the richness of their personal interests and passions. The journey of self-discovery involves exploring the multifaceted layers of one's character, each layer representing a unique aspect of personal interest waiting to be discovered.

They explore areas of interest that align with their missions. Similarly, individuals in self-exploration aim to align their talents with true passions. Recognizing the intersection between innate abilities and genuine interests leads to the discovery of a purposeful path where personal talents and passions harmoniously coexist.

Delving into the passionate depths is a quest for authentic self-expression. Submarines express their capabilities in the ocean's depths, and individuals express their true selves by aligning their talents with passions. This alignment fosters a profound sense of authenticity, allowing individuals to showcase their unique contributions to the world.

Submarines harness the transformative power of oceanic exploration, and similarly, individuals harness the transformative power of their passions. Immersing oneself in what truly excites and drives them creates a positive ripple effect, influencing personal growth, resilience, and the ability to overcome challenges with unwavering enthusiasm.

In the process of delving into passionate depths, individuals discover inherent talents they might not have been aware of. Submarines reveal hidden landscapes, and self-exploration unveils latent talents that, once brought to the surface, contribute to a more comprehensive understanding of personal capabilities.

The alignment of talents with true passions becomes the cornerstone for creating a purpose-driven life. Submarines pursue missions aligned with their capabilities, and individuals, by aligning talents with passions, embark on a mission that resonates with their core values, providing a sense of purpose and direction in life.

Chapter **17**

Emergency Protocols

Submarines have protocols for crises; similarly, we must have strategies for personal emergencies to maintain mental health.

Submarines, the quiet sentinels of the ocean's profundities, are prepared with fastidious conventions to explore emergencies quickly and viably. In a parallel travel, our lives regularly experience individual emergencies—unexpected storms that challenge our mental well-being. Creating methodologies associated to submarine conventions gets to be basic for controlling through these turbulent times.

- **Acknowledging the Reality of Personal Emergencies:**

Submarines, despite their advanced technology, operate in an unpredictable environment. Similarly, life unfolds with uncertainties. Acknowledging the reality of personal emergencies involves embracing the inherent unpredictability of existence, understanding that challenges are not aberrations but integral facets of the human experience.

They do not deny the possibility of crises; they prepare for them. Likewise, individuals must overcome denial and confront the possibility of personal emergencies.

This acknowledgment serves as a powerful antidote to complacency, motivating proactive measures to fortify mental and emotional well-being.

Subs build resilience against external pressures, and individuals can build a resilient mindset. Acknowledging the reality of personal emergencies fosters mental toughness. It lays the foundation for a mindset that views challenges not as insurmountable obstacles but as opportunities for growth and development.

They navigate through shifting oceanic conditions, adjusting their course as needed. Similarly, acknowledging personal emergencies requires a shift in perspective. Instead of perceiving challenges as mere setbacks, individuals can view them as opportunities to learn, adapt, and emerge stronger on the other side.

Also, Submarines are mentally prepared for crisis scenarios. Similarly, individuals acknowledging the reality of personal emergencies engage in mental preparedness. This involves developing a proactive mindset that, rather than dwelling on fear, focuses on preparing oneself for the potential challenges that may arise.

Submarines, despite their robust structures, acknowledge vulnerability. Likewise, recognizing personal emergencies involves honoring one's vulnerability. It encourages individuals to embrace their emotional and mental states authentically, fostering a culture where seeking help and expressing vulnerability are seen as strengths rather than weaknesses.

Subs undergo regular maintenance to prevent breakdowns. Similarly, acknowledging personal emergencies prompts proactive mental health practices.

Regular self-care, mindfulness, and seeking professional support are embraced as ongoing practices, ensuring that mental well-being is not neglected in the face of life's uncertainties.

They navigate with clear intentions, knowing crises may arise. Similarly, acknowledging personal emergencies involves navigating life with intentionality. Individuals, with a clear understanding of the potential challenges, can steer their lives with purpose, making decisions aligned with their values and mental well-being.

- **Establishing a Personal Crisis Response Plan:**

Submarines rely on the collaboration and support of the entire crew during crises. Similarly, individuals should identify their support systems – friends, family, mental health professionals – who can offer assistance during personal emergencies. Establishing a network of reliable connections provides emotional and practical support.

They are equipped with specific mechanisms to cope with crises. Similarly, individuals should delineate coping mechanisms and strategies tailored to their unique needs. This may include mindfulness practices, journaling, or engaging in activities that bring solace and calmness during turbulent times.

Submarines are equipped to detect potential issues before they escalate.

In a personal crisis response plan, individuals should define triggers and warning signs indicating the onset of a crisis.

Understanding these indicators enables timely intervention and the implementation of coping strategies.

Submarines have specialized tools for crisis management. Likewise, individuals can create a crisis toolkit – a set of resources and activities that have proven effective in alleviating stress and maintaining mental well-being. This toolkit may include contact information for support, relaxation techniques, and self-help resources.

They prioritize clear communication during crises. In a personal crisis response plan, individuals should establish communication protocols. This involves outlining how and when to communicate with support networks, ensuring effective and timely sharing of information during challenging situations.

Submarines may call upon experts for specialized assistance. Similarly, individuals should consider seeking professional help as a part of their crisis response plan. This may involve having contact information for mental health professionals or crisis helplines, ensuring access to expert guidance when needed.

They undergo regular reviews and updates to their crisis protocols. Individuals should adopt a similar practice, routinely reviewing and updating their personal crisis response plans. Life circumstances and personal dynamics change, and an evolving plan ensures relevance and effectiveness in addressing current needs.

Submarines engage in drills to practice crisis responses. Likewise, individuals can conduct simulations of potential crisis scenarios. This hands-on practice enhances preparedness and familiarizes individuals with the actions outlined in their crisis response plan, reducing anxiety and facilitating a more efficient response when faced with a real emergency.

- **Prioritizing Mental Health Preparedness:**

Submarines undergo routine checks to assess their operational readiness. Similarly, individuals should engage in regular self-assessment to gauge their mental well-being. This introspective practice involves reflecting on emotions, stress levels, and overall mental health, allowing individuals to identify potential areas of concern before they escalate.

They cultivate resilience to withstand the pressures of crisis situations. Likewise, individuals should focus on building emotional resilience. This involves developing coping mechanisms, practicing mindfulness, and acquiring skills to navigate through challenges with adaptability and strength. Emotional resilience acts as a protective buffer during turbulent times.

Submarines rely on a well-coordinated crew during crises. Similarly, individuals should establish and nurture a robust support network. This network may include friends, family, colleagues, or mental health professionals. Cultivating these connections ensures that individuals have reliable sources of emotional and practical support when facing personal emergencies.

Submarines prioritize clear communication during crises. In mental health preparedness, individuals should encourage open communication about their emotions and challenges. Expressing feelings and concerns to trusted individuals fosters a supportive environment and enables others to offer assistance when needed.

They may engage experts for specialized assistance. Likewise, individuals should be open to seeking professional guidance for mental health. Whether through therapy, counseling, or other mental health services, accessing professional support adds an additional layer of expertise and tailored assistance during challenging times.

Submarines employ specific strategies to cope with crises. Similarly, individuals should develop their own set of coping strategies. These strategies may include activities that bring comfort, relaxation techniques, and hobbies that serve as outlets for stress. Having a repertoire of coping mechanisms enhances mental health preparedness.

They ensure that the crew is educated on crisis protocols. Similarly, individuals should educate those within their support network about mental health awareness. This not only reduces stigma but also ensures that those around them are better equipped to recognize signs of distress and offer meaningful assistance.

Submarines have detailed plans for crisis response. Likewise, individuals should create a personalized crisis response plan for mental health emergencies. This plan outlines steps to be taken, support systems to be contacted, and coping strategies to be implemented. Having a structured approach enhances mental health preparedness.

- **Embracing Adaptability in Crisis:**

Just as submarines encounter dynamic and ever-changing conditions underwater, individuals facing personal crises need to recognize the fluid nature of such situations. Understanding that crises can evolve and take unexpected turns is essential for adapting strategies accordingly.

Submarines have systems that can adapt to different challenges. Similarly, individuals should develop flexible coping mechanisms that can be adjusted based on the specific nature of the crisis. What works in one situation may need modification in another, emphasizing the importance of adaptability in coping strategies.

They may need to explore alternative routes or solutions during unexpected challenges. Likewise, individuals should remain open to alternative approaches and solutions in times of crisis. This may involve seeking different perspectives, considering new strategies, or accessing alternative support systems.

Also, submarines learn from each mission to enhance future responses. Similarly, individuals should view each crisis as an opportunity to learn and adjust their preparedness strategies.

Analyzing past experiences, understanding what worked well, and making necessary adjustments contribute to ongoing adaptability.

Submarines demonstrate resilience by adapting to the uncertainties of the underwater environment. Individuals, too, must cultivate resilience to navigate the uncertainties associated with personal emergencies. Resilience involves bouncing back from setbacks and adjusting one's mindset to effectively cope with challenges.

They adapt communication strategies based on changing conditions. Individuals should employ dynamic communication strategies during personal crises, adjusting the way they express their needs, seek support, and share information depending on the evolving circumstances.

Submarines make timely decisions to address emerging challenges. Individuals should cultivate the ability to make timely decisions during personal crises, considering the evolving nature of the situation and adapting their responses accordingly. Proactive decision-making contributes to effective crisis management.

They maintain a balance between stability and flexibility in their operations. Likewise, individuals need to strike a balance between stability, such as having a well-established crisis response plan, and flexibility, which allows for adjustments based on the specific demands of each crisis.

- **Cultivating Emotional Resilience:**

Submarines understand the importance of resilience in challenging environments. Similarly, individuals should comprehend the concept of emotional resilience, which refers to the ability to adapt positively to adversity, trauma, or significant stress. It involves maintaining mental well-being despite facing difficulties.

They learn and adapt from setbacks during their missions. Likewise, individuals should view setbacks in their personal lives as opportunities for learning and growth. Extracting lessons from challenges contributes to the development of emotional resilience, fostering a mindset that can navigate future adversities.

Submarines have built-in mechanisms to cope with external pressures. Similarly, individuals need to develop effective coping strategies to handle emotional stress. This might involve mindfulness practices, seeking support from others, or engaging in activities that promote mental well-being.

They maintain a positive operational mindset to endure challenges. Individuals should cultivate a positive mindset as a core component of emotional resilience. Optimism, hope, and the ability to find silver linings in difficult situations contribute to the capacity to bounce back from adversity.

Also, submarines demonstrate adaptability to navigate changing conditions.

Emotional resilience requires adaptability in response to life's uncertainties. Being flexible in one's emotional responses, adjusting to unexpected situations, and embracing change contribute to a resilient approach to personal emergencies.

Submarines operate as part of a support network within the naval fleet. Similarly, individuals should establish a robust support network in their personal lives. Having trusted friends, family members, or mental health professionals who can provide emotional support enhances resilience during challenging times.

They operate with precision but also have maintenance periods. Similarly, individuals should recognize the importance of self-compassion. Acknowledging one's own vulnerabilities, practicing self-care, and being compassionate toward oneself during difficult times contribute to emotional resilience.

Chapter **18**

Sustenance and Provisions

Submarines carry limited supplies, reminding us to manage resources and energy for sustaining our inner journeys.

Within the endless scope of the sea, submarines work as wonders of designing, exploring through the profundities with accuracy and reason. One striking viewpoint of submarine missions lies in their restricted supplies. These vessels are prepared with limited assets, carefully overseen to support the group all through their ventures underneath the surface. This characteristic of submarines serves as a significant representation for our individual journeys.

- **Managing Energy Reserves:**

Submarines, functioning in the vast and often treacherous expanse of the ocean, are equipped with protocols meticulously designed for crisis situations. These protocols are the lifelines that guide submariners in navigating through unforeseen challenges, ensuring their safety and the success of their missions. In a parallel manner, individuals encounter the unpredictable currents of life, where personal crises can emerge suddenly, demanding swift and calculated responses.

Much like submarines encounter turbulent waters during their missions, individuals face periods of upheaval and uncertainty in their personal journeys.

These turbulent times can manifest in various forms, such as career setbacks, relationship challenges, or health issues. Developing crisis management strategies becomes essential for effectively navigating through the rough waters of life.

Submarines thrive on the synergy of their crews, each member playing a crucial role in crisis situations. Similarly, in personal development, the support of a well-coordinated team, whether friends, family, or mentors, can be instrumental during challenging times. Building a network of reliable connections enhances one's ability to weather storms and emerge stronger from personal crises.

Preparedness is a cornerstone of submarine operations. Regular drills and simulations ensure that the crew is well-prepared for potential crises. Similarly, in personal development, proactive preparation involves cultivating resilience, acquiring coping mechanisms, and developing a mindset that can adapt to unexpected challenges. This readiness becomes a pillar of strength during times of crisis.

Submariners operate in an environment where visibility is limited, requiring an acute sense of adaptability to the unseen depths. In personal development, life often plunges individuals into the unknown, demanding a similar adaptability to unforeseen circumstances and challenges.

The ability to navigate through uncertainties, much like a submarine navigating the unseen ocean floor, underscores the importance of adaptability in both realms.

The crew of a submarine embodies a mastery of skills crucial for its safe and effective operation. From navigation to crisis management, the precision in executing these skills is paramount. In personal development, the acquisition and refinement of skills—be it communication, resilience, or adaptability—mirror the precision needed in operating a submarine. These skills, when honed, become the tools individuals employ to navigate the complexities of their own lives.

The engine room of a submarine is the heartbeat of its operations, requiring meticulous attention and discipline. Likewise, in personal development, self-discipline serves as the engine room of growth. The commitment to consistent self-improvement, the daily habits that foster progress, and the resilience to stay the course even in turbulent times are akin to the discipline required to keep a submarine's systems functioning optimally.

Submariners engage in continuous learning to stay abreast of evolving technologies and tactics. Similarly, personal development is an ongoing journey marked by a commitment to continuous learning.

Embracing new ideas, acquiring fresh perspectives, and adapting one's approach based on lessons learned form the bedrock of growth. Much like submariners chart new courses based on acquired knowledge, individuals in personal development navigate their journeys with a commitment to lifelong learning.

- **Strategic Resource Allocation:**

In the submerged world beneath the ocean's surface, where resources are finite, submarines must adhere to strategic resource allocation. The confined space demands meticulous planning to ensure the crew's well-being and the successful execution of their mission. Prioritizing essentials such as life support, propulsion systems, and mission-critical functions becomes imperative to sustain the vessel.

Similarly, individuals must navigate the vast expanse of their personal development journey with a keen understanding of strategic resource allocation. In the complex landscape of daily life, time, attention, and emotional energy are limited resources. Intentional allocation is essential to align these resources with core values and aspirations. This strategic approach ensures that personal efforts are directed toward endeavors that contribute significantly to individual growth and fulfillment.

Core functions in submarines align with the vessel's purpose, emphasizing essentials necessary for operation and crew well-being. Mapping these core values ensures that resources are allocated in a manner consistent with the submarine's mission.

Individuals, too, must map their core values, identifying the principles and goals that define their personal mission. This mapping process becomes the compass guiding strategic resource allocation, ensuring that time and energy are invested in endeavors that resonate with one's fundamental beliefs.

In the submerged environment, resource depletion poses a severe risk. Submariners guard against this by carefully monitoring and conserving essential resources to maintain operational integrity.

Individuals must adopt a similar vigilance against resource depletion in their personal lives. The conscious monitoring of time and energy expenditure guards against burnout and ensures sustained momentum in the pursuit of personal goals.

Essentials such as life support systems and critical machinery take precedence in resource allocation within a submarine. Prioritizing these essentials is non-negotiable for the safety and functionality of the vessel.

In personal development, individuals must prioritize essentials aligned with their goals. Whether it's investing time in education, fostering meaningful relationships, or dedicating energy to self-care, recognizing and prioritizing these essentials is vital for holistic personal growth.

Every action within a submarine is aligned with the overarching mission. Strategic resource allocation ensures that each crew member's contribution is directed toward the common goal.

Individuals must align their actions with their aspirations. Strategic resource allocation involves directing efforts and energy toward activities that contribute meaningfully to personal growth and fulfillment.

Adaptability is crucial in submarine operations. Flexibility in resource allocation allows for adjustments based on evolving circumstances and unforeseen challenges.

Similarly, individuals must adopt a flexible approach to resource allocation. Life is dynamic, and the ability to adapt resource allocation based on changing priorities and circumstances is essential for sustained personal development.

Resource allocation in submarines is a collaborative effort. Each crew member plays a role in ensuring that resources are distributed effectively for the collective benefit.

Individuals benefit from collaboration in resource allocation. Seeking support from others, delegating tasks when necessary, and building a network that complements individual strengths contribute to effective resource management.

- **Balancing Tangible and Intangible Resources:**

Submarines exemplify holistic resource management by recognizing the significance of tangible supplies like food, water, and fuel, while also prioritizing intangible factors such as crew morale and mental well-being. This holistic approach ensures that the vessel operates optimally.

Similarly, in personal development, individuals must adopt a holistic perspective.

Balancing tangible elements like physical health, financial stability, and time commitments with intangible aspects like emotional well-being and personal growth creates a comprehensive strategy for navigating life's complexities.

Submarines, with limited resources, optimize their time and attention to prioritize essential functions. Similarly, individuals must be discerning in how they allocate their time and attention. Strategic decisions on where to invest one's focus—whether in career pursuits, relationships, or personal passions—play a crucial role in sustaining and enhancing the quality of life. The ability to prioritize aligns with the submarine's strategy of optimizing resources for maximum effectiveness.

They acknowledge the critical role of crew morale, understanding that emotional reserves contribute to mission success. In the personal realm, emotions are powerful yet finite resources. Managing emotional energy—being aware of emotional well-being, seeking support when needed, and fostering a positive mindset—is integral to maintaining mental health. Individuals must recognize that emotional reserves are valuable resources that, when managed wisely, contribute to resilience and overall well-being.

Just as submarines are vigilant in managing their limited supplies, individuals must practice financial stewardship in their personal lives.

Budgeting, saving, and making thoughtful financial decisions align with the submarine's approach to managing tangible resources. Financial stability becomes a key pillar in supporting personal goals and aspirations, ensuring a smooth journey through the unpredictable currents of life.

Meticulously manage energy reserves to ensure essential functions operate optimally. Similarly, individuals need to manage their energy reserves—physical, mental, and emotional—for sustained personal growth. Recognizing the signs of burnout, adopting self-care practices, and knowing when to recharge are essential aspects of preserving energy. This deliberate approach ensures that individuals can navigate life's challenges with resilience and vitality.

Resource allocation on submarines involves strategic decision-making to ensure mission success. In personal development, strategic decision-making is equally crucial. Individuals must make intentional choices aligned with their values and long-term goals. Whether it's choosing a career path, cultivating meaningful relationships, or pursuing personal passions, strategic decision-making guides the trajectory of the personal journey.

They prioritize resources based on their mission objectives. Similarly, individuals must maintain focus on their core values and aspirations. Aligning actions with values creates a sense of purpose and direction in personal development.

It involves making choices that resonate with one's authentic self, contributing to a more meaningful and fulfilling life.

Submarines exhibit adaptability in resource allocation to respond to dynamic situations. Similarly, individuals must be adaptable in their approach to resource management. Life is inherently unpredictable, and the ability to adjust resource allocation based on changing circumstances is a valuable skill. Adaptability ensures that individuals can navigate the ebb and flow of life with resilience and agility.

- **Long-Term Sustainability:**

Submarines may uncover hidden landscapes in the ocean, much like individuals discovering their unique talents. Exploring one's talents is akin to navigating uncharted territories within oneself, revealing abilities that contribute to personal growth.

In the ocean's depths, submarines rely on anchors for stability. Similarly, individuals can explore and identify their inner strengths, acting as anchors during turbulent times. Understanding and leveraging these strengths enhance the ability to stay grounded amid life's uncertainties.

They navigate undercurrents, and individuals possess the undercurrent of resilience. Delving into this reservoir of resilience allows for the navigation of life's challenges, providing the strength to withstand pressures and emerge stronger from difficult situations.

Submarine journeys may uncover untouched ocean floors. Likewise, exploring personal resources involves delving into hidden potential. By recognizing and nurturing this potential, individuals can unearth new possibilities, fostering personal development and self-discovery.

Also, submarines adapt to changing tides, reflecting the adaptability required in life. Individuals can explore their adaptability—navigating the ebb and flow of experiences, adjusting to circumstances, and learning to thrive in different environments.

Submarines utilize ocean currents for efficient navigation. Similarly, individuals can explore their reservoir of knowledge—constantly learning, evolving, and harnessing intellectual currents that contribute to personal development and a broader understanding of the world.

In the ocean's vastness, echoes are created. Likewise, individuals exploring personal resources can discover the echo of empathy within themselves. Understanding and embracing empathy fosters meaningful connections, enriching the tapestry of personal relationships.

Chapter 19

Critical Systems Maintenance

The integrity of a submarine's systems is crucial, paralleling the need for regular self-care to ensure our well-being.

The complicated apparatus of a submarine works quietly underneath the ocean's surface, its frameworks fastidiously kept up to guarantee ideal usefulness. Essentially, within the complex embroidered artwork of human presence, the astuteness of our physical, mental, and passionate well-being plays a foremost part. The parallel between the cautious support of a submarine's frameworks and the basic of standard self-care underscores the centrality of protecting our all encompassing wellbeing.

- **Holistic Maintenance:**

Submarines, as marvels of engineering, require comprehensive maintenance to ensure their peak performance. This includes the meticulous care of mechanical components, regular checks on electronic systems, and structural evaluations. The synergy among these elements is critical for the submarine's overall integrity. Regular inspections, part replacements, and preventive measures are implemented to address vulnerabilities and sustain the submarine's operational efficiency.

Parallel to the holistic maintenance of submarines, personal well-being encompasses a comprehensive approach to self-care.

It involves nurturing the physical, mental, and emotional dimensions of our being, recognizing their interconnectedness. Just as a submarine's systems rely on each other, our well-being flourishes when we address our physical health, engage in mental stimulation, and foster emotional resilience. Holistic care means understanding that neglecting one facet may impact the overall harmony of our well-being.

In submarines, mechanical, electronic, and structural elements work in harmony; any imbalance affects the vessel's performance. Similarly, our physical, mental, and emotional well-being are interconnected. For instance, regular exercise not only benefits physical health but also has positive impacts on mental and emotional states. Holistic maintenance recognizes that each dimension plays a crucial role, contributing to a balanced and thriving well-being.

Submarines implement preventive measures to avoid breakdowns during critical missions. Regular checks and assessments are conducted to identify potential issues before they escalate. This preventive approach safeguards the submarine's functionality. Likewise, in personal well-being, preventive measures involve proactive self-care practices. Regular exercise, proper nutrition, and stress management act as metaphorical checks, preventing the accumulation of physical and mental health challenges.

For submarines, continuous maintenance is essential for their evolution and longevity. Lessons learned from past missions inform future improvements. Similarly, personal well-being is an ongoing journey of evolution. Reflecting on our experiences, learning from challenges, and adjusting our self-care practices contribute to continuous growth and development. Holistic maintenance recognizes that both submarines and individuals are on a perpetual journey of improvement.

In submarines, an integrated approach ensures that all components work seamlessly. The same principle applies to personal well-being, where an integrated approach addresses physical, mental, and emotional needs. A balanced lifestyle that includes adequate rest, mental stimulation, and emotional support fosters overall health and resilience. Holistic maintenance advocates for an integrated approach to self-care, acknowledging the synergy among different facets.

The integrity of submarines relies on the synergy among mechanical, electronic, and structural components. Similarly, personal well-being flourishes when there is synergy among physical health, mental clarity, and emotional well-being. Recognizing the interdependence of these components allows for a more effective and harmonious approach to self-care.

Both submarines and personal well-being require resilience and adaptability.

Submarines must withstand oceanic pressures and external factors, adapting to dynamic environments. In personal well-being, resilience involves coping with life's challenges and adapting to changes. Holistic maintenance recognizes the importance of cultivating resilience and adaptability to navigate the complexities of submarines and the intricate tapestry of personal development.

- **Preventive Measures for Longevity:**

Regular checks and preventive measures are not mere routine tasks; they are the lifelines that extend the lifespan of these complex systems. The proactive identification of vulnerabilities, timely part replacements, and adherence to maintenance protocols are all geared towards ensuring the sustained functionality of the submarine over the long term.

In the realm of personal well-being, the concept of preventive measures echoes the submarine's approach. Just as submarines require meticulous attention to various systems, our bodies and minds demand proactive care. Engaging in preventive measures becomes paramount for the longevity of our overall well-being. Regular exercise acts as a check on physical health, a well-balanced nutrition plan becomes a replacement for essential elements, and stress management serves as a preventive measure against the wear and tear of mental health.

Submarines meticulously identify vulnerabilities in their systems, understanding that early detection is key to preventing larger issues.

Regular inspections and assessments are conducted to pinpoint potential weaknesses. Similarly, personal well-being benefits from the identification of vulnerabilities. Consistent self-assessment, whether physical or mental, allows individuals to recognize potential health challenges before they escalate, enabling timely intervention and the preservation of well-being.

Submarines adapt to changes in technology and underwater conditions to ensure their longevity. Similarly, personal well-being thrives when individuals adapt to changes in lifestyle and circumstances. Embracing evolving self-care practices and adjusting to the changing demands of life contribute to the adaptability necessary for long-term well-being.

A submarine's longevity is influenced by mindful resource consumption, and personal well-being parallels this through mindful nutrition. What we consume plays a pivotal role in our health, and adopting a mindful approach to nutrition ensures that our bodies receive the essential elements for prolonged vitality. This preventive measure becomes a cornerstone for sustaining energy, resilience, and overall well-being.

Beyond physical aspects, mental resilience is crucial for both submarines and personal well-being. Submarines encounter challenging underwater conditions, and mental resilience practices are integrated into crew training. In personal well-being, consistent mindfulness and stress management practices enhance mental resilience, providing the capacity to navigate life's challenges with a clear and composed mindset.

Submarines don't wait for a breakdown to address issues; they proactively conduct maintenance to prevent potential failures. Likewise, individuals can adopt a proactive approach to their well-being by incorporating regular exercise, mental stimulation, and emotional support into their routines. This proactive maintenance is foundational for the prevention of health challenges and the promotion of longevity.

They engage in continuous learning from past missions to improve future operations. Similarly, personal well-being benefits from a commitment to continuous learning and improvement. Reflecting on past experiences, learning from successes and challenges, and integrating these insights into our self-care practices contribute to the longevity of our overall well-being.

- **Adaptability to Changing Environments:**

Submarines are marvels of engineering designed to adapt seamlessly to the dynamic and unpredictable conditions of the ocean. Their systems are equipped to handle varying pressures, temperatures, and underwater terrains. This adaptability is not just a feature but a necessity, ensuring that submarines remain operational and effective in diverse environments. Whether navigating through deep abyssal plains or near the surface, submarines demonstrate a remarkable ability to adjust to changing conditions.

In a parallel vein, personal well-being thrives on the principle of adaptability to changing environments.

Life is a journey marked by shifting circumstances, unexpected challenges, and evolving landscapes. Regular self-care becomes the anchor that enhances an individual's adaptability. Engaging in practices such as mindfulness, stress management, and a balanced lifestyle equips individuals with the resilience needed to navigate the diverse challenges presented by life's changing environments.

Just as submarines need to be resilient in fluctuating oceanic conditions, individuals benefit from cultivating mindful resilience in the face of life's uncertainties. The ability to bounce back from setbacks, learn from experiences, and adjust one's approach based on changing circumstances contributes to a resilient mindset. This adaptability ensures that individuals not only survive but thrive in the ever-shifting landscapes of personal and professional life.

Submarines undergo adaptations during different phases of their missions. Similarly, individuals experience various life stages, each presenting unique challenges. Adaptable self-care practices recognize the changing needs of well-being across different stages of life. Whether facing the demands of a busy career, navigating parenthood, or transitioning into retirement, individuals can tailor their self-care routines to suit the specific environments they find themselves in.

The ocean's unpredictability requires submarines to exhibit emotional agility in decision-making.

Similarly, personal well-being benefits from emotional agility—a capacity to navigate and understand one's emotions. This adaptability in emotional responses allows individuals to maintain mental equilibrium, make sound decisions, and foster healthy relationships, even in challenging environments.

Submarines showcase flexibility in their operations, and personal well-being draws a parallel through flexible self-care practices. Flexibility in self-care means adapting routines to fit changing schedules, embracing new wellness trends, and adjusting goals based on evolving priorities. This flexibility ensures that self-care remains relevant and effective in different life contexts.

They encounter different operational requirements, and personal adaptability is crucial in navigating career changes. For individuals, career shifts often come with unique stressors and adjustments. Consistent self-care becomes a stabilizing force, promoting mental and emotional well-being as individuals navigate the challenges and opportunities associated with changing professional environments.

Also, submarines undergo holistic adaptation to varied underwater conditions, and individuals can embrace a holistic approach to adaptability in their personal lives. This involves not only mental and emotional resilience but also physical well-being. A holistic self-care routine addresses the interconnectedness of these dimensions, ensuring comprehensive adaptability to the changing environments individuals encounter.

- **Continuous Monitoring and Adjustment:**

Continuous monitoring involves the use of advanced technologies and human expertise to track the performance of various components. Whether it's checking pressure levels, assessing navigation systems, or monitoring energy consumption, submarines engage in a proactive approach to ensure that every element functions optimally. Additionally, adjustments and calibrations are made in real-time based on the data gathered, preventing potential issues from escalating.

In a parallel context, personal well-being requires a similar commitment to continuous monitoring and adjustment. Regular self-assessment is akin to the monitoring systems of a submarine. Individuals need to introspect, evaluate their physical and mental states, and identify areas that may need attention. This self-awareness serves as the foundation for making informed adjustments in various aspects of life. It involves adapting lifestyle choices, modifying habits, and reprioritizing commitments in response to the ever-changing circumstances of personal and professional life.

Just as submarines employ advanced tools for monitoring, individuals can use mindful self-assessment as a powerful tool for well-being. This involves being attuned to one's emotions, energy levels, and overall state of mind. Regular check-ins with oneself allow for the identification of potential areas of stress, fatigue, or imbalance. This mindfulness serves as an early warning system, prompting individuals to make necessary adjustments before issues escalate.

Submarines make adjustments to their operations based on real-time data, and individuals must do the same with their lifestyles. This may involve adjusting sleep patterns, modifying dietary choices, or incorporating regular exercise. Lifestyle adjustments are a proactive measure to address the daily demands and challenges that impact an individual's physical and mental well-being.

Continuous monitoring in personal well-being extends to mental health. Regular self-reflection helps individuals identify signs of stress, anxiety, or other mental health challenges. Adjustments in this context may involve seeking professional support, practicing mindfulness techniques, or making changes in daily routines to prioritize mental health.

They actively manage stress through continuous monitoring, and individuals can adopt a proactive stress management approach. This includes recognizing stress triggers, implementing stress-reducing activities, and adjusting the pace of life to prevent chronic stress. Proactive stress management ensures a healthier and more resilient mental state.

Just as submarines adjust their course based on changing conditions, individuals need flexibility in goal-setting. Continuous monitoring of personal goals allows for realistic adjustments in response to evolving priorities, timelines, or unforeseen challenges. Flexibility in goal setting ensures that individuals can navigate the dynamic landscape of personal and professional aspirations.

Chapter **20**

The Dark Ocean

Submarines navigate the profound darkness of the sea, akin to facing the darkness within ourselves and overcoming our fears.

Submarines, those enigmatic vessels of the sea, embody the essence of venturing into the profound darkness beneath the ocean's surface. As they navigate through the murky depths, guided by advanced technologies and the expertise of their crews, submarines reflect a journey that resonates beyond the confines of the aquatic world. This exploration into the profound darkness draws a compelling parallel to the introspective expedition each individual undertakes within themselves. Just as submarines pierce through the obscurity of the ocean, individuals face the challenge of confronting the darkness within – a realm where fears, uncertainties, and uncharted emotions reside.

- **The Abyss of Self-Reflection:**

Submarines venture into an enigmatic abyss beneath the ocean's surface, a realm characterized by darkness and mystery. Similarly, when individuals embark on the journey of self-reflection, they traverse the enigmatic depths of their inner landscapes—unveiling the complexities of thoughts, emotions, and memories that often elude the clarity of everyday perception.

As submarines confront the abyss, individuals, in moments of self-reflection, confront the obscured realities of their lives.

It is a confrontation with aspects of the self that may be overlooked or intentionally kept in the shadows—an acknowledgment that is crucial for holistic self-awareness.

The abyss serves as a metaphor for the depth of our inner landscapes. In the absence of external influences, the inner world unfolds like a vast and intricate ocean floor, housing thoughts and emotions that demand exploration and understanding. The depth represents the layers of one's consciousness waiting to be unraveled. Submerged in the abyss, submarines navigate in darkness. Similarly, during self-reflection, individuals explore the recesses of their minds and emotions in the absence of the external "light" of distractions. It is in this darkness that profound revelations and introspective insights often come to light.

Submarines find themselves free from the influences of external factors as they delve into the abyss. Likewise, self-reflection requires a withdrawal from the external noise of daily life, providing individuals with the solitude necessary for introspective contemplation.

Just as submarines move in silence through the abyss, the process of self-reflection often unfolds in internal silence. This silence is a canvas for listening to the whispers of one's thoughts, understanding the nuances of emotions, and gaining clarity amid the quietude.

Submarines navigating the abyss unveil hidden complexities of the ocean floor.

Similarly, individuals, in their quest for self-awareness, unveil the intricate complexities of their personalities, confronting the multifaceted nature of their thoughts, emotions, and experiences.

The abyss symbolizes a journey beyond surface realities. Similarly, self-reflection is a plunge beyond superficial layers, encouraging individuals to delve into the profound depths of their being—a journey that unveils the richness and intricacy hidden beneath the surface.

- **The Murkiness of Unresolved Fears:**

Submarines, in their navigation through the enigmatic depths, face the challenges of maneuvering through murkiness, akin to the internal exploration individuals undertake during moments of introspection. The metaphorical darkness within the self often echoes the ambiguities, uncertainties, and anxieties concealed beneath the surface layers of consciousness, patiently awaiting acknowledgment and resolution.

Just as submarines delve into the obscured depths of the ocean, individuals embark on an internal voyage where the murkiness symbolizes the complexities of unresolved fears. These fears, much like elusive sea creatures lurking in the shadows, have the potential to influence emotions, decisions, and overall well-being. Confronting this murkiness becomes an essential aspect of personal growth, requiring the courage to face and address the fears that linger in the unexplored corners of the mind.

The murkiness of unresolved fears may manifest as persistent doubts, insecurities, or past traumas that cast shadows on one's inner landscape. Introspection becomes a metaphorical dive into these murky waters, necessitating a deliberate effort to bring these fears to the surface. It involves peeling back the layers of avoidance or suppression and allowing the light of self-awareness to illuminate the hidden recesses where fears reside.

Acknowledging these unresolved fears is a crucial step, akin to submarines recognizing the challenges posed by navigating through murky waters. The internal acknowledgment opens the door to understanding the origins and triggers of these fears, providing valuable insights into the complexities of one's psyche. Like a submarine adjusting its course to navigate through the darkness, individuals can begin the process of adapting and addressing their fears with intentionality.

Just as submarines employ advanced sonar and navigation systems to navigate through the murkiness, individuals can utilize self-awareness and mindfulness as their guiding tools. Cultivating these mental tools enables a clearer understanding of the fears, allowing for intentional and informed decision-making in addressing and mitigating their impact. The process involves patiently deciphering the signals within, much like a submarine interpreting sonar readings to navigate safely.

Addressing the murkiness of unresolved fears requires a commitment to self-compassion and vulnerability.

It involves creating an environment within oneself that encourages open exploration and acceptance of the emotions and experiences that contribute to the darkness. Just as submarines rely on a well-coordinated crew, individuals may seek support from trusted friends, family, or mental health professionals to navigate through these internal waters.

The journey through the murkiness of unresolved fears is not a solitary endeavor but a shared human experience. Embracing this shared aspect fosters empathy and connection, recognizing that everyone, like submarines navigating through the depths, contends with their unique set of fears and uncertainties. By collectively acknowledging and addressing these fears, individuals contribute not only to their own growth but also to the broader tapestry of shared understanding and resilience.

- **Sonar of Self-Awareness:**

Much like submarines relying on advanced sonar technology to navigate through the darkness of the ocean, individuals can cultivate their own form of self-awareness, serving as a guiding sonar in the intricate landscapes of the subconscious. This metaphorical sonar becomes a powerful tool, allowing individuals to navigate through the depths of their inner world, shedding light on aspects that might otherwise remain concealed.

Submarines use sonar systems to emit sound waves and interpret the echoes, providing them with crucial information about the surrounding environment. Similarly, individuals can develop self-awareness as a mental sonar, emitting their attention inward to gain insights into their thoughts, emotions, and instincts. This intentional self-reflection becomes a mechanism to decipher the echoes of one's internal experiences, helping to unravel the complexities that may be hidden from conscious awareness.

The process of developing a sonar of self-awareness involves tuning into inner cues and signals, much like submarines tuning their sonar to detect subtle variations in the underwater landscape. It requires a conscious effort to listen to the whispers of one's emotions, the subtle shifts in mood, and the underlying motivations that shape behavior. By honing this internal sonar, individuals can illuminate the otherwise dark corners of their minds, gaining a clearer understanding of their beliefs, desires, and fears.

Navigating the subconscious with a sonar of self-awareness also involves recognizing the importance of instincts. Submarines depend on their crew's instincts, honed through training and experience, to interpret sonar readings effectively. Similarly, individuals can trust their instincts as a valuable component of self-awareness. Intuitive feelings and gut reactions often provide valuable information about the alignment of actions with inner values and the authenticity of personal choices.

Just as submarines adjust the frequency and sensitivity of their sonar to adapt to different underwater conditions, individuals can refine their self-awareness to suit the nuances of their internal landscapes. This adaptability allows for a deeper exploration of thoughts and emotions, facilitating a more nuanced understanding of the self. It involves fine-tuning the mental sonar to be receptive to subtle changes and shifts in the internal environment.

The sonar of self-awareness serves not only as a tool for personal exploration but also as a guide for decision-making. Submarines use sonar to make informed navigational decisions, and individuals can use self-awareness to make conscious and intentional choices aligned with their values. This heightened awareness provides clarity in navigating life's challenges, helping individuals stay true to themselves amidst the complexities of the external world.

Developing and utilizing the sonar of self-awareness is an ongoing practice. Submarines continuously monitor and adjust their sonar systems, and similarly, individuals can engage in regular self-reflection and introspection to refine their self-awareness. Cultivating this internal guidance system empowers individuals to navigate the vast and often mysterious depths of their own consciousness, promoting personal growth, authenticity, and a deeper connection with the self and the world.

- **Facing the Unknown:**

Much like submarines that venture into uncharted waters, individuals embark on a parallel journey of self-discovery, where the unknown territories lie within the depths of their own emotions, memories, and fears. The profound nature of this internal exploration mirrors the uncertainty and unpredictability encountered by submarines in unexplored sea regions, creating a narrative of facing the unknown with courage and curiosity. Submarines navigate through vast expanses of uncharted waters, relying on advanced technologies and strategic planning to confront the challenges that arise. Similarly, individuals delve into the unexplored realms of their psyche, armed with introspection, self-awareness, and a willingness to confront the mysteries that lie within. The journey involves a recognition that, like the ocean depths, the human mind is complex, with layers waiting to be unraveled.

Stepping into the unexplored territories of one's emotions, memories, and fears requires a mindset akin to submariners approaching uncharted waters—resilient, adaptable, and prepared for unexpected discoveries. It involves a deliberate decision to confront the unknown aspects of the self, acknowledging that the richness of personal growth often lies in the uncharted territories of the mind.

Just as submarines employ sonar to navigate through the darkness of the ocean, individuals can develop their own form of self-awareness as a guiding mechanism.

This internal sonar involves tuning into inner cues, emotions, and instincts to navigate through the intricacies of the subconscious. The awareness acts as a guiding light, shining upon the otherwise concealed aspects of the self and aiding in deciphering the nuances of one's inner landscape.

The journey of facing the unknown within oneself is a profound expedition that requires openness to the uncertainties that come with self-discovery. It involves confronting emotions that may have been buried, exploring memories that may have shaped one's identity, and acknowledging fears that may have influenced decision-making. Each step in this internal exploration mirrors the submarines' navigation through uncharted waters—each turn revealing new facets, challenges, and opportunities for growth.

Embracing the unknown within oneself is an act of courage and self-acceptance. It requires a willingness to navigate through the murkiness of uncertainties, trusting that the insights gained will contribute to personal understanding and resilience. Much like submarines overcoming challenges in uncharted waters, individuals find strength in the process of facing the unknown within, emerging with a deeper understanding of themselves and the complexities that shape their inner worlds.

- **Navigating Emotional Turbulence:**

Much like submarines skillfully navigate through underwater currents, individuals traverse the intricate landscape of emotional turbulence within. The ability to navigate these emotional currents involves a nuanced approach, akin to submariners navigating through the unpredictable movements beneath the ocean's surface. It requires cultivating emotional intelligence, understanding the ebbs and flows of feelings, and steering through challenges with resilience and adaptability.

Submarines, equipped with advanced technologies to detect and respond to underwater currents, exemplify the importance of awareness in navigating complex environments. Similarly, individuals can cultivate emotional intelligence—a heightened awareness of their own emotions and those of others—as a powerful tool to navigate the dynamic currents of their internal world. This self-awareness becomes the compass guiding individuals through the often unpredictable emotional landscape.

Emotional turbulence, much like underwater currents, is a natural part of the human experience. Just as submarines are designed to withstand and maneuver through the challenges posed by underwater currents, individuals can develop strategies to navigate the complexities of their emotions. This involves acknowledging and understanding the diverse range of emotions, recognizing their origins, and embracing them as valuable signals that provide insights into one's inner state.

Chapter **21**

Surface Intervals

Submarines occasionally resurface for air, analogous to the importance of taking breaks and connecting with the world for balance.

Within the profundities of the sea, submarines explore through the obscure, typified in an environment of significant haziness. In any case, indeed these wonders of designing, planned to investigate concealed depths, recognize the basic got to reemerge occasionally. Developing into the open discuss, submarines draw a parallel to a crucial perspective of human existence—the need of taking breaks and reconnecting with the world for inward   harmony.

Fair as submarines rise to the surface to renew their oxygen supplies, people as well require moments of relief to revive their mental, enthusiastic, and physical resources. This reemerging isn't just a pause but a think act of self-care, recognizing the significance of keeping up a fragile adjust within the confront of life's ceaseless requests.

- **Oxygenation of the Mind and Spirit:**

Ascending to the surface is a strategic maneuver for submarines, a moment when they breach the water's edge to welcome the influx of fresh air. This act is not merely a necessity for sustaining the vessel but a calculated step to replenish the crucial oxygen stores within.

In the confined underwater environment, where every breath is a valuable resource, resurfacing becomes a lifeline. The functionality of the submarine, the well-being of its crew, and the success of its mission hinge on this deliberate act of ascent.

Analogously, individuals experience a comparable need for resurfacing in their lives. Taking breaks, stepping away from the routine, and connecting with the world become opportunities to breathe, both literally and metaphorically. In the ebb and flow of daily existence, these moments of respite serve as a breath of fresh air for the mind and spirit. Just as submarines require oxygen for their operational vitality, individuals require moments of mental rejuvenation. These breaks offer a chance to inhale clarity, exhale stress, and recharge mental faculties. In this oxygenated space, creativity flourishes, and a renewed sense of purpose and direction emerges.

- **Preventing Emotional Stagnation:**

In the world of submarines, prolonged submersion can create an environment where emotional strain may gradually accumulate among the crew. The confined spaces, the isolation from external stimuli, and the intense nature of their responsibilities can contribute to a sense of emotional fatigue over time. Recognizing the potential impact on the crew's well-being, submariners and naval protocols acknowledge the importance of periodic resurfacing as a countermeasure.

This intentional break from the underwater realm serves not only to replenish vital resources but also to address the emotional well-being of the crew.

Similarly, in the personal sphere, continuous engagement without breaks may lead to emotional stagnation. The routine demands of daily life, constant responsibilities, and unrelenting stressors can create a sense of monotony and emotional fatigue. Taking breaks and resurfacing metaphorically become essential strategies to disrupt this cycle. These breaks allow individuals to step away from routine, engage with different facets of life, and introduce a sense of novelty. By doing so, they prevent emotional stagnation and create opportunities for rejuvenation.

- **Building Connections with the External Environment:**

For submarines, resurfacing is not merely a physical act but a strategic move that opens avenues for communication. Breaking through the water's surface allows submarines to establish connections with other vessels and command centers. This communication is vital for receiving updates, coordinating maneuvers, and ensuring alignment with broader naval strategies. Resurfacing, in this context, becomes a dynamic process of engagement with the external environment, fostering collaboration and synergy.

In the realm of personal well-being, taking breaks plays a similar role in building connections with the external environment.

Stepping away from the demands of routine life provides individuals with opportunities to engage socially, connect with nature, or simply appreciate their surroundings. Social interactions, outdoor activities, or moments of contemplation in natural settings contribute to a holistic sense of well-being. These connections act as a source of support, inspiration, and perspective, enriching the individual's emotional landscape.

- **Assessment and Course Correction:**

For submarines, resurfacing is a critical phase that goes beyond mere replenishment. It marks a moment for assessment and course correction. Submarine commanders utilize the time above water to evaluate the vessel's performance, assess the accuracy of navigation, and ensure alignment with mission objectives. Any necessary adjustments to the course, tactics, or systems are made during this phase, optimizing the submarine's readiness for future operations.

Similarly, in the realm of personal well-being, breaks serve as a parallel opportunity for assessment and course correction. Taking breaks provides individuals with a pause from the hustle and bustle of daily life, allowing for introspection and self-assessment. During these moments of respite, individuals can reflect on their goals, evaluate their emotional and mental well-being, and consider whether their current life trajectory aligns with their aspirations.

This self-awareness enables them to make informed decisions and necessary adjustments to steer their lives in a direction that promotes overall well-being.

- **Recharging Physical Energy:**

The process of resurfacing for submarines is not only about assessing and adjusting course but also a moment to tap into external sources of energy. Submarines, equipped with solar panels, leverage this time above water to harness solar power, which is then used to recharge the vessel's batteries. This strategic utilization of renewable energy ensures that the submarine's power reservoirs are replenished, contributing to sustained functionality during subsequent dives.

In the context of personal well-being, the analogy holds true as breaks provide individuals with an opportunity to recharge their physical energy. Much like submarines accessing solar power, individuals require moments of rest and relaxation to replenish their own energy stores. Adequate sleep, leisure activities, and periods of downtime play a crucial role in preventing physical fatigue and burnout. These breaks become essential for maintaining overall health, enhancing resilience, and ensuring individuals have the vitality needed to navigate the challenges of their daily lives.

- **Enhancing Social Connections:**

Surface time allows for team-building activities and enhanced collaboration among crew members. Taking breaks facilitates participation in group activities, workshops, or collaborative projects, fostering a sense of community and teamwork in personal and professional spheres.

Crew members may communicate with family during resurfacing, strengthening familial connections. Breaks provide valuable moments for spending quality time with family, building and nurturing strong emotional bonds.

Crew interactions during surfaced periods contribute to the development of strong friendships and camaraderie. Breaks offer opportunities to connect with friends, share experiences, and build a supportive network that adds richness to life.

Resurfacing provides a chance for naval vessels to engage in joint exercises and social events. Taking breaks allows participation in social events, networking activities, and community gatherings, fostering connections beyond immediate circles.

Senior crew members may provide mentorship to junior members during surfaced periods. Breaks offer the chance to seek mentorship or guidance from experienced individuals, contributing to personal and professional growth.

Surface time may involve engagement with local communities during port visits. Breaks create opportunities for community involvement, volunteering, and contributing to social causes, enhancing a sense of purpose and connection.

International collaboration during surfaced periods allows for cultural exchange. Taking breaks can involve travel and exposure to different cultures, broadening perspectives and enriching personal experiences.

Communication technology is utilized during surfaced periods for connection. Breaks enable the use of digital communication tools, fostering connections with individuals globally, maintaining relationships across distances.

Crew support systems are reinforced during surfaced times. Taking breaks reinforces personal support systems, ensuring that individuals have a network to lean on during challenging times.

Crews may celebrate achievements during surfaced periods. Breaks provide moments for personal celebrations, fostering a positive and joyful mindset.

- **Cultivating Mindfulness:**

Resurfacing allows crew members to witness the vastness and beauty of the open sea. Taking breaks in natural settings enhances mindfulness. Whether it's a walk in the park or enjoying the serenity of a garden, connecting with nature promotes a sense of calm and presence.

Crew members may engage in specific breathing protocols during resurfacing. Breaks provide an opportunity for mindful breathing exercises. Techniques like deep breathing or meditation contribute to relaxation and mental clarity.

Resurfacing offers a view of the sky and potential inspiration for creativity. Engaging in artistic activities during breaks, such as drawing, painting, or playing a musical instrument, promotes mindfulness and self-expression.

Crew members may reflect on the successful completion of a mission during resurfacing. Breaks allow for gratitude reflection, acknowledging positive aspects of life, fostering a positive mindset, and contributing to mental well-being.

Resurfacing involves limited digital communication. Taking breaks can include a digital detox. Disconnecting from screens and technology promotes mindfulness by reducing external distractions.

Resurfacing brings crew members into the sunlight, a moment worth savoring. Breaks offer moments for savoring positive experiences—whether it's enjoying a favorite meal, sipping a cup of tea, or relishing a beautiful sunset.

Crew members may explore the submarine's deck during resurfacing.

Breaks can include mindful walking. Paying attention to each step and the surrounding environment brings attention to the present moment.

Resurfacing could be a time for crew members to record experiences.

Breaks offer an opportunity for reflective journaling, allowing individuals to process thoughts and emotions, promoting self-awareness.

- **Preserving Overall Health:**

Resurfacing allows crew members to engage in physical activities on the deck. Breaks are an opportunity for physical exercise, whether it's a quick workout, stretching, or a short walk. Regular movement supports physical health and overall well-being.

Resurfacing often involves replenishing supplies, including food and water. Breaks provide a chance to focus on nutrition and hydration. Consuming healthy meals and staying hydrated during breaks supports overall health and energy levels.

Crew members may establish sleep routines during resurfacing periods.

Breaks should include prioritizing quality sleep. Adequate rest is essential for mental and physical health, contributing to improved mood, cognitive function, and overall well-being.

Resurfacing offers crew members a break from high-stress situations.

During breaks, incorporating stress reduction techniques, such as mindfulness, meditation, or deep breathing exercises, supports mental health and resilience.

Crew members benefit from camaraderie during resurfacing. Breaks are an opportunity to connect with social support networks. Spending time with friends, family, or colleagues fosters a sense of belonging and positively impacts mental health.

Resurfacing allows crew members to engage in recreational activities.

Breaks should include time for hobbies and recreational pursuits. Pursuing activities that bring joy and fulfillment contributes to overall life satisfaction.

Periodic assessments are conducted to ensure the submarine's health.

Taking breaks provides individuals with the time to schedule and attend regular health check-ups. Proactive health management is vital for early detection and prevention of potential issues.

Crew members may engage in mental exercises during resurfacing.

Breaks can include activities that stimulate the mind, such as reading, puzzles, or learning new skills, promoting cognitive health.

Resurfacing allows for moments of relaxation. Breaks should incorporate leisure activities and relaxation. Whether it's enjoying a hobby or simply unwinding, these moments contribute to stress relief and mental well-being.

Resurfacing provides an opportunity for crew reflection. Breaks are a time for personal reflection, allowing individuals to assess their overall health, set goals, and make adjustments to support a healthy and balanced lifestyle.

Chapter 22

Sonar Contacts and Making Connections

Submarines detect nearby entities using sonar, resembling how we form connections with others that reflect aspects of our inner selves.

Within the significant profundities of the sea, submarines explore through obscurity and segregation, depending on progressed sonar frameworks to identify nearby entities. This prepare isn't as it were a confirmation to the accuracy of innovation but moreover an interesting relationship to the way human creatures frame associations with others. Our connections frequently serve as sonar signals, reflecting perspectives of our internal selves. Fair as submarines disentangle the submerged environment, we, as well, interpret our interpersonal associations to pick up experiences into our feelings, values, and individual development.

- **Sonar of Shared Values:**

Submarines utilize sonar to identify echoes that align with their surroundings. In human connections, shared values create harmony in principles. Individuals resonate with those who share similar ethical, moral, and philosophical beliefs, fostering a sense of unity and understanding.

Sonar aids submarines in building trust by recognizing familiar patterns. In interpersonal connections, shared values play a crucial role in establishing trust and rapport. Trust forms the foundation of meaningful relationships, allowing individuals to rely on one another and feel secure in their connection.

Submarines use sonar for cohesive navigation. Similarly, shared values contribute to cohesive team dynamics in personal and professional settings. When individuals within a group align in their values, it promotes cooperation, collaboration, and a shared vision, enhancing overall group effectiveness.

Sonar helps submarines navigate different depths in the ocean. In relationships, shared values assist in navigating the various dimensions of connection. Whether in friendships, partnerships, or professional collaborations, having shared values allows individuals to explore deeper levels of understanding and intimacy.

Submarines interpret sonar signals for effective communication. Likewise, shared values create resonance in communication between individuals. When values align, communication becomes more open, honest, and meaningful, fostering a deeper connection and mutual understanding.

Sonar helps submarines distinguish between objects, preventing collisions. Shared values serve a similar purpose in relationships, acting as a guide for conflict resolution.

When conflicts arise, a foundation of shared values provides a framework for understanding and resolving differences.

Submarines use sonar to adapt to different underwater environments. Similarly, shared values contribute to cultural and social alignment. Connecting with others who share similar values helps individuals navigate diverse social and cultural landscapes with greater ease and understanding.

Sonar echoes reveal changes in the underwater environment. In connections formed around shared values, the evolving resonance becomes echoes of personal growth. Relationships that reflect our inner values also mirror our journey of self-discovery and development.

Submarines rely on sonar for sustained navigation. Shared values ensure the sustainability of connections. When connections are rooted in shared values, they are more likely to withstand the tests of time, evolving and adapting without compromising the core principles that brought individuals together.

- **Echoes of Empathy:**

Submarines use sonar to distinguish between different materials in the underwater environment. Similarly, empathy allows individuals to tune into the emotional frequencies of others. This capacity to understand and resonate with diverse emotions fosters a deeper connection based on emotional intelligence.

Sonar creates resonance by analyzing underwater signals. In human connections, empathy generates emotional resonance. When individuals demonstrate empathy, it creates a shared emotional experience, fostering a connection that goes beyond surface-level interactions.

Subs utilize sonar for effective communication underwater. Empathy serves as a tool for effective communication in relationships. Understanding the emotions and perspectives of others enhances communication, promoting clarity and reducing misunderstandings.

Sonar in submarines involves the ability to distinguish subtle underwater signals. Likewise, empathy allows individuals to discern nuanced emotions. Cultivating compassionate connections based on empathy involves recognizing and responding to the subtleties of others' feelings.

They navigate complex underwater terrains using sonar. In connections built on empathy, individuals navigate the intricate emotional depths of themselves and others. This skill becomes particularly crucial in understanding and supporting others during challenging times.

Also, sonar aids submarines in building trust through understanding their surroundings. Empathy contributes to building trust in relationships. When individuals feel understood and heard, it fosters a sense of trust and reliability, creating a foundation for strong connections.

Submarines use sonar to avoid collisions and conflicts. Empathy plays a pivotal role in conflict resolution. When conflicts arise, the ability to empathize with others' perspectives allows for more constructive discussions and resolutions, preventing emotional collisions.

Moreover, sonar helps submarines work cohesively as a team. Empathy fosters a culture of support in personal and professional environments. When individuals practice empathy, it creates an atmosphere where everyone feels understood, supported, and valued.

Sonar echoes reflect changes in the underwater environment. In connections based on empathy, the evolving resonance becomes echoes of personal and collective growth. Empathetic connections contribute to individuals' ongoing journey of understanding themselves and others more deeply.

Subs use sonar globally for navigation. Expanding empathy on a global scale contributes to collective understanding. Fostering empathy not only in individual connections but also on a broader scale can lead to a more compassionate and interconnected world.

- **Depth of Emotional Bonds:**

Submarines gauge distances using sonar in the ocean's depth. Similarly, emotional bonds can be quantified by the proximity individuals feel to one another emotionally. The closer the emotional connection, the more profound and impactful the relationship.

Sonar in submarines measures the understanding of the underwater environment. Emotional bonds can be measured by the depth of mutual understanding between individuals. The ability to comprehend each other's emotions and perspectives contributes to the depth of the connection.

Subs navigate through varying depths in the ocean. In relationships, emotional bonds allow individuals to navigate through the diverse emotional depths within themselves and each other. This navigation requires an understanding of the intricacies that make the connection unique.

Also, sonar aids submarines in building trust through reliable distance measurements. In emotional bonds, trust deepens as individuals consistently show understanding, reliability, and emotional support. The depth of trust forms a solid foundation for lasting connections.

Submarines detect echoes to understand the underwater environment. Emotional bonds echo shared experiences. The depth of these bonds is often revealed through shared memories, milestones, and challenges, creating echoes that resonate within the relationship.

Sonar in submarines helps explore the vulnerabilities of the ocean's depths. Emotional bonds allow individuals to explore vulnerabilities together. The depth of connection is often tested and strengthened when individuals share their fears, insecurities, and innermost feelings.

Submarines endure varying depths, reflecting their resilience. Emotional bonds become a measure of resilience in relationships. The ability to withstand challenges, conflicts, and changes without compromising the depth of connection showcases the strength and durability of the bond.

In addition, Sonar measures depths for accurate navigation. Emotional bonds deepen through emotional intimacy. The willingness to share personal thoughts, feelings, and aspirations contributes to the profound nature of the connection.

Subs resonate with the underwater environment. Emotional bonds resonate within the depths of individuals. The resonance reflects a shared emotional frequency, where both individuals feel understood, valued, and emotionally connected.

Furthermore, sonar sustains depth over extended distances. Emotional bonds that endure over time reflect a sustained depth in long-term connections. The ability to maintain and even deepen emotional closeness over the years is a testament to the enduring nature of the bond.

Subs connect globally through sonar technology. Emotional bonds, when deep and profound, can contribute to a sense of global connectivity. Individuals who share deep emotional connections may feel a broader sense of interconnectedness, fostering empathy and understanding on a global scale.

- **Navigating Personal Growth:**

Submarines use sonar to identify underwater features. Human connections serve as mirrors reflecting personal strengths. Interactions with others can highlight areas where individuals excel, fostering a positive sense of self-awareness and reinforcing one's capabilities.

Sonar helps submarines identify navigational challenges. Likewise, human connections assist in identifying areas for personal development. Constructive feedback and insights from others can point to opportunities for growth and self-improvement.

Subs navigate through various underwater landscapes. Human connections aid in navigating the emotional terrain of personal growth. Relationships provide emotional support, guidance, and a sense of security as individuals navigate through challenges and triumphs.

Sonar mapping assists submarines in understanding underwater dynamics. Human connections help map interpersonal dynamics. By engaging with diverse individuals, individuals gain insights into different perspectives, enhancing their interpersonal skills and enriching their personal growth journey.

Submarines measure depth during navigation. Human connections, especially deep and meaningful ones, add depth to personal growth. Interactions that go beyond surface-level conversations contribute to a richer understanding of oneself and others, fostering personal development.

Also, submarines benefit from collective sonar data. Similarly, personal growth is often accelerated through shared experiences. Learning from the collective wisdom of those in our social circles provides valuable insights, enabling individuals to glean lessons from a broader range of experiences.

Sonar helps submarines adapt to changing underwater conditions. Human connections assist in adapting to changing life circumstances. Friends, mentors, and family members can provide guidance and support during transitions, contributing to adaptive personal growth.

Sonar echoes aid submarines in navigation. In personal growth, echoes of encouragement from meaningful connections resonate deeply. Positive affirmations, support, and encouragement from others create a supportive environment that fuels an individual's belief in their ability to grow and evolve.

Submarines navigate with a growth mindset using sonar. Human connections, especially those grounded in mutual respect, foster a growth mindset. Encouraging each other's aspirations, celebrating achievements, and collectively embracing a mindset of continuous improvement contribute to shared personal growth.

Subs use sonar to navigate through different underwater environments. Similarly, human connections expose individuals to diverse perspectives. Engaging with people from varied backgrounds and experiences broadens one's understanding, fostering personal growth through a more inclusive worldview.

- **Reflecting Shadows of Self-Discovery:**

Submarines use sonar to identify hidden obstacles. Similarly, connections may act as mirrors revealing unexplored talents. Interacting with others can bring attention to latent skills and abilities, encouraging individuals to explore new facets of themselves.

Sonar reveals hidden structures beneath the ocean's surface. Human connections prompt introspection by unveiling aspects of ourselves. The shadows in relationships serve as cues for self-reflection, encouraging individuals to explore their motivations, values, and personal narratives.

Subs use sonar to navigate around blind spots. Connections in our lives act as mirrors, revealing personal blind spots. Interactions can bring awareness to areas where individuals might have limited self-awareness, fostering a deeper understanding of their own perspectives and biases.

Also, sonar helps submarines navigate through underwater depths. Human connections assist in navigating emotional depths. The shadows in relationships may encompass unexplored emotions and vulnerabilities, guiding individuals to delve into their emotional landscapes for a more profound understanding of themselves.

Chapter 23

Defensive Mechanisms

Submarines have defenses against threats, similar to our psychological defenses protecting our ego and identity.

In the complicated profundities of the human mind, a complex interaction of feelings, encounters, and self-perceptions unfurls, reminiscent of the concealed world underneath the ocean's surface. Fair as submarines explore the profundities with an cluster of protections to upset potential dangers, the human intellect utilizes mental guards to protect the inner self and protect the astuteness of one's personality. This perplexing move between defenselessness and assurance shapes the forms of our mental scenes, impacting how we see ourselves, lock in with the world, and climate the storms of life.

- **Denial as Protective Armor:**

Within the realm of denial, individuals may selectively retrieve memories that align with their preferred narrative. This allows them to filter out information that challenges their established beliefs or threatens their self-image, reinforcing the protective barrier of denial.

Denial can involve a temporal displacement of threatening realities. Individuals may acknowledge the existence of challenges but postpone their emotional engagement with these issues, creating a buffer of time that temporarily shields them from the immediate impact of distressing truths.

Denial, much like the compartmentalization of submarines, can take on different forms. Individuals may compartmentalize aspects of their lives, denying challenges in specific domains while maintaining awareness in others. This selective denial enables a semblance of control over the perceived threats.

In the age of digital connectivity, individuals may seek out echo chambers that reinforce their denial. Online communities or social circles that share similar perspectives act as amplifiers, solidifying the protective armor of denial by surrounding individuals with like-minded voices.

Also, denial can become institutionalized, manifesting in societal or cultural norms that discourage open acknowledgment of certain challenges. In such cases, individuals may adopt denial as a shared defense mechanism, aligning with collective beliefs to maintain a cohesive social identity.

Projection, an extension of denial, involves attributing one's own denied qualities to others. This mechanism not only shields the individual from acknowledging personal vulnerabilities but also projects these denied aspects onto external sources, preserving a sense of righteousness and moral high ground.

In addition, denial often intertwines with rationalization. Individuals may construct elaborate rationalizations to justify their denial, creating a cognitive framework that reinforces the belief that distancing oneself from threatening realities is a logical and reasonable response.

Peripheral denial involves acknowledging threats at a surface level while downplaying their significance. Individuals engaging in this form of denial may acknowledge challenges but minimize their impact, creating a superficial awareness that maintains a veneer of control over the perceived threats.

Denial can lead to emotional detachment from threatening realities. Individuals may consciously or unconsciously detach emotionally from distressing truths, creating a numbness that shields them from the emotional turbulence associated with acknowledging challenging aspects of their lives.

Furthermore, denial can become intertwined with one's identity. Individuals may resist acknowledging threats that challenge the core aspects of their identity, leading to a more profound and entrenched form of denial that safeguards the very foundations of the self.

Denial may follow cyclical patterns, resurfacing periodically to shield the individual from recurrent threats. Understanding these cycles is crucial for recognizing the habitual nature of denial and initiating steps toward a more adaptive and open approach to challenging realities.

- **Projection: Shifting the Threat External:**

Submarines may deploy countermeasures to divert threats away from vital areas. Similarly, individuals, through projection, displace the responsibility for their internal conflicts onto external factors. By attributing negative emotions or challenges to external circumstances, they alleviate the burden of personal accountability. Projection serves as a tool to preserve a positive self-image. By projecting undesirable qualities onto others, individuals can maintain the illusion of their own moral superiority or competence. This defense mechanism helps shield the ego from acknowledging personal flaws.

Subs deploy countermeasures to avoid direct confrontation with threats. Similarly, projection allows individuals to avoid internal conflicts by externalizing them. This deflection strategy aids in evading self-reflection and the potential discomfort associated with addressing one's own issues.

Also, projection can be a mechanism to preserve relationships. Instead of acknowledging personal shortcomings, individuals project their insecurities onto others. This can help avoid conflict within relationships and maintain a facade of harmony.

Projection contributes to the creation of a distorted reality. By attributing their own fears or undesirable traits to external sources, individuals distort their perception of reality. This distorted lens serves as a protective measure against facing the uncomfortable truths within.

Submarines externalize threats to minimize the impact on critical systems. Similarly, projection allows individuals to externalize their internal anxieties. By attributing anxiety to external factors, individuals can attempt to regain a sense of control over their emotional well-being.

Projection involves a degree of self-deception. Individuals may deceive themselves into believing that external factors are the primary source of their distress, providing temporary emotional comfort. This self-deception shields them from the harsh reality of internal struggles.

In addition, projection acts as a psychological defense against overwhelming emotions. When individuals face intense internal conflicts, projecting these conflicts onto external elements provides a buffer, preventing emotional overwhelm and allowing for a semblance of emotional stability.

- **Rationalization: Crafting Protective Narratives:**

Submarines employ intellectual strategies for defense, analyzing threats with precision. In psychology, intellectualization involves creating emotional distance by overemphasizing logic and reason. Individuals may focus on facts and detached analysis, avoiding the emotional impact of a situation to protect themselves.

They may retreat to known locations for safety; similarly, regression is a defense mechanism where individuals revert to previous, often less mature, behaviors. This retreat to familiar patterns provides comfort during times of stress, serving as a protective mechanism against overwhelming emotions.

Subs redirect threats away from critical areas; individuals, through displacement, transfer emotions from a source that feels threatening to a safer one.

This redirection of emotional response allows for a more manageable expression of feelings while safeguarding the core aspects of one's identity.

Submarines compartmentalize sections for different functions; individuals use compartmentalization as a defense by separating conflicting thoughts or emotions into distinct mental compartments. This helps maintain a semblance of order and control, safeguarding the overall sense of self.

They may reverse certain actions for defense; undoing, in psychology, involves symbolic acts of reversal to counteract unacceptable thoughts or behaviors. Individuals may engage in rituals or behaviors aimed at undoing perceived wrongs, providing a psychological defense against guilt or anxiety.

Subs minimize potential threats; individuals, through minimization, downplay the significance of challenging situations. By diminishing the importance of a threat, individuals protect their self-esteem and maintain a positive self-perception.

They isolate sensitive equipment; individuals, through the isolation of affect, separate emotions from thoughts as a defense mechanism. This separation allows individuals to intellectually engage with challenging situations while minimizing the emotional impact.

Also, submarines may deploy countermeasures; similarly, reaction formation involves expressing the opposite of threatening feelings.

Individuals may outwardly display attitudes or behaviors that are contrary to their true emotions, creating a defensive façade to protect their internal state.

- **Compartmentalization: Segregating Threats:**

Compartmentalization helps preserve cognitive harmony. By segregating conflicting thoughts or emotions, individuals maintain a semblance of mental order and coherence. This separation allows them to avoid the discomfort of cognitive dissonance.

Submarines compartmentalize to protect critical systems; similarly, individuals compartmentalize to protect core beliefs about themselves. This defense mechanism enables individuals to shield their fundamental self-concept from challenges or threats, maintaining a stable and positive self-image.

In addition, compartmentalization is a strategy for managing cognitive dissonance. When faced with conflicting thoughts or emotions, individuals may compartmentalize to reduce the discomfort of holding contradictory beliefs. This helps in maintaining a sense of mental equilibrium.

Subs have compartments for various functions; likewise, individuals may compartmentalize to adapt to diverse roles. This allows individuals to navigate different aspects of their lives without allowing conflicts from one domain to spill into another.

Compartmentalization enhances focus and functionality. By isolating specific thoughts or emotions, individuals can concentrate on the task at hand without being overwhelmed by conflicting internal dynamics. This can contribute to increased productivity and efficiency.

Submarines use compartments to limit damage from potential breaches; similarly, individuals compartmentalize to limit emotional contamination. This involves containing negative emotions or threatening thoughts to prevent them from infiltrating other aspects of one's psyche.

Moreover, compartmentalization can contribute to relationship stability. Individuals may use this defense mechanism to avoid letting personal conflicts spill over into their relationships, thus preserving the stability of their social connections.

Also, compartmentalization is an adaptive coping mechanism. It allows individuals to navigate complex emotional landscapes by creating mental partitions, reducing the emotional load and facilitating a more controlled approach to challenging situations.

As well, compartmentalization may involve temporal separation, allowing individuals to focus on different emotions at distinct times. This can be a strategic approach to avoid emotional overwhelm and deal with conflicting feelings gradually.

Subs balance conflicting needs in different compartments; similarly, individuals may use compartmentalization to balance conflicting priorities. This helps in managing various aspects of life without allowing one area to jeopardize another.

- **Regression: Seeking Safety in Familiar Territory:**

Regression provides comfort through familiar behaviors. Individuals may revert to earlier stages of behavior that were more comfortable or less challenging, seeking solace in the known and predictable aspects of their past.

Submarines retreating to safer depths mirror individuals reconnecting with past coping mechanisms. Regression may involve revisiting strategies or behaviors that were effective in the past, providing a sense of security during times of perceived threat.

As well, regression aims to reduce stress and anxiety. By returning to familiar territories, individuals may experience a decrease in the emotional burden associated with the present situation, finding relief in the simplicity of previously mastered behaviors.

Regression offers a temporary escape from the complexities of the present reality. Individuals may use this defense mechanism to momentarily distance themselves from the challenges or threats they face, creating a psychological refuge in familiar and less demanding mental spaces.

Subs retreating to safer depths conserve energy; similarly, individuals may use regression to preserve mental energy. This defense mechanism allows individuals to redirect their focus to less demanding mental states, conserving resources for dealing with immediate stressors.

Also, regression may involve nostalgia for a perceived safer time. Individuals may engage in nostalgic thoughts or behaviors to create a protective shield against the uncertainties of the present, finding reassurance in memories of a perceived simpler or less threatening past.

Regression can be an attempt to reestablish a sense of control. By returning to familiar behaviors or thought patterns, individuals regain a sense of mastery over their actions, contributing to a feeling of control in the face of perceived threats.

Submarines retreat to safer depths, resembling childlike responses; individuals may exhibit childlike behaviors during regression. This can involve seeking comfort, reassurance, or protection in ways reminiscent of earlier stages of emotional development.

Chapter **24**

Fuel and Propulsion

The energy that powers a submarine is comparable to the motivation and drive necessary for personal growth.

Setting out on a travel of individual development is associated to the complicated operations of a submarine impelled through the profundities of the sea. Much like a submarine requires a vigorous vitality source to explore the submerged field, people on the way of self-discovery and advancement require a wellspring of inspiration and drive. The cooperative energy between the vitality impelling a submarine and the internal driving force driving individual development reveals a embroidered artwork of parallels, where both endeavors explore through challenges, overcome resistance, and endeavor for ceaseless progression.

- **Powering Forward Through Challenges:**

Underwater environments can be hostile, with submarines facing resistance and challenges. Their energy systems enable them to navigate through adversity.

In personal growth, challenges and setbacks are inevitable. Motivation serves as the resilient force, empowering individuals to persevere and navigate through life's adversities.

Submarines encounter unseen obstacles beneath the ocean's surface. Their energy systems provide the power needed to overcome these internal challenges.

Similarly, personal growth involves facing internal obstacles such as self-doubt and limiting beliefs. Motivation becomes the force that propels individuals past these hurdles toward self-improvement.

Water resistance poses a continual challenge. Submarines use their energy to push against this resistance, moving forward despite the opposing force.

Life's complexities create resistance to personal development. Motivation acts as the force that propels individuals forward, allowing them to push against the resistance posed by external circumstances.

External pressures, such as changes in water pressure, require submarines to adapt. Their energy systems facilitate this adaptability.

External pressures in life, such as societal expectations or unforeseen challenges, necessitate adaptation. Motivation enables individuals to adapt and navigate through changing circumstances.

Underwater terrains are complex, requiring strategic navigation. Submarines utilize their energy systems for precise and strategic movements.

Navigating the complexities of personal growth demands strategic thinking. Motivation serves as the driving force, guiding individuals with precision through the intricate landscape of self-discovery.

Unseen underwater currents can affect submarines. Their energy systems persistently propel them forward against these unseen forces.

Unseen forces, such as unforeseen life events, can impact personal development. Motivation acts as a persistent force, propelling individuals forward despite uncertainties and unforeseen challenges.

Maintaining momentum is crucial for submarines when facing challenges. Their energy systems ensure continuous forward movement.

In personal development, challenges can disrupt momentum. Motivation becomes the driving force that sustains momentum, allowing individuals to keep moving forward despite obstacles.

Maneuvering through underwater obstacles requires precision. Submarines use their energy systems to navigate with accuracy.

Precision in personal growth involves setting and achieving specific goals. Motivation provides the necessary energy for individuals to navigate with precision toward their desired outcomes.

Challenges in underwater terrains are harnessed for strategic maneuvers. Submarines use their energy to navigate challenges effectively.

Challenges in personal development can be transformative. Motivation harnesses these challenges, turning them into opportunities for growth and self-discovery.

- **Endurance for Prolonged Journeys:**

Propelled by powerful engines, submarines counteract water resistance and navigate through challenging underwater terrains. The thrust generated by their energy systems helps them overcome obstacles.

Similarly, in personal growth, challenges act as resistance. Motivation serves as the thrust that propels individuals forward, enabling them to navigate through life's complexities and overcome obstacles on their developmental journey.

Underwater terrains are intricate and filled with unseen obstacles. Submarines, powered by their energy systems, navigate through these complexities with precision to reach their destinations.

Personal growth involves navigating the intricate landscape of one's life. Motivation acts as the guiding force, allowing individuals to navigate through the complexities of self-discovery and overcome challenges with resilience and determination.

Efficient energy use is crucial for submarines. They employ energy-efficient maneuvers to navigate through challenging conditions, optimizing their propulsion systems for effective movement.

In personal growth, individuals must use their motivation efficiently. Strategic and purposeful actions, aligned with one's goals and values, optimize the energy invested in navigating life's challenges, ensuring effective progress.

Long missions require sustainable energy consumption. Submarines carefully manage their energy resources to ensure they endure the extended underwater journeys.

The pursuit of personal growth is a marathon, not a sprint. Motivation acts as the sustainable energy source that individuals tap into for the long haul, ensuring they endure and thrive over the extended journey of self-improvement.

Submarines need resilience to endure the challenges of the deep sea. They must withstand pressure, adapt to changing conditions, and remain operational despite external adversities.

Similarly, personal growth requires resilience. Motivation becomes the driving force that empowers individuals to endure hardships, adapt to life's changes, and remain steadfast in their commitment to personal development.

To endure prolonged journeys, submarines strategically conserve energy, optimizing their systems to avoid depletion.

Motivation necessitates strategic energy conservation in personal growth. Individuals must prioritize self-care, balance effort with rest, and strategically conserve their motivational energy to avoid burnout and ensure sustained progress.

Varied underwater terrains demand adaptability in energy use. Submarines adjust their propulsion systems to navigate through different conditions effectively.

Life's journey presents diverse terrains. Motivation allows individuals to adapt their energy for different life stages, challenges, and opportunities, ensuring they endure and thrive in varied circumstances.

- **Optimizing Energy Efficiency:**

Strategic resource allocation is vital for submarines to prioritize essentials and maximize efficiency in their operations.

Similarly, in personal development, strategic resource allocation involves prioritizing time, effort, and attention to activities that align with individual goals, ensuring optimal efficiency in the pursuit of growth.

Balancing tangible supplies with intangible factors like crew morale is critical for submarine operations.

Individuals need to balance tangible investments, such as time and effort, with intangible aspects like mental well-being and emotional health to foster a holistic and efficient personal growth journey.

Regular maintenance is essential for submarines to ensure peak performance and longevity.

Just as submarines need maintenance, individuals benefit from regular self-care and reflection to maintain peak mental, emotional, and physical performance in their pursuit of personal growth.

Continuous monitoring and adjustments are made to maintain the optimal performance of a submarine.

Regular self-assessment and adjustments in lifestyle, habits, and priorities are crucial for maintaining overall well-being and ensuring continued progress in personal development.

Submarines explore the depths of the ocean for untapped resources.

Motivation drives individuals to explore their untapped potentials, pushing beyond comfort zones to discover hidden talents and strengths that contribute to personal growth.

Mental resilience is vital for submarines to navigate challenging conditions.

Motivation acts as a source of mental resilience, helping individuals navigate life's challenges and setbacks with determination, ultimately contributing to sustained personal growth.

- **Navigating Inner Depths:**

Underwater currents pose challenges to submarines, requiring adaptability in navigation.

Motivation enables individuals to adapt to emotional currents within themselves, navigating through the ebbs and flows of emotions during the personal growth journey.

Submarines encounter cognitive challenges in navigating complex underwater terrains.

Motivation serves as the guiding force for individuals to navigate cognitive challenges, such as changing perspectives, overcoming limiting beliefs, and enhancing cognitive abilities in the pursuit of personal development.

Submarines must withstand underwater pressure.

Motivation acts as a force against the pressure of setbacks, enabling individuals to persevere through challenges and maintain progress on their personal growth journey.

Submarines explore uncharted territories beneath the ocean's surface.

Motivation propels individuals to explore uncharted emotional territories within themselves, uncovering aspects of their character and emotions that contribute to a more profound understanding of self.

Submarines engage in self-reflection to navigate through complex underwater landscapes.

Motivation facilitates the process of self-reflection, allowing individuals to negotiate the depths of their thoughts, beliefs, and values, contributing to personal growth and self-awareness.

Submarines use navigation systems to align with a predetermined course.

Motivation aligns with personal values, acting as a compass that guides individuals on a predetermined course toward meaningful goals and aspirations.

Submarines tap into internal power sources for energy.

Motivation, when rooted in intrinsic factors, becomes a powerful internal source driving individuals to explore their inner depths and foster personal development.

Submarines face the unknown in unexplored underwater territories.

Motivation empowers individuals to embrace the unknown aspects of self-discovery, encouraging them to venture into unexplored psychological landscapes and uncover hidden potentials.

- **Resistance from External Pressures:**

Submarines encounter unforeseen challenges in the darkness, necessitating adaptability.

Motivation fuels adaptability in personal development. The ability to adjust course, learn from unexpected turns, and remain resilient in the face of uncertainty becomes a defining characteristic of the growth journey.

The murkiness of dark waters mirrors the ambiguity submarines face in their journeys.

Motivation serves as inner guidance amidst life's uncertainties. It becomes a source of clarity and strength, helping individuals make decisions aligned with their values and aspirations, even in challenging and ambiguous situations.

Submarines constantly explore the potential of the ocean's depths for resources and information.

Motivation drives individuals to continuously explore their potential, pushing boundaries, and seeking new opportunities for learning and self-discovery.

Subs need to use mental resources efficiently for navigation and operation.

Also, motivation prompts individuals to use mental resources efficiently, directing focus and attention toward meaningful goals and self-improvement, optimizing cognitive efforts in the journey of personal growth.

Submarines build resilience to withstand external pressures.

Motivation contributes to the building of emotional resilience. It involves bouncing back from setbacks, learning from experiences, and fortifying the emotional foundation for future challenges in the personal development journey.

Chapter **25**

Buoyancy Control

Submarines adjust buoyancy for depth control, just as we must find balance between groundedness and aspiration in life.
Exploring the profundities of life mirrors the complicated move of submarines underneath the ocean's surface. Submarines, with their capacity to alter buoyancy for exact profundity control, offer a captivating allegory for the sensitive harmony we must strike between groundedness and yearning. Life, just like the tremendous sea, presents changed territories, and our travel requires a nuanced understanding of when to stay ourselves to the show and when to rise towards modern statures. This fragile adjust, much like a submarine's control of buoyancy, shapes the forms of our individual development, versatility, and the interest of desires.

- **The Art of Buoyancy Adjustment:**

The adjustment of buoyancy in submarines demands precision, as even slight changes can influence their depth.
Similarly, finding balance in life requires a meticulous approach. Small adjustments in our thoughts, behaviors, and priorities can significantly impact our overall well-being and direction.
Buoyancy control involves managing the delicate balance between air and water in ballast tanks.
Life, too, is a delicate balance of elements. Integrating the airy aspirations with the grounded realities is key to maintaining equilibrium. It involves harmonizing dreams and practicality for a well-rounded existence.
Adjustments are crucial when submarines transition between different underwater environments.
Similarly, adapting our metaphorical buoyancy means recognizing the changing landscapes of our lives. Flexibility in our approach allows us to navigate transitions, adjusting our mindset and actions accordingly.
External water pressure necessitates careful buoyancy management.
Life often exerts external pressures. Balancing our metaphorical buoyancy involves navigating societal expectations, external demands, and unforeseen challenges while staying true to our core values and aspirations.
Continuous adjustments are made to ensure submarines maintain their desired depth.
Finding balance is an ongoing process. Regular self-reflection and adjustments are necessary to stay aligned with our evolving goals, personal growth, and the ever-changing dynamics of our lives.
Cooperative efforts are crucial for buoyancy adjustments in submarines.
Relationships play a vital role in our balance. Cooperative endeavors with others—family, friends, and colleagues—can provide support and assistance in navigating the challenges and joys of life.
Emotions are integral to our existence. Balancing emotional buoyancy involves acknowledging and processing feelings, understanding their influence, and ensuring they contribute positively to our overall well-being.
Adjustments in buoyancy are made to achieve specific mission objectives.
Similarly, our life's mission and goals require adjustments. Aligning our metaphorical buoyancy with our aspirations involves setting clear objectives, adapting strategies, and persevering through challenges to achieve meaningful outcomes.

- **Grounded Anchors in Present Realities:**

Ballast anchors submarines to the ocean floor, providing stability.
Being grounded involves anchoring ourselves to our core values. These values act as anchors, providing stability and guiding our decisions in the unpredictable currents of life.
Anchored submarines appreciate the current water conditions for stability.
Groundedness in the present requires appreciating current circumstances. It involves cultivating gratitude for what we have, fostering contentment, and finding joy in the present moment.
Anchored submarines maintain stability in a fixed position.
Establishing routines and habits can act as anchors in our daily lives, providing stability and a sense of order amidst the ever-changing currents of external events.
Anchored submarines are present in a specific location.
Being grounded necessitates mindful presence. It involves fully engaging in the current moment, appreciating the nuances of our surroundings, and fostering a deeper connection with the present.
Anchored submarines remain resilient against changing tides.
Also, groundedness enables resilience in the face of life's uncertainties. Like anchored submarines, individuals anchored in their values can weather the changing tides with strength and adaptability.

Ballast allows submarines to balance stability with flexibility.

Being grounded involves striking a balance between stability and flexibility. While anchored in values, individuals remain open to adaptability, allowing them to navigate the ebb and flow of life.

Anchored submarines tap into the ocean's depth for stability.

Grounded individuals connect with their inner wisdom. They delve into their depths, drawing on self-awareness and intuition for stability and guidance in decision-making.

Anchored submarines draw on past experiences for stability.

Moreover, groundedness involves learning from the past. Individuals anchored in the present apply lessons from previous experiences, using them as a foundation for stability and growth.

Anchored submarines find stability as a source of peace.

Also, groundedness brings a sense of inner peace and joy. Being anchored in the present allows individuals to find stability, leading to a deeper appreciation of life's simple pleasures.

Ballast anchors submarines to the natural environment.

Grounding can involve connecting with nature. Spending time outdoors, appreciating the natural world, and immersing oneself in the environment contribute to a sense of groundedness and well-being.

- **Aspiring to New Depths:**

Adjusting buoyancy enables submarines to ascend towards goals.

Balancing groundedness with aspiration involves setting meaningful goals. Individuals anchor themselves in the present while aspiring to reach new heights through well-defined objectives.

Buoyancy adjustment signifies adaptability for growth.

A growth mindset aligns with aspiration. Being grounded doesn't mean stagnation; it involves a continuous journey of learning, embracing challenges, and aspiring to grow beyond one's current capabilities.

Adjusting buoyancy allows submarines to dream of new depths.

Balancing groundedness with aspiration encourages individuals to dare to dream. It involves envisioning a future filled with possibilities and channeling motivation towards turning those dreams into reality.

Adjusting buoyancy requires understanding the environment.

Aspiring to new depths involves seeking knowledge. Grounded individuals stay connected with reality while aspiring to learn and explore new ideas, perspectives, and skills.

Adjusting buoyancy is guided by curiosity about the environment.

Balancing groundedness with aspiration is fueled by curiosity. Grounded individuals remain curious about the world, asking questions, seeking new experiences, and staying open to the wonders that life has to offer.

Buoyancy adjustment aids submarines in maneuvering through different depths.

Personal development is a key aspect of aspiring to new depths. Individuals grounded in the present strive for continuous self-improvement, exploring their potential and evolving into better versions of themselves.

Adjusting buoyancy helps submarines navigate challenging underwater conditions.

Balancing groundedness with aspiration involves facing challenges with resilience. Grounded individuals embrace difficulties as opportunities for growth, navigating through obstacles with determination and strength.

Buoyancy adjustment requires flexibility in response to changing conditions.

Aspiring to new depths demands flexibility. Grounded individuals remain adaptable, adjusting their plans and strategies as they pursue new aspirations and navigate the dynamic currents of life.

Adjusting buoyancy can involve innovative technologies.

Balancing groundedness with aspiration encourages innovation. Grounded individuals seek creative solutions, think outside the box, and contribute to progress while staying rooted in their values.

Submarines exploring new depths inspire others in maritime endeavors.

Individuals balancing groundedness with aspiration inspire those around them. By pursuing their dreams with determination and resilience, they become beacons of motivation for others on their own journeys.

- **Navigating Turbulent Waters:**

Navigating turbulent waters requires submarines to adapt their buoyancy.

Similarly, in the face of life's uncertainties and challenges, individuals must adapt to changing circumstances. Adjusting one's mental buoyancy allows for flexibility in responding to unexpected events and turbulent times.

Buoyancy adjustments ensure submarines maintain stability in turbulent conditions.

Balancing groundedness with aspiration involves maintaining inner stability amidst chaos. Grounded individuals remain resilient, drawing on their core values and principles to navigate through turbulent periods without losing their sense of self.

Navigating turbulent waters requires the efficient use of a submarine's energy and propulsion systems.

Similarly, individuals navigating life's storms must efficiently utilize their inner strength. This involves drawing on personal resilience, determination, and the motivation to weather turbulent times and emerge stronger on the other side.

Turbulent waters may exert forces on submarines.

Balancing groundedness with aspiration means resisting the pull of negativity during turbulent periods.

Grounded individuals actively counter negative influences, maintaining a positive outlook and steering their course towards constructive goals.

Buoyancy adjustments maintain the stability of submarines by controlling their position.

Grounded individuals find stability in their values. During turbulent times, they anchor themselves in their core beliefs, ensuring that their actions and decisions align with their fundamental principles.

Adjusting buoyancy involves altering the submarine's position in the water.

Balancing groundedness with aspiration requires adjusting perspectives during turbulent times. Individuals may need to shift their viewpoint, reevaluate priorities, and adopt a flexible mindset to navigate challenges more effectively.

Navigating turbulence demands a calm and calculated approach.

Grounded individuals remain calm amidst life's storms. They cultivate emotional resilience, allowing them to navigate turbulent waters with a composed demeanor, making rational decisions even in challenging situations.

In challenging conditions, submarines may rely on external guidance.

During turbulent times, seeking support and guidance is essential. Grounded individuals recognize the value of connecting with others, seeking advice, and leaning on their support network to navigate through difficulties.

Turbulent conditions provide valuable data for navigation.

Balancing groundedness with aspiration involves learning from turbulent experiences. Individuals use challenges as opportunities for growth, extracting valuable lessons that contribute to their personal development and resilience.

Buoyancy adjustments enable submarines to embrace changes in water conditions.

Navigating turbulent waters in life requires embracing change as an opportunity. Grounded individuals see challenges as catalysts for growth, understanding that turbulent times can lead to positive transformations and new possibilities.

Chapter 26

Periscope Perspective

Periscopes allow a view above the surface; this symbolizes the ability to gain broader perspectives on our lives.

In the complex world of submarines, periscopes develop as basic rebellious, advertising a interesting vantage point to watch the world over the ocean's surface while submerged underneath. So also, within the complex embroidered artwork of our lives, the allegory of a periscope resonates deeply. This device symbolizes the significant capability to raise our perspectives, rising above the prompt circumstances and picking up broader viewpoints that can enlighten the way of our individual travel.

- **Rising Above Challenges:**

Periscopes are employed by submarines to elevate their viewpoint, aiding in the identification of potential obstacles or threats.

Gaining broader perspectives enhances our problem-solving abilities. It allows us to approach challenges with a heightened sense of creativity and innovation, exploring solutions from angles that might not be immediately apparent when immersed in the midst of difficulties.

Submarines use periscopes to navigate challenges resiliently, adapting to the dynamic underwater environment.

Gaining broader perspectives fosters resilience in the face of adversity. It encourages a mindset that perceives challenges as opportunities for growth, enabling individuals to bounce back from setbacks and navigate life's complexities with greater tenacity.

Periscopes allow submariners to spot opportunities even in challenging underwater conditions.

Broader perspectives enable us to recognize hidden opportunities within challenges. It prompts a shift in focus from the difficulties themselves to the potential growth and positive outcomes that can emerge from navigating and overcoming those challenges.

Submariners learn from underwater challenges to enhance their navigation skills.

Gaining broader perspectives encourages a reflective approach to setbacks. It invites individuals to view challenges as learning experiences, extracting valuable lessons that contribute to personal development and resilience in the face of future obstacles.

Periscopes provide a clearer view in uncertain underwater environments, aiding in navigation.

Broader perspectives instill confidence in navigating uncertainty. By adopting a comprehensive view of life's uncertainties, individuals can approach the unknown with a sense of assurance, knowing that they possess the capacity to adapt and find solutions.

Submarines use periscopes for informed decision-making in challenging conditions.

Gaining broader perspectives contributes to more informed decision-making. It allows individuals to consider a multitude of factors, weigh various options, and make choices that align with their long-term goals, even in the face of adversity.

Clear visibility with periscopes contributes to submariners' emotional well-being during challenges.

Gaining broader perspectives positively impacts emotional well-being. It enables individuals to see beyond the immediate stressors, fostering emotional resilience and a sense of well-being even in the midst of life's challenges.

Successful navigation through challenges builds a foundation for future missions.

Gaining broader perspectives in challenging times contributes to the foundation of future success. The lessons learned, resilience cultivated, and insights gained become integral components of an individual's growth trajectory, preparing them for the challenges and triumphs that lie ahead.

- **Surveying Opportunities on the Horizon:**

Submarines strategically plan their movements based on observations through periscopes.

Gaining broader perspectives involves strategic planning for personal growth. It encourages individuals to envision their future, set meaningful goals, and navigate towards opportunities that align with their values and aspirations.

Submarines use periscopes to identify potential threats in their surroundings.

Broader perspectives aid in identifying potential threats in our lives. It prompts individuals to be vigilant and proactive in recognizing challenges that may hinder personal development, allowing for timely adjustments and proactive measures.

Subs use periscopes to look forward, emphasizing a forward-thinking approach.

Gaining broader perspectives fosters a forward-thinking mindset. It encourages individuals to focus on future opportunities, fostering a positive outlook that drives personal growth and a proactive response to life's challenges.

They continuously learn from the information gathered through periscopes.

Broader perspectives encourage a commitment to continuous learning. Individuals who actively seek new knowledge and insights are better equipped to identify opportunities on the horizon, adapting and evolving with the changing landscape of their personal and professional lives.

Submarines aim to maximize their potential for successful navigation through clear visibility.

Gaining broader perspectives maximizes the potential for personal success. It enables individuals to make choices that align with their strengths, values, and aspirations, creating a path that leads to fulfillment and achievement of their goals.

Subs adapt to changing conditions based on periscope observations.

Broader perspectives enhance adaptability. Individuals who can see beyond immediate circumstances are better equipped to adapt to changing environments, seize opportunities, and navigate through life's twists and turns with resilience.

Also, submarines use periscopes for communication and coordination with other vessels.

Gaining broader perspectives involves building strategic alliances. Forming connections with others who share similar goals and values provides a collaborative network that enhances the exploration of opportunities and shared growth.

Submarines use periscopes proactively to anticipate and respond to changes.

Broader perspectives foster a proactive mindset. Individuals who actively seek opportunities on the horizon are better prepared to anticipate changes, make proactive decisions, and steer their lives in directions that lead to personal fulfillment and success.

- **Understanding Interconnectedness:**

Submarine periscopes offer a glimpse of the interconnected world above, highlighting the immediate surroundings and beyond.

Broader perspectives enable individuals to recognize the ripple effect of their actions. Understanding how personal choices impact not only immediate circumstances but also the broader context of life emphasizes the interconnected nature of our decisions and their far-reaching consequences.

The periscopes reveal the surface world where relationships, vessels, and landscapes are connected.

Also, broader perspectives encourage the appreciation of relationships as interconnected threads in the fabric of life. It prompts individuals to value connections, understanding that relationships contribute to the richness and complexity of their personal journey.

Subs use periscopes to navigate through the social dynamics of the ocean's surface.

Broader perspectives aid in navigating social dynamics. Understanding the interconnected web of social relationships allows individuals to engage with others authentically, fostering meaningful connections and collaborations.

Periscopes provide insights into the environmental conditions above the waterline.

Broader perspectives cultivate environmental consciousness. It prompts individuals to consider the interconnectedness between their lives and the environment, encouraging sustainable practices and a sense of responsibility towards the larger ecosystem.

Submarines balance their position relative to other vessels for collective well-being.

Broader perspectives aid in balancing personal aspirations with collective well-being. Individuals recognize that their journey is intertwined with the journeys of others, fostering a sense of responsibility for the greater good and contributing to the well-being of the collective.

They use periscopes to gain visual information about the world above, fostering awareness.

Understanding the interconnected nature of human experiences allows individuals to empathize with the joys and struggles of others, fostering compassion and a deeper connection to the human experience.

Periscopes reveal the diversity of the world above the surface.

Perspectives encourage the embrace of diversity. Individuals understand the interconnected tapestry of varied cultures, perspectives, and experiences, fostering an inclusive mindset that enriches their own personal growth journey.

Submarine periscopes provide a view of vessels contributing to the larger narrative of the sea.

Perspectives enable individuals to recognize their role in contributing to the larger narrative of life. It encourages a sense of purpose and the understanding that each person's journey is a unique thread in the intricate tapestry of the human experience.

- **Navigating Ethical Decision-Making:**

Submarines assess potential consequences when using periscopes for surveillance to make informed decisions. Gaining broader perspectives involves evaluating the consequences of our actions. Ethical decision-making requires individuals to consider the impact of their choices on themselves, others, and the broader community, fostering a thoughtful and responsible approach.

Subs, when using periscopes, consider the presence of other vessels and entities in the surrounding area.

Broader perspectives prompt individuals to consider multiple stakeholders in ethical decision-making. Recognizing the interconnectedness of relationships and communities emphasizes the importance of considering the well-being of various parties affected by a decision.

Also, submarines align surveillance practices with ethical principles and national values.

Gaining broader perspectives involves aligning actions with personal and societal values.

Ethical decision-making requires individuals to uphold principles that reflect integrity, justice, and respect for others, contributing to the cultivation of a moral compass.

Submarines aim for transparency in their surveillance activities.

Perspectives encourage transparency in decision-making. Ethical considerations involve openness and honesty, ensuring that individuals are accountable for their choices and fostering trust within relationships and communities.

They may seek guidance from commanders and experts for ethical decision-making.

Ethical decision-making involves recognizing one's limitations and being open to input from mentors, experts, and trusted individuals, enhancing the quality of choices made.

Subs learn from ethical challenges encountered during surveillance operations.

Broader perspectives prompt individuals to learn from ethical dilemmas. Ethical decision-making involves a continuous process of reflection and growth, allowing individuals to evolve in their understanding of moral principles and navigate future dilemmas with increased wisdom.

They may engage in discussions about ethical considerations in their operations.

Ethical decision-making involves engaging in meaningful conversations with others, promoting understanding, and collectively shaping ethical norms within communities and society.

Submarines balance individual actions with collective ethical standards.

Gaining broader perspectives requires individuals to balance personal ethics with collective values. Ethical decision-making involves navigating the tension between individual convictions and the shared ethical framework of a community, promoting harmony and cohesion.

Chapter **27**

Command and Control

Leadership within a submarine is critical, as is self-leadership in directing our life's course.
Leadership, whether inside the limited spaces of a submarine or the tremendous scope of our individual ventures, stands as a basic constrain forming the course of activity and the achievement of destinations. Inside the submarine's metal dividers, a well-defined progression coordinates facilitated endeavors for a common mission. Additionally, within the endless sea of our lives, the concept of self-leadership rises as a directing guideline, controlling us through challenges and openings.

- **Hierarchical Structure:**

The hierarchical structure in submarines aligns with core principles and protocols, ensuring unity of purpose. In self-leadership, aligning with core values establishes a personal hierarchy that guides decision-making. Understanding and adhering to these fundamental values provide a compass for navigating life's complexities, fostering coherence and purpose.

Submarine leaders prioritize goals and objectives based on mission requirements.

Self-leadership involves prioritizing personal goals and objectives. By understanding our life's mission and setting clear priorities, we can navigate challenges more effectively, directing our efforts towards meaningful accomplishments.

The hierarchical structure streamlines decision-making in submarines, ensuring prompt and effective responses.

In self-leadership, an organized internal hierarchy aids effective decision-making. Prioritizing values and goals helps streamline choices, reducing indecision and enabling individuals to make decisions that align with their overarching life vision.

Leaders within a submarine delegate responsibilities according to expertise and roles.

Self-leadership involves delegating responsibilities within ourselves. Acknowledging our strengths and weaknesses allows us to allocate our energy and resources efficiently, fostering a balanced and sustainable approach to personal growth.

Effective leaders in submarines exhibit a high degree of self-awareness to lead with insight.

Self-leadership requires cultivating self-awareness. Understanding our strengths, weaknesses, and triggers enables us to navigate challenges, make informed decisions, and continuously evolve as individuals.

Submarine leaders adapt to dynamic underwater conditions, making real-time decisions.

Self-leadership involves adaptability. Life is dynamic, and individuals must adjust their internal hierarchy to navigate changing circumstances, demonstrating resilience and flexibility in the face of challenges.

Resilience is crucial for submarine leaders to navigate unforeseen challenges.

Also, self-leadership requires building a resilient mindset. Embracing challenges as opportunities for growth, learning from setbacks, and maintaining a positive outlook contribute to a resilient internal leadership approach, enhancing the ability to overcome adversity.

Subs leaders undergo continuous training and development to stay effective.

Moreover, self-leadership involves a commitment to continuous learning and personal development. Embracing a mindset of growth and seeking opportunities for self-improvement ensures that individuals evolve and stay effective in directing their life's course.

Effective leaders in submarines inspire motivation and discipline among the crew.

Self-leadership requires inspiring motivation and discipline within oneself. Setting clear goals, maintaining focus, and cultivating intrinsic motivation are essential aspects of leading one's life purposefully and with dedication.

- **Clear Communication:**

Leaders in submarines articulate mission goals clearly to ensure everyone understands their role.

Clear communication involves articulating personal goals. Defining and expressing individual aspirations, whether short-term or long-term, enhances clarity of purpose and provides a roadmap for personal development.

Submarine leaders establish expectations for the crew's performance.

Self-leadership necessitates setting internal expectations. Clearly defining personal standards, values, and expectations ensures a cohesive internal structure, fostering a sense of accountability and commitment to one's chosen path.

Effective communication within a submarine involves navigating complex technical dialogues.

Also, self-leadership requires navigating internal dialogues. Developing the skill to communicate with oneself about thoughts, emotions, and motivations facilitates a deeper understanding of one's inner dynamics, contributing to informed decision-making.

Subs leaders use feedback to improve operations and address challenges.

In self-leadership, a feedback loop is crucial for personal growth. Regular self-reflection, seeking constructive feedback, and adjusting strategies based on personal assessments contribute to continuous improvement and development.

Effective leaders in submarines understand and navigate the emotions of the crew.

Self-leadership involves cultivating emotional intelligence. Recognizing, understanding, and effectively managing one's emotions contribute to a more harmonious internal dialogue, fostering resilience and adaptability.

Leaders ensure communication resonates with the values of the crew and the mission.

In self-leadership, effective communication aligns with personal values. Expressing oneself in a manner consistent with core beliefs fosters authenticity and integrity in navigating life's complexities.

Also, leaders mediate conflicts within the crew for optimal functioning.

Self-leadership involves negotiating inner conflicts. Effectively communicating with conflicting aspects of oneself, such as desires and responsibilities, promotes internal harmony and reduces cognitive dissonance.

Clear communication aids decisive actions during critical situations.

In self-leadership, clear internal communication facilitates decisive decision-making. Clarity of thought and purpose reduces ambiguity, enabling individuals to make informed choices aligned with their values and goals.

Leaders foster positive relationships among the crew.

Moreover, self-leadership involves fostering positive intrapersonal relationships. Establishing a constructive and supportive dialogue with oneself cultivates a sense of self-trust and self-compassion, contributing to overall well-being.

Leaders encourage crew members to reflect on their roles and performance.

Self-leadership embraces self-reflection. Clear communication with oneself encourages introspection, providing insights into personal strengths, areas for improvement, and the alignment of actions with one's aspirations.

- **Team Collaboration:**

Team collaboration in submarines involves integrating the expertise of each crew member into a cohesive unit.

In self-leadership, recognizing and integrating the various roles within oneself — be it the strategist, motivator, or caretaker — leads to a more cohesive and unified approach to personal development.

Diverse skills and roles are recognized and utilized for effective teamwork.

Self-leadership involves recognizing one's inner diversity. Acknowledging and appreciating the diverse aspects of one's personality and skills contribute to a more comprehensive understanding of oneself.

Effective collaboration in submarines requires understanding and navigating the emotions of team members.

In self-leadership, leveraging emotional intelligence enhances collaboration with oneself. Understanding and navigating one's own emotions foster self-awareness and contribute to better internal collaboration.

Each member shares responsibility for the success of the submarine's mission.

Self-leadership involves taking shared responsibility for personal success. Recognizing that every internal aspect plays a role in achieving personal goals fosters a sense of accountability and shared responsibility within oneself.

Team collaboration in submarines requires adaptability to different roles and responsibilities.

In self-leadership, being adaptable to the changing internal landscape — adjusting to different emotions, circumstances, and roles — enhances the ability to navigate life's challenges effectively.

Effective communication is crucial for team collaboration in submarines.

Self-leadership involves constructive communication within oneself. Communicating thoughts, feelings, and aspirations internally fosters clarity and ensures that each aspect is aligned with the overall mission of personal development.

Leaders in submarines address conflicts within the team promptly.

In self-leadership, addressing internal conflicts is essential. Promptly recognizing and resolving conflicts between different aspects of oneself contributes to internal harmony and supports the pursuit of personal goals.

Team members in submarines balance autonomy with interdependence.

Self-leadership involves balancing autonomy and interdependence within oneself. Recognizing when to rely on personal strengths and when to seek support from various internal aspects contributes to a well-rounded approach to personal growth.

Leaders cultivate a positive culture within the submarine crew.

In self-leadership, fostering a positive internal culture involves nurturing self-compassion, resilience, and a growth mindset. Cultivating a positive internal environment contributes to a more supportive and conducive atmosphere for personal development.

Recognizing and celebrating achievements boosts team morale.

Self-leadership involves celebrating personal achievements. Acknowledging and appreciating one's progress and successes contributes to motivation and a positive mindset in the journey of self-development.

- **Mission Clarity:**

The mission of a submarine is rooted in specific values and objectives.

In self-leadership, defining personal values establishes the foundation for the mission. Identifying core values provides a compass for decision-making and ensures alignment with one's authentic self.

Submarines set clear objectives for each mission, providing a roadmap for success.

In self-leadership, setting clear personal goals acts as a roadmap for the journey. Specific, measurable, achievable, relevant, and time-bound (SMART) goals provide clarity and direction in personal development.

Submarine missions align with broader strategic goals and purposes.

Also, self-leadership involves aligning personal missions with life's purpose. Clarifying how personal goals contribute to a meaningful and purposeful life ensures that each action aligns with a greater sense of purpose.

Subs leaders continuously assess the mission's progress and adjust strategies as needed.

In self-leadership, continuous self-assessment is crucial. Regularly evaluating personal goals, values, and aspirations allows for adjustments, ensuring that the mission remains relevant and aligned with evolving circumstances.

Submarine missions may require adaptability to unforeseen challenges.

Moreover, self-leadership involves adaptability to life's changes. Being open to adjusting goals and strategies in response to unexpected events or personal growth insights ensures a resilient approach to life's journey.

Subs leaders integrate lessons learned from previous missions into future strategies.

In self-leadership, integrating lessons learned from personal experiences is essential. Reflection on past achievements and challenges contributes to continuous improvement and informs future decisions.

Chapter **28**

Hull Integrity

The strength of a submarine's hull is vital to withstand pressure, similar to the strong core values and identity we need in life.

In the mysterious depths of the ocean, where the pressures are immense and the environment unforgiving, submarines stand as marvels of engineering. Among their critical components, the strength of a submarine's hull is paramount. This robust structure not only protects the vessel from the relentless pressure of the surrounding water but also ensures its resilience and ability to navigate through challenging underwater terrains. In a profound parallel, the analogy of a submarine's hull finds resonance in our personal lives. Much like the submarine's structural integrity, our core values and identity act as the sturdy hull that shields us from the pressures of life, providing the strength needed to withstand challenges, uncertainties, and the tests of time.

- **Foundation of Resilience:**

The submarine's hull acts as a barrier, resisting the external pressures of the surrounding ocean, safeguarding the vessel's internal systems.

Our core values and identity function as a shield against external influences that may attempt to compromise our authenticity.

This protective barrier preserves our internal integrity, allowing us to stay true to our principles amidst external demands and expectations.

The hull's construction ensures stability in stormy waters, preventing the submarine from being tossed about uncontrollably.

Similarly, when our identity is rooted in robust values, we remain steadfast in the face of life's storms. Challenges and uncertainties may arise, but a strong sense of self provides stability, preventing us from being easily swayed by the turbulence of external circumstances.

The resilience of the hull contributes to the mental and emotional endurance of the submarine's crew, even in challenging underwater conditions.

In life, a foundation of core values enhances our mental and emotional endurance. When facing adversity, the principles that define us become a source of inner strength, enabling us to navigate difficulties with resilience and grace.

While the hull is sturdy, it possesses a degree of flexibility, allowing the submarine to adapt to changing underwater dynamics.

Our core values offer a similar balance of strength and flexibility. They provide a stable framework for decision-making, yet they are adaptable enough to accommodate the evolving nature of life. This balance ensures resilience without compromising the authenticity of our identity.

The robustness of the hull instills confidence in the submarine crew, assuring them that the vessel can withstand the challenges of the deep.

Similarly, a strong sense of identity grounded in core values fosters confidence in our decision-making. We navigate life with assurance, knowing that our choices align with our fundamental beliefs, contributing to a sense of purpose and direction.

The resilience of the hull sets an example for the entire submarine crew, inspiring confidence and unity.

In life, embodying our core values becomes an inspiration to others. When our identity is built on a resilient foundation, our actions speak volumes, influencing those around us positively and fostering a sense of collective strength.

The hull, as the foundation of resilience, serves as an internal guide for the submarine's navigation through challenging waters.

Our core values and identity act as an internal compass, providing guidance in navigating the complexities of life. They offer a reference point for ethical choices, ensuring that our actions align with the principles that define us.

The robust hull contributes to emotional stability in the submarine, fostering a sense of security among the crew.

Core values and a strong identity contribute to emotional stability in life.

They provide a sense of inner security, helping us manage emotions effectively and navigate the emotional nuances of various life situations.

- **Steadfast in Stormy Waters:**

The construction of the submarine hull is designed to ensure stability, preventing the vessel from being tossed about uncontrollably in stormy waters. The hull acts as a reliable anchor, allowing the submarine to navigate through turbulent conditions with a greater sense of control.

Much like the submarine's hull, our identity, firmly anchored in core values, provides stability in the midst of life's storms. When faced with challenges, uncertainties, or adversities, a strong sense of self becomes the stabilizing force that allows us to weather the turbulence without losing our direction or composure.

Life often presents emotional storms—times of intense feelings, conflicts, or difficult decisions. A robust identity grounded in core values becomes our emotional anchor, helping us navigate through turbulent emotions with resilience and grace.

Just as the submarine hull prevents drift in stormy seas, a solid core identity prevents emotional drift. It ensures that, even in challenging emotional situations, we maintain a sense of purpose and direction, avoiding being carried away by the tumultuous waves of intense feelings.

Chaos and unpredictability characterize stormy waters, both in the ocean and in life. Our grounded identity acts as a center of gravity, allowing us to remain centered amidst chaos. This internal stability becomes a source of strength, guiding us through uncertain and challenging times.

Stormy waters demand adaptability, and the submarine hull showcases the ability to adapt without losing its foundational strength. Similarly, a resilient identity allows for adaptability in life's changing circumstances, enabling us to adjust course while remaining true to our core values.

Storms, whether literal or metaphorical, can be emotionally taxing. A strong identity fosters emotional resilience, helping us endure difficult times with a positive mindset and providing the emotional fortitude to overcome adversity.

In stormy waters, maintaining inner calm is crucial for effective navigation. Likewise, a strong identity rooted in core values fosters inner calmness, offering a serene internal space even amid life's chaos, enabling thoughtful decision-making and constructive responses.

- **Elevating Mental and Emotional Endurance:**

The resilience of the submarine's hull is instrumental in elevating the mental and emotional endurance of its crew. The structural integrity of the hull ensures that the crew can endure the pressures and challenges of the underwater environment without succumbing to emotional strain.

in life, a foundation of core values acts as a cornerstone in elevating mental and emotional endurance. When anchored in principles that define our character, we gain the mental fortitude to endure challenging situations and the emotional resilience to navigate through turbulent times with steadfastness.

Adversity is an inevitable part of life, and the mental and emotional toll it takes can be significant. Just as the submarine's hull allows the crew to cope with the adversities of the underwater world, a strong sense of identity and values equips us to cope with life's challenges without succumbing to despair.

Pressure situations, whether underwater or in daily life, demand mental focus. The resilience of the submarine's hull ensures that the crew can maintain focus despite external pressures. Similarly, a foundation in core values helps us stay focused on our goals and principles, even in the face of external challenges.

The underwater environment poses stress and uncertainty for submarine crews. Likewise, life brings its share of stress and uncertainties. A resilient identity, rooted in core values, becomes a stabilizing force that helps us overcome stress and navigate through uncertain times with a sense of purpose.

The mental and emotional endurance cultivated through a strong foundation of values enhances problem-solving abilities.

Just as the submarine's crew relies on their mental resilience to address challenges, individuals grounded in core values are better equipped to find constructive solutions in the face of life's complexities.

Life often requires adaptation to changing circumstances. The mental and emotional endurance developed through core values fosters positive adaptation. It enables individuals to navigate changes with a positive mindset, embracing growth and learning from experiences.

Resilience is a key component of enduring challenges. The mental and emotional endurance derived from a foundation in core values contributes to building a resilient mindset. This mindset allows individuals to bounce back from setbacks, learn from failures, and approach life with optimism.

- **Flexibility Without Compromise:**

The submarine's hull, although sturdy, is designed with a degree of flexibility. This flexibility is crucial for adapting to the dynamic and changing conditions of the underwater environment without compromising the overall strength of the vessel.

Similarly, our core values offer a delicate balance of strength and flexibility. They serve as a stable and reliable framework that guides decision-making and actions. Yet, these values are adaptable, allowing us to navigate the ever-changing dynamics of life while maintaining the authenticity of our identity.

Life is marked by constant change, and our ability to adapt is paramount. The flexibility embedded in our core values allows us to navigate life's twists and turns without abandoning our principles. It enables us to adjust to new circumstances while holding true to the fundamental aspects of our identity.

Challenges often demand a resilient response. The flexibility derived from core values ensures that we can face challenges with adaptability. This resilience allows us to endure difficulties, learn from them, and emerge stronger without compromising the fundamental aspects of who we are.

Life is inherently ambiguous, and uncertainty is a constant companion. The flexibility within our core values equips us to navigate ambiguity with grace. It provides the agility to make decisions, even in uncertain situations, while maintaining a clear ethical and moral compass.

Flexibility in our values fosters an open-minded approach. It encourages us to consider different perspectives, learn from diverse experiences, and grow as individuals. This open-mindedness allows for personal development without rigidly adhering to preconceived notions.

The adaptability of core values supports a growth mindset. It encourages us to embrace challenges as opportunities for growth and learning. This mindset enables us to evolve and refine our values based on experiences, ensuring a continuous and meaningful personal development journey.

In interpersonal relationships, flexibility in core values promotes collaboration. It allows for mutual understanding, compromise, and growth within relationships without compromising the foundational principles that define our character.

- **Fostering Confidence in Decision-Making:**

The robust construction of the submarine's hull serves as a foundation for confidence among the crew. This confidence stems from the assurance that the vessel is well-equipped to withstand the challenges posed by the deep sea.

In a parallel manner, a strong sense of identity rooted in core values fosters confidence in our decision-making. Our decisions are guided by a clear understanding of our fundamental beliefs and principles, providing a sense of purpose and direction in navigating the complexities of life.

Confidence in decision-making arises from the alignment of our choices with core values. When our decisions resonate with the principles that define us, there is a deep-seated assurance that we are staying true to ourselves and acting in accordance with our ethical and moral compass.

Life often presents complex situations that require decisive action. The confidence derived from core values provides clarity amid this complexity. It enables us to make decisions with a clear understanding of what matters most to us, even in the midst of uncertainty.

Confidence is not just about making the right decisions but also about resilience in the face of challenges. The strength drawn from core values instills the confidence to confront adversity, learn from setbacks, and persist with a positive outlook.

A strong identity rooted in core values empowers autonomy in decision-making. It allows individuals to trust their judgment, make choices that align with their principles, and take ownership of the consequences, fostering a sense of empowerment and self-reliance.

Confidence in decision-making extends to interpersonal relationships. Consistency in aligning choices with core values builds trust with others. It establishes a reputation for reliability and integrity, contributing to positive and meaningful connections.

Confidence is not rigid; it adapts to evolving circumstances. The flexibility within core values allows for confident decision-making even in situations that demand adaptation. This adaptability ensures that confidence remains a dynamic and resilient aspect of self-leadership.

Chapter 29

Salvage and Recovery Operations

Submarines can perform salvage missions, akin to our ability to learn from past experiences and recover from setbacks.

Submarines, with their progressed innovation and capabilities, are not as it were wonders of designing underneath the ocean's surface but too serve a basic part in rescue missions. These missions include recouping profitable resources or amending unanticipated challenges. In a allegorical sense, our lives are too checked by rescue missions – minutes when we must draw upon our versatility, learn from past encounters, and recuperate from mishaps. This perplexing parallel between submarines and human encounters highlights the significant capacity to rescue lessons from the profundities of our claim presence.

- **Navigating the Abyss of Adversity:**

Resilience is crucial for submarines facing the challenges of the abyss during salvage missions. The vessel must withstand pressure and adapt to the ever-changing underwater landscape.

In life's abyss, resilience becomes our ally. Confronting adversity necessitates developing inner strength, adaptability, and the ability to withstand the pressures that come with unexpected challenges.

Salvage operations often take submarines to unexplored depths where recovery efforts demand careful navigation through unfamiliar territories.

Life's adversities may lead us to uncharted emotional or situational depths. Salvaging lessons involves courageously exploring these unexplored territories within ourselves, uncovering hidden strengths and insights.

Salvage missions require meticulous planning and reflection to recover lost assets effectively.

Navigating the abyss of adversity prompts deep self-reflection. Examining our experiences, understanding the root causes of challenges, and learning from setbacks contribute to a more effective salvage of valuable life lessons.

Salvage efforts often encounter the unknown, requiring submarines to adapt quickly to unexpected conditions.

Life's abyss presents uncertainties. Salvaging lessons involves cultivating the ability to adapt to the unknown, embracing change, and transforming challenges into opportunities for personal growth.

In the abyss, darkness prevails, and submarines rely on advanced technology to navigate and salvage.

Facing adversity often feels like traversing through darkness. Salvaging lessons includes finding the light within, tapping into our inner resources, and using our resilience to navigate challenges and emerge stronger on the other side.

Salvage missions require a delicate balance between control and surrender to the forces of the underwater environment.

Navigating life's abyss involves a similar balance. Salvaging lessons requires discerning when to assert control and when to surrender, recognizing that some challenges are beyond our immediate influence.

Salvage operations are collaborative efforts, relying on the coordinated actions of the submarine crew.

Navigating personal adversity often involves teamwork. Seeking support from friends, family, or professionals can enhance our ability to salvage lessons, providing diverse perspectives and shared experiences that contribute to growth.

Successful salvage missions leave submarines strengthened, equipped to face future challenges.

Learning from the depths of adversity contributes to personal growth. Just as submarines emerge stronger from successful salvage missions, individuals can use their recovered insights to build resilience and face life's uncertainties with newfound strength.

- **Recovering Lost Opportunities:**

Resilience is crucial for submarines facing the challenges of the abyss during salvage missions. The vessel must withstand pressure and adapt to the ever-changing underwater landscape.

In life's abyss, resilience becomes our ally. Confronting adversity necessitates developing inner strength, adaptability, and the ability to withstand the pressures that come with unexpected challenges.

Salvage operations often take submarines to unexplored depths where recovery efforts demand careful navigation through unfamiliar territories.

Life's adversities may lead us to uncharted emotional or situational depths. Salvaging lessons involves courageously exploring these unexplored territories within ourselves, uncovering hidden strengths and insights.

Salvage missions require meticulous planning and reflection to recover lost assets effectively.

Navigating the abyss of adversity prompts deep self-reflection. Examining our experiences, understanding the root causes of challenges, and learning from setbacks contribute to a more effective salvage of valuable life lessons.

Salvage efforts often encounter the unknown, requiring submarines to adapt quickly to unexpected conditions. Life's abyss presents uncertainties. Salvaging lessons involves cultivating the ability to adapt to the unknown, embracing change, and transforming challenges into opportunities for personal growth.

In the abyss, darkness prevails, and submarines rely on advanced technology to navigate and salvage.

Facing adversity often feels like traversing through darkness. Salvaging lessons includes finding the light within, tapping into our inner resources, and using our resilience to navigate challenges and emerge stronger on the other side.

Salvage missions require a delicate balance between control and surrender to the forces of the underwater environment.

Navigating life's abyss involves a similar balance. Salvaging lessons requires discerning when to assert control and when to surrender, recognizing that some challenges are beyond our immediate influence.

Salvage operations are collaborative efforts, relying on the coordinated actions of the submarine crew.

Navigating personal adversity often involves teamwork. Seeking support from friends, family, or professionals can enhance our ability to salvage lessons, providing diverse perspectives and shared experiences that contribute to growth.

Successful salvage missions leave submarines strengthened, equipped to face future challenges.

Learning from the depths of adversity contributes to personal growth. Just as submarines emerge stronger from successful salvage missions, individuals can use their recovered insights to build resilience and face life's uncertainties with newfound strength.

- **Adapting to Unforeseen Circumstances:**

Salvage operations require efficient allocation of resources, adjusting plans based on the dynamic underwater environment.

Adapting to unforeseen circumstances in life involves wise resource allocation. Being flexible with our time, energy, and resources allows us to address unexpected challenges effectively and make the most of our capabilities.

Salvage missions often encounter unpredictable challenges, necessitating a mindset of readiness for the unknown.

Life's unforeseen circumstances are inherently unpredictable. Embracing the uncertainty with an open mind and a readiness to face the unknown enables individuals to navigate challenges more gracefully and with greater resilience.

Unforeseen circumstances demand real-time, innovative problem-solving during salvage missions.

Adapting to unexpected situations in life requires a capacity for innovative problem-solving. Thinking creatively and finding novel solutions contribute to a proactive approach when faced with challenges.

Salvage operations require a solution-focused mindset to address challenges promptly and effectively.

When confronted with unforeseen circumstances in life, maintaining a solution-focused approach is crucial. Instead of dwelling on problems, individuals can channel their energy into identifying and implementing solutions, fostering a more positive and proactive outlook.

The underwater environment is dynamic, requiring continuous learning and adaptation during salvage missions.

Adapting to unforeseen circumstances in life necessitates learning agility. Being open to acquiring new knowledge, skills, and perspectives enables individuals to navigate changing environments and emerge stronger from unexpected experiences.

Salvage missions may evoke emotional challenges for the crew, requiring emotional resilience to navigate the complexities.

Adapting to unforeseen circumstances in life involves navigating emotional resilience. Building emotional strength allows individuals to cope with unexpected twists, maintaining composure and mental well-being during challenging times.

Salvage operations often involve collaboration among crew members to adapt to unforeseen challenges.

Life's unexpected circumstances can benefit from collaborative adaptation.

Seeking support from others, sharing insights, and collaborating on solutions enhance the collective ability to adapt and overcome unforeseen challenges.

Salvage missions require a balance between maintaining stability and embracing flexibility to navigate challenging conditions.

Adapting to unforeseen circumstances in life involves finding the right balance between stability and flexibility. While rooted in core values and principles, individuals must be adaptable to effectively navigate unexpected changes and uncertainties.

- **Turning Setbacks into Strengths:**

Salvage missions foster a growth mindset among the crew, encouraging continuous learning and improvement. Embracing setbacks in life with a growth mindset allows individuals to see challenges as opportunities for learning and development. Viewing setbacks as a pathway to improvement fosters resilience and a positive outlook.

Effective salvage operations involve adapting strategies based on lessons learned from setbacks.

Similarly, in life, setbacks necessitate the development of adaptive strategies. Assessing what went wrong, adjusting approaches, and incorporating newfound insights contribute to building resilience and enhancing one's ability to overcome future challenges.

Setbacks during salvage missions stimulate the crew's problem-solving skills, leading to innovative solutions. In life offer opportunities to enhance problem-solving skills. Individuals learn to analyze situations critically, identify root causes, and develop effective strategies to overcome obstacles, ultimately strengthening their problem-solving capabilities.

Overcoming setbacks requires determination and perseverance in salvage missions.

Learning from setbacks in life fosters determination and perseverance. The ability to persist in the face of challenges, fueled by a resilient mindset, becomes a source of strength that propels individuals forward in their personal and professional pursuits.

Salvage missions extract valuable lessons from setbacks to inform future operations.

Setbacks in life offer profound lessons. Extracting insights from challenges allows individuals to grow wiser, refine their decision-making, and navigate future endeavors with a greater understanding of potential pitfalls and opportunities.

Also, setbacks may evoke emotional challenges for the crew, necessitating emotional resilience.

Learning and growing from setbacks in life involve the development of emotional resilience.

Managing and overcoming emotional challenges associated with setbacks contribute to an individual's overall well-being and adaptability.

Addressing setbacks in salvage missions requires a focus on solutions rather than dwelling on problems.

Cultivating a solution-oriented mindset in response to setbacks is crucial. Individuals who proactively seek solutions, rather than dwelling on difficulties, empower themselves to overcome setbacks and drive positive change in their lives.

Successful salvage missions embrace change and adapt to unforeseen circumstances.

Turning setbacks into strengths in life involves embracing change and adapting to new circumstances. Individuals who welcome change as an inherent part of their journey are better equipped to navigate setbacks and transform challenges into opportunities for personal growth.

Overcoming setbacks contributes to the overall resilience and identity of the submarine.

Individuals who learn and grow from setbacks cultivate a resilient identity. Setbacks become integral to the narrative of personal development, shaping individuals into more resilient, adaptable, and capable beings.

Chapter **30**

Echo Soundings and Feedback

Submarines use echo soundings to understand their environment, just as we benefit from feedback to comprehend our impact on others.

In the depths of the ocean, where sunlight wanes and visibility is obscured, submarines employ a remarkable mechanism known as echo soundings. These sophisticated sonar systems emit sound waves, probing the surrounding darkness and capturing the reflections to create a detailed map of the underwater terrain. In this intricate dance of sonar pulses and echoes, submarines navigate through the enigmatic depths with precision and awareness. Strikingly similar is the role of feedback in our human interactions—a complex interplay of communication where the echoes of our actions and words provide insights into the depths of our impact on others. As submarines rely on echo soundings to fathom their surroundings, we, too, depend on feedback to comprehend and navigate the complex social and emotional landscapes that define our interconnected lives.

- **Navigating the Unseen Depths:**

Echo soundings assist submarines in identifying potential collisions with underwater obstacles.

Feedback plays a crucial role in helping individuals identify potential collisions in their relationships. Constructive feedback allows for course correction, preventing misunderstandings and conflicts before they escalate.

Submarines adjust their communication based on echo soundings to ensure optimal understanding.

Understanding how our words and actions are perceived enables us to adjust our communication style, fostering clearer and more effective interactions.

Echo soundings reveal the presence of objects hidden beneath the surface, aiding navigation.

Feedback serves as a tool to uncover hidden emotions and unspoken thoughts in interpersonal relationships. Understanding the emotional undercurrents allows for more empathetic and authentic connections with others.

Also, echo soundings prompt course corrections to avoid obstacles and stay on the right path.

Feedback facilitates course correction in relationships. It provides an opportunity to reflect on behavior, make adjustments, and ensure that our actions align with our intentions, contributing to healthier and more fulfilling connections.

Moreover, echo soundings contribute to the submarine crew's awareness of their surroundings.

Feedback enhances self-awareness by offering external perspectives on our behavior. It allows individuals to see themselves more objectively, fostering personal growth and a deeper understanding of how they impact those around them.

Echo soundings help submarines avoid misinterpreting underwater features.

Furthermore, feedback is instrumental in preventing misinterpretations in relationships. Clarity gained through feedback ensures that our intentions are accurately conveyed, reducing the likelihood of misunderstandings.

Echo soundings assist submarines in navigating complex underwater environments.

Feedback is invaluable in navigating the intricate dynamics of social relationships. Understanding how our actions are perceived by others allows us to navigate social nuances with sensitivity and awareness.

Also, echo soundings contribute to the crew's understanding of the emotional landscape underwater.

Feedback fosters the development of emotional intelligence. It provides insights into how our words and actions impact the emotions of others, fostering empathy and the ability to navigate social situations with emotional awareness.

The use of echo soundings supports continuous improvement in navigation techniques.

Feedback is a catalyst for continuous improvement in personal growth. Embracing feedback as a tool for learning ensures that individuals are on a path of continual self-refinement, adapting to evolving circumstances and deepening their understanding of themselves and their impact on others.

- **Creating a Mental Map:**

Echo soundings assist submarines in understanding the underwater currents. This helps them anticipate and navigate through the dynamic nature of the ocean.

Feedback in our personal interactions acts as a compass for emotional currents. Understanding how our expressions impact others emotionally allows us to navigate through social landscapes with empathy and consideration.

Submarines often adjust the frequency of their sonar to optimize communication and reduce interference.

Feedback aids us in adjusting our communication frequencies. By understanding how our message is received, we can fine-tune our expressions, ensuring clarity and resonance in our interactions.

Echo soundings reveal the composition of the seabed, helping submarines identify areas of strength and potential hazards.

Feedback illuminates our hidden strengths and weaknesses. Understanding how our qualities are perceived allows us to leverage strengths and work on areas that may need improvement.

Echo soundings require submarines to be aware of their own signals and how they might bounce back.

Also, feedback fosters self-awareness. By comprehending the reflections of our actions, we gain insights into our own behavior, leading to personal growth and development.

Coordinated efforts are crucial in interpreting echo soundings for navigation.

Moreover, feedback fosters collaboration in social settings. It encourages open communication, mutual understanding, and collaborative problem-solving, enhancing the dynamics of relationships.

Submarines continuously learn from echo soundings and adapt their navigation strategies accordingly.

Feedback promotes continuous learning. It encourages us to adapt our behaviors based on experiences, ensuring ongoing personal and interpersonal development.

- **Adjusting Trajectory with Real-Time Data:**

Adjusting trajectory in submarines ensures they navigate through diverse underwater landscapes.

Real-time feedback assists in navigating the social seascape. By adjusting our trajectory based on immediate responses, we can effectively navigate various social contexts and tailor our interactions accordingly.

Echo soundings prompt submarines to make course corrections to avoid obstacles.

Real-time feedback facilitates course corrections in relationships. Understanding the impact of our actions allows us to navigate relationship dynamics with agility, avoiding potential misunderstandings and conflicts.

Adjusting trajectory enhances the effectiveness of submarines in their missions.

Real-time feedback enhances interpersonal effectiveness. It provides valuable insights into how our words and actions influence others, enabling us to refine our approach for more impactful and positive interactions.

Submarines optimize their path for mission success based on immediate data.

Also, real-time feedback aids in optimizing personal development. It allows individuals to tailor their learning experiences, adapting to challenges, and ensuring continuous growth on their unique life journey.

Adjustments prevent misinterpretation of underwater features.

By actively responding to feedback, individuals can mitigate misunderstandings, ensuring that their intended message aligns with the received message.

Adaptability builds trust in submarine operations.

Real-time adjustments build trust in relationships. Adapting based on feedback demonstrates a willingness to understand and respond to others, fostering trust and strengthening interpersonal bonds.

Trajectory adjustments keep submarines aligned with mission objectives.

Real-time feedback assists in staying aligned with personal and professional goals. It ensures that actions and decisions remain congruent with overarching objectives, fostering a sense of purpose and direction.

Furthermore, real-time data empowers proactive decision-making in submarines.

Real-time feedback empowers proactive decision-making in personal and professional realms. It allows individuals to anticipate potential challenges, make informed decisions, and navigate their paths with foresight and intention.

- **Detecting Undercurrents and Emotional Nuances:**

Echo soundings contribute to fine-tuning navigation based on underwater features.

Feedback aids in fine-tuning communication skills. Understanding the emotional nuances and adjusting communication styles based on feedback ensures more effective and empathetic interpersonal connections.

Echo soundings heighten awareness of the underwater environment, fostering empathy for the surroundings.

Feedback heightens empathy. By discerning emotional undercurrents and subtle cues, individuals develop a greater sense of empathy, enhancing their ability to connect with others on a deeper, more meaningful level.

Also, echo soundings cultivate awareness of the undersea environment, contributing to social intelligence.

Feedback cultivates social awareness. It enables individuals to navigate social situations with greater understanding, contributing to the development of social intelligence and interpersonal acumen.

Detecting undercurrents helps submarines avoid potential conflicts in their path.

By detecting emotional undercurrents, assists in conflict resolution. It provides valuable insights into the root causes of conflicts, allowing individuals to address issues with greater understanding and find constructive resolutions.

Echo soundings contribute to a deeper understanding of the ocean's features.

Understanding emotional nuances and adapting based on feedback fosters more profound connections in personal and professional relationships.

Echo soundings detect features beyond visible surfaces.

Feedback helps recognize non-verbal cues. It allows individuals to perceive subtle expressions, gestures, and body language, adding depth to their comprehension of communication.

Furthermore, echo soundings allow submarines to adapt to changing underwater dynamics.

Feedback enables individuals to adapt to evolving social dynamics. Understanding emotional undercurrents facilitates adaptability, ensuring individuals can navigate changing interpersonal landscapes with grace.

Echo soundings contribute to a comprehensive understanding of the ocean's depths.

By detecting emotional nuances, contributes to a comprehensive understanding of personal relationships, nurturing a foundation for meaningful connections and mutual growth.

- **Maintaining Course Alignment:**

Echo soundings prevent submarines from deviating off course, ensuring integrity in navigation.

Feedback strengthens personal integrity. By aligning actions with values and adjusting based on feedback, individuals fortify their commitment to ethical conduct, fostering a sense of integrity in their personal and professional endeavors.

Echo soundings contribute to precision in underwater navigation.

Also, feedback refines decision-making precision. It provides the necessary data points for individuals to make informed choices, reducing uncertainties and contributing to more accurate and thoughtful decision-making.

Echo soundings contribute to learning about the underwater environment.

Feedback cultivates a learning mindset. It encourages individuals to embrace continuous improvement, learn from experiences, and adapt behaviors based on insights gained through feedback, fostering a growth-oriented approach.

Chapter 31

Propeller and Direction

The propeller's importance in steering a submarine mirrors the role of personal decisions in steering our life's direction.

The significant world underneath the ocean's surface may be a domain of puzzle, where submarines noiselessly navigate through the profundities, exploring perplexing scenes with a sense of reason and accuracy. At the heart of these submerged vessels lies a basic component—the propeller. This modest however significant gadget moves the submarine forward, dictating its direction and guaranteeing control within the endless scopes of the submerged world. Much just like the propeller's part in directing a submarine, our individual decisions play an similarly pivotal part in controlling the heading of our lives. Life's travel could be a endless region, abounding with conceivable outcomes and challenges. Within the complicated move of choices, our choices act as propellers, moving us forward and deciding the course we chart through the unexplored regions of our presence.

- **Propulsion as the Driving Force:**

The propeller harnesses the energy generated within the submarine's systems to create thrust.

Personal decisions harness the energy within us—our passions, motivations, and desires—to create momentum.

Each decision becomes a deliberate channeling of personal energy toward specific goals, driving us forward in our life's journey.

The propeller's thrust is directed with precision to navigate the submarine in a chosen direction.

Personal decisions are intentional vectors. They represent the directed thrust of our aspirations, goals, and values, ensuring that the trajectory of our life aligns with our chosen direction.

The propeller initiates the forward movement of the submarine, overcoming the resistance of water.

Personal decisions act as initiators of forward movement in our lives. They propel us past obstacles, challenges, and inertia, ensuring that we move with purpose and determination.

The speed of the propeller influences the velocity of the submarine's movement through the water.

The velocity of our personal journey is influenced by the speed and decisiveness of our decisions. Swift and well-considered choices can accelerate our progress toward goals, enhancing the overall velocity of our life's trajectory.

Continuous rotation of the propeller ensures consistent propulsion.

Consistent personal decisions maintain continuous propulsion in our lives.

The regularity of thoughtful decision-making contributes to sustained progress, preventing stagnation and promoting a dynamic and evolving life path.

The propeller balances power and control to navigate effectively.

Personal decisions involve a delicate balance between exerting power and maintaining control. Decisions should be powerful enough to drive us forward but controlled enough to navigate challenges and avoid unintended consequences.

The propeller dynamically responds to changes in water currents and external factors.

Personal decisions must dynamically respond to external forces and changing circumstances. Being adaptable and responsive ensures that our decisions remain effective in navigating the unpredictable currents of life.

Efficient propulsion minimizes resource consumption and maximizes effectiveness.

Efficient personal decisions optimize the use of our internal resources—time, energy, skills—ensuring that we propel ourselves forward effectively while minimizing unnecessary consumption of valuable resources.

The propeller drives the submarine toward its mission objectives and destinations.

Personal decisions drive us toward personal fulfillment and the achievement of our life's objectives. Each choice becomes a conscious step in the direction of a purposeful and satisfying life journey.

- **Precision in Navigation:**

In uncharted underwater terrains, propellers ensure that submarines navigate with precision, avoiding obstacles and unknown dangers.

Personal decisions act as our guiding force through uncharted territories in life. With precision, each decision becomes a navigational tool, helping us navigate through uncertainties and challenges, avoiding pitfalls along the way.

Submarines strategically use propellers to respond to the underwater landscape, making calculated adjustments for optimal navigation.

Personal decisions involve strategic thinking. Like a submarine's propeller responding to the underwater landscape, our decisions respond to the intricate landscape of our lives. Strategic decision-making ensures that we adapt to changing circumstances and make adjustments aligned with our overarching goals.

Propellers aid in avoiding collisions with underwater obstacles, contributing to the overall safety of the submarine.

Personal decisions, when made with precision, help us avoid collisions with detrimental paths. Navigating through life's challenges requires careful consideration, ensuring that our decisions align with our values and contribute to our well-being.

Propellers allow submarines to navigate through intricate underwater environments, where precise course charting is essential.

In complex life environments, personal decisions are the compass guiding our course. Each decision becomes a marker on our life map, ensuring that we navigate through the intricacies of relationships, career choices, and personal growth with precision and intention.

Propellers enable submarines to respond to changing underwater currents, adjusting their trajectory accordingly.

Life is dynamic, and personal decisions must respond to changing currents. Like a submarine's propeller adjusts to underwater currents, our decisions adapt to evolving circumstances, ensuring that we stay on course despite the unpredictable nature of life.

Propellers provide the means for submarines to maneuver effortlessly through challenging underwater conditions.

Personal decisions, when executed with precision, allow us to maneuver through life's challenges with grace and efficiency. Each decision becomes a tool for overcoming obstacles and navigating through difficulties, contributing to our overall resilience.

Submarines integrate external feedback and data to adjust propeller speed and direction for precise navigation.

Personal decisions benefit from external feedback. Integrating insights from experiences and feedback from others enhances our decision-making process, contributing to a more accurate and refined navigation through life.

Propellers contribute to navigating emotional nuances in the underwater environment.

Personal decisions navigate emotional terrain. Understanding the emotional implications of our decisions adds another layer of precision, ensuring that our choices align with our emotional well-being and contribute positively to our life journey.

- **Adaptability in Changing Currents:**

The propeller is the powerhouse, generating thrust to propel the submarine through the water. Its rotation creates forward motion, serving as the primary force behind the submarine's mobility.

Personal decisions act as the driving force in life, generating momentum and propelling us forward. Each decision becomes a source of energy that propels us toward our goals and aspirations. The power to move our lives lies within the choices we make.

Propellers provide precise control, allowing submarines to navigate through challenging underwater terrains. The ability to control the speed and direction of the propeller ensures accurate navigation.

Personal decisions enable precise navigation through the complexities of life. With each decision, we chart a course, navigate obstacles, and steer toward the destinations that align with our values. Precision in decision-making enhances the likelihood of reaching our desired outcomes.

Submarines adapt to changing currents by adjusting the propeller's speed and direction. This adaptability is crucial for maintaining control and stability.

Personal decisions require adaptability. Just as submarines adjust their propellers to changing currents, our decisions must adapt to the evolving circumstances, ensuring we stay on course despite life's unpredictable currents. The ability to pivot and adjust is a hallmark of effective decision-making.

Propellers respond to external forces, adjusting to ensure the submarine remains on its intended course. This responsiveness is essential for overcoming resistance from the surrounding environment.

Personal decisions must also respond to external forces such as challenges, opportunities, and unexpected events. The ability to adapt our decisions to external factors ensures that we can navigate through life's twists and turns with resilience and agility.

The continuous rotation of the propeller generates momentum, propelling the submarine forward with sustained energy.

Personal decisions, when made consistently in alignment with our goals, generate momentum in our lives. Each positive decision contributes to the overall momentum, creating a powerful force that propels us towards success and fulfillment.

Submarines use the propeller to steer through the depths of the ocean, maintaining control in challenging environments.

Personal decisions act as our steering mechanism through the depths of life. They empower us to navigate through challenges, make course corrections when needed, and stay in control of our direction despite the uncertainties that may arise.

Propellers optimize the use of resources to generate efficient thrust, ensuring the submarine operates effectively.

Personal decisions should optimize the use of our resources, including time, energy, and skills. Efficient decision-making maximizes our potential and propels us toward our objectives with effectiveness and purpose.

The propeller significantly influences the overall course of the submarine. Its efficiency and effectiveness determine the success of the mission.

Personal decisions exert a profound influence on the overall course of our lives.

The cumulative impact of our choices shapes the trajectory of our journey, influencing our experiences, relationships, and the fulfillment of our life's purpose. Each decision is a building block in the construction of our life's narrative.

- **Efficiency in Resource Utilization:**

Propellers are designed for sustainable energy management, ensuring that the conversion of power into motion is not only efficient but also sustainable over the long term.

Sustainable energy management in personal decisions involves considering the long-term impact of choices. Opting for decisions that align with our values and contribute positively to our well-being ensures a sustainable and enduring journey through life.

Propellers are streamlined to minimize resistance in the water, allowing the submarine to move forward with minimal hindrance.

Personal decisions, when well-considered and aligned with our goals, can minimize resistance in our life's path. Making choices that align with our values and aspirations reduces friction, enabling a smoother and more fulfilling journey.

Consistency in the operation of propellers is essential for maintaining steady motion. Irregularities can affect the overall performance.

Consistency in personal decision-making is crucial for sustained progress.

Regularly aligning our choices with our values and goals creates a rhythm that propels us forward, contributing to the achievement of long-term objectives.

The continuous rotation of propellers contributes to the overall momentum of the submarine, ensuring a constant forward motion.

Consistent, well-aligned personal decisions contribute to the overall momentum of our lives. Each positive choice adds to the cumulative force that propels us toward our aspirations, creating a powerful and enduring sense of progress.

Propellers are designed to adapt to variations in water conditions, ensuring effective propulsion in different environments.

Personal decisions should possess adaptability to navigate through diverse life situations. Being open to adjusting our choices based on the circumstances ensures that we can continue to move forward, even in challenging and unpredictable environments.

Chapter **32**

The Engine Room

The power center of a submarine, paralleling the heart and mind's role in driving personal transformation.

Submarines unveil a realm of intricate machinery and sophisticated systems, each component playing a pivotal role in the vessel's functionality. Among these, the power center stands as the heartbeat, the pulsating core that breathes life into the submarine, propelling it through the depths with purpose and precision. In a striking parallel, the human experience too harbors its own power center, an amalgamation of the heart and mind, orchestrating the symphony of personal transformation. This intricate interplay mirrors the dynamic relationship between the submarine's power center and its operational prowess.

- **Fusion of Forces:**

Within the submarine's power center, a harmonious integration of energy sources, from conventional engines to advanced technologies, contributes to the generation of propulsive force.

In the realm of personal transformation, a similar synergy emerges as emotional and intellectual energies converge. The heart's emotive currents and the mind's analytical prowess blend together, creating a potent force propelling individuals toward self-discovery and growth.

The submarine's energy integration mirrors the resonance of emotional currents within the heart, providing a parallel to the propulsion generated by emotional forces.

Personal transformation resonates with emotional currents, much like the energy integration in a submarine. Emotions become a driving force, propelling individuals forward and infusing the journey with passion and purpose.

The intellectual component of the power center aligns with the mind's analytical capabilities, providing the necessary thrust for precise navigation.

Intellectual prowess, akin to the analytical functions of the mind, propels individuals forward in their personal growth journey. The mind's capacity to navigate complexities and make informed decisions serves as a vital force in the transformative process.

The unified propulsion generated by diverse energy sources working together ensures the submarine's efficient movement.

Personal transformation gains momentum when the heart and mind operate in unison. The unified propulsion of emotional and intellectual forces propels individuals forward with clarity, coherence, and a sense of purpose.

A balanced mix of energy sources contributes to the stability and efficiency of the power center.

Balance in personal transformation is achieved through a nuanced interplay of emotions and intellect. A harmonious blend ensures stability, resilience, and adaptability in navigating life's challenges and opportunities.

The power center dynamically adapts to varying energy demands, optimizing performance in diverse operational conditions.

Personal transformation necessitates dynamic adaptation. The ability to adjust emotional and intellectual energies based on evolving circumstances ensures that individuals optimize their performance on the journey of self-discovery.

In overcoming underwater challenges, the power center propels the submarine with resilience and precision.

Personal challenges become transformative opportunities when met with the resilience generated by the fusion of emotional and intellectual forces. The heart and mind, working in tandem, provide the impetus needed to navigate and grow through life's trials.

The power center evolves through continuous advancements in technology, ensuring optimal performance over time.

Personal transformation, like the evolution of a power center, is an ongoing process. Embracing continuous learning, insights, and adaptations ensures that the fusion of emotional and intellectual forces propels individuals toward sustained growth and development.

- **Symbiotic Collaboration:**

Various components within the submarine's power center collaborate in a symbiotic manner, ensuring the optimal conversion and utilization of diverse energy streams.

The heart and mind, like interconnected energy streams, collaborate in a symbiotic dance. Emotions infuse depth and color into intellectual pursuits, while intellect guides and shapes the emotional landscape. This collaboration forms the foundation for a rich and balanced transformative existence.

Each component's contribution enhances the overall efficiency of the power center, much like emotional depth enriches intellectual pursuits.

Emotions, akin to a component in the power center, bring depth and nuance to intellectual endeavors. The infusion of passion, empathy, and subjective experience enhances the quality and meaningfulness of intellectual pursuits.

Certain components in the power center guide and shape the overall energy landscape.

Intellect acts as a guiding influence, shaping the emotional landscape. Rational thinking and analytical capabilities provide a framework for understanding and navigating the complex terrain of emotions, ensuring a balanced and purposeful transformative journey.

Symbiotic collaboration leads to a harmonious balance in energy utilization, optimizing the overall performance of the power center.

The collaboration between the heart and mind fosters a harmonious balance. Emotional and intellectual energies, when working in tandem, contribute to the optimization of personal growth, resilience, and well-being.

Components dynamically adapt to changing conditions, ensuring efficient operation in various circumstances.

The heart and mind dynamically adapt to life's challenges. Emotional resilience and intellectual flexibility enable individuals to navigate uncertainties, adjusting their responses and strategies based on evolving circumstances.

Components share a common objective of optimizing energy utilization for effective propulsion.

The heart and mind share a common objective in personal transformation — the optimization of emotional and intellectual energies for effective personal propulsion. The shared commitment to growth and well-being forms the core of the symbiotic collaboration.

Different components mutually enrich each other's functionalities within the power center.

The collaboration between the heart and mind leads to mutual enrichment. Emotional experiences enrich intellectual understanding, and intellectual insights contribute to a deeper comprehension of emotional states, creating a holistic and enriched transformative experience.

Symbiotic collaboration ensures the optimal utilization of each component's strengths for efficient operation.

The heart's strengths, including intuition and empathy, synergize with the mind's analytical capabilities. This optimal utilization of strengths ensures that emotional and intellectual energies complement each other, fostering a transformative journey marked by wisdom, compassion, and personal growth.

- **Heartbeat of Passion:**

The rhythmic throb of the power center serves as a pulsating energy source, symbolizing the passion driving the submarine's activities.

In individuals, the heartbeat of passion emanates from the fusion of emotional and intellectual energies. This pulsating source propels them forward, infusing vitality into their pursuits and steering them towards their aspirations.

The rhythmic activities of the power center resonate with a sense of purpose, aligning with the submarine's mission.

The heartbeat of passion aligns with personal missions and goals. It creates a resonance within individuals, harmonizing their emotional and intellectual energies in pursuit of a meaningful and purposeful life journey.

The power center's rhythmic beat signifies resilience, adapting to challenges in the underwater environment.

The heartbeat of passion embodies emotional resilience. It allows individuals to adapt to life's challenges, bouncing back from setbacks, and maintaining a steady rhythm in the face of adversity.

The power center's activities involve a harmonic fusion of diverse components to generate power.

Heartbeat of passion represents a harmonic fusion of emotional and intellectual elements. The interplay of these components generates the power needed for personal growth, creativity, and transformative experiences.

Rhythmic beat hints at the creative impulses within the power center, essential for innovative navigation.

Passionate heartbeats fuel creative impulses within individuals. The synergy of emotions and intellect sparks innovation, enabling them to navigate through the complexities of life with ingenuity and imagination.

The rhythmic activities of the power center are synchronized for optimal efficiency.

The heartbeat of passion seeks a synchronized harmony between emotions and intellect. This alignment enhances personal efficiency, allowing individuals to make decisions, express themselves, and navigate life's complexities with coherence and balance.

Rhythmic vibrations express the energy coursing through the power center.

The heartbeat of passion serves as expressive vibrations of an individual's inner energy. It communicates enthusiasm, determination, and the vibrant force that propels them forward in their life journey.

Rhythmic beat is the lifeline of the submarine's vitality, ensuring sustained propulsion.

The heartbeat of passion is the lifeline of an individual's vitality. It ensures sustained energy for personal growth, resilience, and the pursuit of a purpose-driven life.

- **Mind as Navigation System:**

The power center's intricate calculations and precision are akin to a submarine's navigation system, ensuring accurate movement in underwater terrains.

The mind engages in cognitive calculations, processing information, analyzing situations, and making decisions. This cognitive precision is crucial for navigating the complexities of personal transformation with accuracy and foresight.

Power center allows for precise adjustments to the submarine's course, adapting to changing underwater dynamics.

Mind serves as a course adjustment mechanism in life. It enables individuals to adapt to evolving circumstances, make informed decisions, and navigate through the dynamic currents of personal growth with agility and resilience.

The power center processes vast amounts of data to optimize energy utilization and efficiency.

Mind, as an information processing hub, assimilates knowledge, experiences, and emotions. This processing capability is instrumental in optimizing personal energy, enhancing efficiency, and facilitating informed choices in the journey of self-discovery.

Precision is paramount in the power center's decisions to ensure effective propulsion.

The mind's precision in decision-making is essential for effective personal propulsion. Clear, well-calculated decisions guide individuals forward, aligning their actions with their values and aspirations in the pursuit of personal transformation.

Power center navigates the intricate mental terrains of underwater environments.

The mind serves as the navigator of mental terrains in personal transformation. It explores the complexities of thoughts, emotions, and beliefs, guiding individuals through the depths of self-awareness and growth.

The power center adapts to changing underwater currents to maintain optimal performance.

The mind's adaptability to emotional currents is crucial. Navigating personal transformation requires an understanding of one's emotional landscape and the ability to adapt to changing feelings, fostering emotional intelligence and resilience.

Strategic planning ensures the power center's efficiency in various operational conditions.

Mind engages in strategic planning for personal growth. It formulates goals, envisions aspirations, and strategizes the steps needed for transformative journeys, ensuring adaptability to different life conditions.

Continuous learning and system upgrades enhance the power center's capabilities.

The mind's continuous learning and growth enhance personal capabilities. Embracing new knowledge, experiences, and perspectives serves as a mental upgrade, enriching the navigation system for a more profound and transformative life journey.

Chapter **33**

Decompression and Adjustment

Understanding the need for decompression when surfacing parallels the need for adjusting to life changes.

One of the critical processes for submarines, much like our own adaptation to life's challenges, is decompression upon resurfacing. Decompression serves as a vital transitional phase, allowing submarines to adjust gradually to the change in pressure. Similarly, in the tapestry of our lives, we encounter various moments that demand a parallel decompression – a nuanced adjustment to transitions, be they professional, personal, or existential. Understanding the need for decompression when surfacing is not merely a nautical concept; it is a profound metaphor for our journey through the ebbs and flows of life.

- **Emotional Equilibrium:**

Decompression protocols in submarines prioritize the mental well-being of the crew. As they ascend to the surface, the controlled pace ensures that emotional equilibrium is maintained, minimizing the impact of pressure changes on crew members' mental states.

Life changes are often accompanied by a cascade of emotions – excitement, fear, uncertainty. In the human experience, decompression aligns with the need to navigate and embrace this emotional complexity.

It involves acknowledging and understanding the diverse range of feelings that arise during periods of change. Rapid resurfacing can lead to decompression sickness, akin to emotional overload. Submarine decompression ensures that emotional adjustments occur gradually, preventing overwhelming feelings among the crew.

In life, emotional balance during transitions is crucial for fostering resilience. Decompression becomes a metaphor for creating a supportive environment that allows individuals to process emotions, fostering the resilience needed to face new challenges.

The synchronized nature of submarine decompression aligns the emotional states of the entire crew. It fosters a sense of unity and shared experience as they collectively adapt to the changing conditions.

While life changes impact individuals uniquely, the concept of decompression in personal growth emphasizes the importance of individual emotional navigation. It involves recognizing, understanding, and managing one's emotions to achieve a state of equilibrium during transitions.

Decompression strategies in submarines actively address stress and anxiety. The gradual ascent allows crew members to release accumulated stress and tension, contributing to a more relaxed emotional state.

Similarly, in life, decompression involves creating emotional space for adaptation. By finding emotional equilibrium, individuals create an environment where they can adapt to new circumstances with a clear and focused mind, enhancing their capacity for effective decision-making and personal growth.

- **Preventing Overwhelm:**

Submarines employ gradual decompression to prevent decompression sickness, a physiological risk associated with rapid ascent. This careful approach protects the crew's physical well-being.

Life changes, akin to rapid ascent, can induce psychological overwhelm. Applying the principle of decompression in personal development involves managing the pace of change to prevent mental and emotional exhaustion.

Decompression in submarines involves incremental pressure adjustment to match external conditions. This approach allows the crew's bodies to acclimate to changes without abrupt stress on internal systems.

Similarly, in life, the principle of preventing overwhelm during transitions involves incremental adaptation. Taking small, manageable steps allows individuals to adjust to new circumstances without feeling inundated by the magnitude of change.

Submarines release pressure gradually during ascent to ensure a controlled and steady adaptation.

This approach prevents the sudden release of built-up pressure, reducing the risk of adverse physiological effects.

In life changes, a controlled release of emotional tension is vital. Decompression becomes a metaphor for allowing emotions to surface gradually, preventing an overwhelming flood of feelings that can impede the adjustment process.

The gradual decompression process ensures the safety of the entire submarine crew. Collective well-being takes precedence over individual speed, emphasizing the importance of a cohesive and supportive team.

In personal development, considering collective well-being during social changes is essential. Applying the principle of preventing overwhelm extends to the social sphere, promoting a supportive environment where individuals can navigate transitions together, enhancing the overall resilience of the community.

- **Integration of Lessons Learned:**

Submarine decompression serves as a designated time for crew members to reflect on the completed mission. This reflection allows them to process experiences and gather insights.

Life changes similarly demand reflection. Decompression in personal growth involves intentional introspection, providing individuals with the opportunity to reflect on the impact of changes and derive valuable insights.

Crew members use decompression to discuss challenges encountered during the mission. This collective discussion facilitates learning from experiences and finding ways to address future challenges.

Life changes often present challenges. Decompression in personal development involves learning from these challenges, understanding the lessons they offer, and incorporating newfound wisdom into one's approach to life.

The decompression process on a submarine is a collaborative debriefing session. Crew members share their perspectives, fostering a collective understanding of the mission's intricacies.

In personal growth, decompression involves sharing experiences with trusted individuals. This collaborative sharing creates a supportive environment, where insights are exchanged, and the collective wisdom of the group contributes to individual development.

During decompression, crew members engage in strategic planning for future missions. This forward-thinking approach ensures that lessons learned contribute to improved future performance.

In personal development, decompression includes strategic planning for the future. Individuals use insights gained from life changes to set goals, plan for personal growth, and navigate future challenges with greater resilience and purpose.

- **Acknowledging Transition Phases:**

in submarines involves gradually reducing pressure to prevent adverse effects. This phased approach ensures a controlled transition for the vessel and its crew.

Life changes, like career shifts or personal transformations, often unfold gradually. Acknowledging and understanding the gradual nature of these transitions helps individuals adapt with greater ease, fostering a smoother journey through change.

Submarines ascend in a controlled manner during decompression. This controlled ascent prevents physiological issues, ensuring the well-being of the crew.

Similarly, in personal growth, a mindful and controlled ascent involves navigating life changes with intention. This approach helps individuals avoid overwhelming adjustments, fostering a sense of control and well-being.

Crew members' vital signs are closely monitored during decompression. This monitoring ensures that any signs of distress are promptly addressed.

In life changes, self-monitoring becomes crucial. Individuals need to pay attention to their emotional well-being, adjusting their pace and seeking support if signs of emotional distress arise during transitions.

Decompression involves the support of the entire submarine team. Each member plays a role in ensuring a smooth transition for the entire crew.

Personal transitions benefit from a support network. Acknowledging transition phases in life includes seeking support from friends, family, or mentors, creating a collaborative environment that eases the journey through change.

- **Balancing Physical and Mental Well-being:**

Decompression in submarines includes restoring optimal oxygen levels for the crew. This step is crucial for their physical well-being after being in an environment with reduced oxygen pressure.

In life changes, restoring balance is essential. This involves identifying areas that may have been neglected during transitions and taking intentional steps to restore equilibrium, whether in work-life balance, relationships, or personal pursuits.

During decompression, the submarine team reflects on the mission. This collective reflection fosters camaraderie and allows for shared insights.

Life transitions benefit from personal reflection. Individuals can use moments of decompression to reflect on their journey, learn from experiences, and set intentions for personal growth.

Submarines gradually return to normal pressure after decompression. This gradual return minimizes the impact on the vessel and its systems.

Similarly, individuals undergoing life changes can benefit from a gradual reintegration into their 'normal' routines. This phased approach allows for adjustment and minimizes the potential stress associated with abrupt shifts.

Psychological debriefing is part of decompression for submarines. This practice helps crew members process the emotional aspects of their mission.

Emotional processing is crucial in life transitions. Individuals can engage in practices like journaling, therapy, or conversations with trusted confidantes to process and understand the emotional dimensions of their evolving circumstances.

Decompression strengthens team bonds in submarines. The shared experience fosters a sense of unity among crew members.

Personal transitions provide opportunities to build connections. Whether through shared experiences or reaching out to new communities, individuals can enhance their support systems and establish new connections during times of change.

- **Facilitating Adaptation:**

Submarine decompression involves a reorientation to surface conditions. This process helps the crew adjust to the differences between the underwater and surface environments.

Life's decompression involves readjusting to external realities.

Whether after a significant life event or a period of intense focus, individuals benefit from a deliberate reorientation to the external factors influencing their lives.

Decompression in submarines prevents barotrauma, the physical damage caused by pressure changes. This precautionary measure safeguards the structural integrity of the vessel.

Life's decompression safeguards mental well-being. By taking preventive measures such as self-care, seeking support, and maintaining mental health practices, individuals protect their psychological integrity during transitions.

During decompression, submarine crews monitor vital signs to ensure the health of each member. This meticulous observation helps identify any signs of distress.

Life's decompression involves self-monitoring and awareness. Individuals can benefit from paying close attention to their own well-being, recognizing signs of stress or imbalance, and taking proactive steps for self-care.

Instruments on submarines may need recalibration after decompression. This ensures their accuracy in providing essential data for the vessel's operation.

Similarly, life's decompression involves recalibrating personal instruments – skills, knowledge, and perspectives.

Individuals can align these elements to ensure their effectiveness in navigating the new terrain of their lives.

Decompression ensures the submarine's structural integrity. This comprehensive check ensures that the vessel remains sound and capable of withstanding future missions.

Life's decompression involves strengthening personal foundations. Individuals can engage in self-reflection and assessment to fortify their emotional, mental, and physical foundations, enhancing their resilience for future endeavors.

Chapter **34**

Underwater Repairs

The ability to make repairs while submerged reflects our need to address issues even when in the depths of hardship.

In the complex move between the profound secrets of the ocean's profundities and the versatile soul of human presence, a captivating parallel emerges— the capacity to create repairs whereas submerged within the unforgiving submerged domain. Submarines, the quiet gatekeepers of the profound, explore through challenges with a exceptional capacity for repair and adjustment. In a allegorical sense, this mirrors the fundamental human ought to address issues indeed when submerged within the profundities of hardship. Life's turbulent waters regularly toss unexpected challenges our way, requesting an immovable commitment to repair the harms, repair the breaks, and rise more grounded from the profundities of misfortune.

- **Precision in Diagnosis:**

Submarines utilize cutting-edge diagnostic systems, including sonar and sophisticated sensors, to pinpoint issues with unparalleled precision.

In the human experience, addressing life's challenges begins with adopting a similarly advanced approach. Utilizing introspection, mindfulness, and perhaps seeking professional guidance, individuals can enhance their ability to diagnose issues with precision.

Sonar technology in submarines enables them to navigate through underwater complexities, detecting even subtle anomalies.

Like sonar guiding submarines through the depths, introspection acts as the human sonar. It allows individuals to navigate the intricate landscape of their thoughts and emotions, revealing subtle nuances that may contribute to challenges.

Submarines focus on identifying the root causes of malfunctions to address issues comprehensively.

Addressing life challenges requires a parallel focus on identifying root causes. Delving beneath surface-level symptoms allows individuals to understand the underlying issues, enabling more effective and sustainable solutions.

Submarines explore the depths of the ocean to identify issues; a metaphor for deep introspection.

Personal growth involves delving into the depths of one's thoughts and emotions. This profound introspection is essential for identifying areas that require attention and nurturing.

Submarines may deploy robotic arms equipped with precision tools for intricate repairs.

Just as submarines use precision tools, individuals can employ mental health tools such as therapy, mindfulness practices, or journaling for meticulous self-repair.

Submarines use advanced systems to gauge the emotional well-being of the crew during repairs.

Emotional intelligence becomes the diagnostic instrument in personal growth. Understanding and managing emotions play a pivotal role in addressing issues and fostering a healthy emotional state.

Submarines may involve collaboration among crew members to diagnose and address complex issues.

Interpersonal challenges often benefit from collaborative diagnosis. Seeking insights from trusted friends, family, or professionals can provide diverse perspectives for a more comprehensive understanding.

Submarines embrace technology for efficient diagnosis; humans can leverage technology for personal growth, such as self-help apps or online resources.

In the contemporary world, technology offers tools for self-discovery and growth. Utilizing apps, online courses, or virtual support communities can enhance the precision of personal diagnosis and growth.

Submarines continuously monitor systems even after repairs to ensure sustained functionality.

Similarly, individuals must adopt a continuous monitoring mindset for personal wellness. Regular self-check-ins and ongoing self-reflection contribute to sustained mental and emotional health.

Submarines use feedback from systems to refine their diagnostic processes.

Individuals can incorporate feedback from life experiences, learnings, and personal growth efforts to refine their diagnostic approaches. A willingness to adapt based on life's feedback enhances the precision of addressing future challenges.

- **Adaptability of Materials:**

Submarines employ materials engineered for resilience, capable of withstanding extreme underwater pressures.

In life, facing challenges requires adopting resilient strategies. Individuals must cultivate mental and emotional resilience, choosing coping mechanisms that endure the pressures of adversity.

Submarines utilize materials resistant to corrosion in the harsh underwater environment.

In navigating life's challenges, individuals benefit from cultivating emotional resilience that resists the corrosive effects of stress, negativity, and setbacks.

Materials in submarines must be flexible to allow for maneuverability and adjustments in challenging underwater conditions.

Flexibility is key in facing life's uncertainties. Individuals need adaptable approaches that allow for maneuvering through changing circumstances, making adjustments as needed.

Submarines showcase adaptability in choosing materials; similarly, individuals should adopt adaptable coping mechanisms.

Coping mechanisms should be adaptable to different life situations. What works in one circumstance may need adjustment in another, requiring individuals to choose strategies that flex with the challenges they face.

Materials are reinforced to ensure endurance under pressure.

Endurance in life's challenges requires personal reinforcement. Individuals must reinforce their mental and emotional well-being to withstand the pressures encountered on their life journey.

Materials used in repairs are chosen for compatibility to ensure stability in the submarine's structure.

Stability in life demands choosing strategies and habits that are compatible with one's values and goals. Compatibility ensures a stable foundation for navigating challenges.

Submarines often use composite materials for holistic strength.

Holistic strength in individuals involves a composite approach to well-being—addressing mental, emotional, and physical aspects. This comprehensive strength contributes to adaptability in the face of life's challenges.

Submarine materials are selected based on the specific underwater environment.

Life challenges come in various environments; individuals must adapt their strategies to the specific context, choosing coping mechanisms that align with the challenges they encounter.

Sustainable materials contribute to the longevity of submarine repairs.

Sustainable well-being practices contribute to the longevity of personal growth. Individuals benefit from adopting habits and coping mechanisms that are sustainable over the long term.

Innovation in materials ensures submarines are equipped for future challenges.

Facing the unknowns of the future, individuals should cultivate innovative approaches to challenges, continuously adapting and evolving in their personal growth journey.

- **Timely Response to Leaks:**

Submarines prioritize the rapid identification of leaks for timely intervention.

Likewise, in life, individuals must develop the skill of swiftly identifying challenges or issues, enabling proactive responses before they escalate.

Once a leak is identified, submarines engage in proactive problem-solving to address the issue promptly.

Responding to life's leaks requires proactive problem-solving. Individuals need to tackle challenges head-on, seeking solutions rather than allowing problems to fester.

Swift responses to leaks prevent further damage and escalation of issues within the submarine systems.

Timely responses in life prevent challenges from escalating, minimizing the potential impact on mental, emotional, or physical well-being.

Submarines aim to mitigate the impact of leaks on critical systems to ensure the vessel's overall functionality.

Addressing leaks in life involves mitigating the impact on personal systems—mental, emotional, and physical—ensuring a smoother continuation of one's overall well-being.

Submarine crews are trained in crisis management to handle leaks efficiently.

Life requires individuals to develop crisis management skills, enabling them to navigate unexpected challenges with resilience and composure.

Swift responses in submarine repairs involve timely decision-making to implement necessary actions.

Timely decision-making is essential in life. Individuals must make decisions promptly when faced with challenges, choosing courses of action that align with their well-being.

Resources are strategically allocated to address leaks effectively.

Addressing life's leaks involves the strategic allocation of personal resources—time, energy, and attention—to ensure an efficient and effective response.

Submarines learn from past responses to improve future leak management.

Individuals benefit from learning from their past responses to life's challenges, refining their approach and enhancing their ability to handle future leaks.

Crew members maintain emotional resilience during crisis responses.

Responding to life's leaks requires emotional resilience. Individuals must cultivate the ability to stay composed and emotionally resilient in the face of challenges.

Submarines engage in continuous improvement of response strategies.

Life demands continuous improvement. Individuals should consistently refine their problem-solving and response mechanisms, adapting to new challenges and growing from each experience.

- **Collaboration in Complex Repairs:**

Complex repairs in submarines involve utilizing the diverse skills and expertise of different crew members.

Life's challenges often benefit from collaborative efforts, where individuals can leverage the diverse skills and perspectives of others to address complex issues.

Team coordination is crucial for successful complex repairs in submarines.

Collaborative efforts in life require effective team coordination. Individuals must work in tandem with others, ensuring smooth communication and synergy in addressing intricate challenges.

Crew members share their knowledge and expertise to contribute to the success of complex repairs.

In life, collaboration involves sharing knowledge and expertise with others. The collective wisdom derived from diverse perspectives enhances problem-solving capabilities.

Dividing tasks among crew members ensures efficiency in complex repair processes.

Collaborative efforts often involve a division of labor. Individuals can assign specific tasks or responsibilities to team members, optimizing the overall effectiveness of problem-solving.

Crew members synergize their problem-solving approaches to address complex issues effectively.

Collaborative problem-solving in life requires synergy. Combining different approaches and strategies from various individuals enhances the overall effectiveness of addressing intricate challenges.

Open communication is vital for successful collaboration in submarine repairs.

Effective collaboration in life necessitates open communication. Individuals must express their thoughts, ideas, and concerns transparently, fostering an environment of trust and cooperation.

Crew members provide mutual support to ensure the success of complex repairs.

Collaboration involves mutual support in life. Individuals can lean on each other for encouragement, assistance, and guidance, enhancing the overall effectiveness of problem-solving efforts.

The entire crew takes ownership of complex repair challenges.

Collaborative efforts in life require a collective sense of problem ownership. Individuals work together, taking responsibility for addressing challenges and achieving shared goals.

Collaborative environments may face conflicts, necessitating effective resolution skills.

Life's collaborations may encounter conflicts, and individuals must possess effective conflict resolution skills to navigate disagreements and maintain a harmonious working relationship.

Successful complex repairs are celebrated as a collective achievement.

Collaborative successes in life should be celebrated collectively. Acknowledging the contributions of each team member fosters a positive and supportive collaborative environment.

Chapter **35**

Dynamic Positioning

Maintaining a submarine's position requires skill, as does maintaining our stance in the face of life's currents.

Navigating the vast expanse of the ocean's depths, submarines possess a unique ability to maintain their position in the face of dynamic currents. This skill is a testament to the intricate balance of technology, precision, and strategic decision-making that submarines employ. In a parallel narrative, our journey through life presents a metaphorical ocean, where we, like submarines, encounter various currents—challenges, changes, and uncertainties. The art of maintaining a submarine's position finds resonance in the delicate dance of maintaining our stance amidst the currents of life. The ability to stand firm, adapt, and navigate challenges demands a skillful interplay of resilience, self-awareness, and strategic decision-making.

- **Adaptive Stability:**

Submarines employ cutting-edge stabilizing mechanisms such as gyroscopes and control surfaces to counteract the turbulence of underwater currents.

These mechanisms showcase the submarine's ability to remain steady and maintain its position despite the unpredictable nature of the ocean.

Life often presents turbulent situations, akin to the unpredictability of underwater currents. Challenges, uncertainties, and changes create a dynamic environment.

Developing adaptive stability in life involves acknowledging and navigating through these turbulent currents without losing one's balance or composure.

Submarines strike a balance between flexibility and resilience, ensuring they can adapt to changing conditions while maintaining a robust stance.

Similarly, individuals must find a delicate equilibrium between being flexible enough to adapt to life's changes and resilient enough to withstand the pressures of challenges.

Underwater currents vary in intensity and direction, requiring submarines to dynamically adjust their stabilizing systems.

Life's challenges are dynamic and multifaceted. Adaptive stability involves recognizing the ever-changing nature of difficulties and adjusting one's approach accordingly.

Submarines continuously adjust their stabilizing mechanisms based on real-time feedback and environmental conditions.

In life, the ability to make ongoing adjustments is crucial. This involves staying attuned to changing circumstances, learning from experiences, and adapting strategies accordingly.

Submarines exhibit a fluid response to changing underwater conditions, showcasing their adaptability.

Individuals need a fluid and adaptable mindset to respond effectively to life's challenges. Rigidity can lead to instability, while adaptability ensures a smoother navigation through turbulent times.

Submarines navigate the ebb and flow of underwater currents without being destabilized.

Life's journey involves navigating through the ebb and flow of circumstances. Adaptive stability enables individuals to move through the highs and lows without losing their footing.

Submarine crews develop the skill of adaptive stability through training and hands-on experience in different ocean conditions.

Similarly, individuals develop adaptive stability through the experiences life presents. Each challenge becomes an opportunity to refine the skill of balancing flexibility and resilience.

Submarines showcase not just structural but also psychological resilience in maintaining stability.

Life's challenges often require psychological resilience. Developing a resilient mindset contributes to adaptive stability, allowing individuals to navigate difficulties with emotional strength.

Submarines strategically respond to unpredictable underwater currents to maintain stability.

In life, strategic responses involve thoughtful decision-making and proactive measures to counteract the unpredictable nature of challenges, ensuring a stable and resilient stance.

- **Strategic Decision-Making:**

Submarines employ strategic decision-making to adjust their position in response to various environmental factors such as water currents, depth, and potential threats.

This strategic navigation ensures the submarine remains on course, highlighting the importance of informed decision-making in challenging conditions.

Life presents a dynamic landscape, akin to the ever-changing underwater environment submarines navigate. Strategic decision-making in life involves understanding the nuances of different situations, foreseeing potential challenges, and adapting one's position to navigate the complexities of personal and professional realms.

Submarines rely on environmental awareness to make decisions about their position, considering factors such as temperature, pressure, and terrain.

Similarly, individuals must cultivate awareness of their surroundings in life. Understanding the external factors influencing their journey enables more informed and strategic decision-making.

Submarines demonstrate foresight by planning their route and adjusting position in anticipation of future challenges.

Foresight and planning are crucial in life's journey. Strategic decision-making involves envisioning potential obstacles, planning for contingencies, and adjusting one's path to proactively address upcoming challenges.

Submarines assess risks in their environment to make decisions that mitigate potential dangers.

Life, too, requires constant risk assessment. Strategic decision-making involves evaluating risks, understanding consequences, and adjusting one's position to minimize potential negative impacts.

Submarines engage in course correction, altering their trajectory to align with their objectives.

Individuals must be open to course correction in life. Strategic decision-making includes recognizing when adjustments are necessary, whether in career paths, relationships, or personal goals.

Submarines strategically allocate resources to optimize their position, ensuring efficient navigation.

Strategic decision-making in life involves optimizing resources such as time, energy, and skills. Efficient resource utilization contributes to maintaining a stable and successful position.

Submarines adapt to external forces like ocean currents, using strategic decisions to navigate these influences.

Life's external forces, such as societal changes or economic shifts, necessitate adaptability. Strategic decision-making allows individuals to navigate these forces, making informed adjustments to maintain stability.

Submarines consider long-term objectives in their strategic decisions to ensure sustained success.

Life planning involves a long-term vision. Strategic decision-making aligns with overarching life goals, steering individuals toward a fulfilling and purpose-driven future.

Submarines exhibit flexibility in decision-making, adjusting their position based on real-time information.

Flexibility in life's decisions is vital. Strategic decision-making requires adaptability, allowing individuals to pivot when necessary and respond effectively to changing circumstances.

Submarines learn from past decisions, incorporating experience into their strategic approach.

Life's journey involves learning from past choices. Strategic decision-making includes reflecting on experiences, understanding the outcomes of previous decisions, and applying these insights to improve future strategies.

Submarines often involve collaboration in decision-making, leveraging the expertise of the crew.

Collaboration in life's decisions is valuable. Strategic decision-making may involve seeking advice, considering diverse perspectives, and engaging in collaborative efforts to enhance the quality of choices.

Submarines align decisions with their mission objectives. Personal values similarly guide strategic decision-making.

Decisions in life should align with personal values and principles. Strategic decision-making involves ensuring that one's choices align with their core beliefs and contribute to overall well-being.

Submarines employ innovative problem-solving in decision-making, addressing challenges with creative solutions.

Life's challenges often demand creative solutions. Strategic decision-making involves thinking innovatively, finding unique approaches to address problems, and adapting to novel situations.

Submarines continuously adapt their decisions based on evolving conditions, showcasing a commitment to ongoing strategic adjustments.

Life is dynamic, requiring continuous adaptation. Strategic decision-making involves recognizing the need for ongoing adjustments, staying agile in the face of change, and navigating the complexities of an ever-evolving journey.

- **Continuous Monitoring:**

Submarines continuously monitor their surroundings, emphasizing the importance of self-reflection in personal growth.

Life requires vigilant self-reflection. Continuous monitoring of our thoughts, emotions, and actions allows for self-awareness, facilitating personal development and informed decision-making.

Submarines scan the underwater environment for potential threats or opportunities.

Similarly, life demands an environmental scan. Continuous monitoring of external factors, societal changes, and emerging trends enables individuals to adapt to the evolving landscape and make informed decisions.

Submarines integrate feedback loops for real-time adjustments.

Life benefits from feedback integration. Continuous monitoring of feedback, whether from personal experiences or external sources, provides valuable insights for ongoing improvements and adjustments in various aspects of life.

Submarines maintain situational awareness for precise positioning.

Life's currents demand situational awareness. Continuous monitoring of the current life situation allows individuals to make timely adjustments, navigate challenges, and align their actions with their goals.

Submarines require emotional intelligence in monitoring crew dynamics.

Life parallels this need for emotional intelligence. Continuous monitoring of emotional states, both within oneself and in others, contributes to effective communication, relationship-building, and overall well-being.

Submarines align with their mission and core values for continuous precision.

Continuous monitoring of decisions against core values is essential in life. It ensures that actions remain aligned with personal values, fostering authenticity and long-term satisfaction.

Submarines learn from ongoing monitoring, adapting strategies for improved performance.

Life involves continuous learning. Monitoring experiences, adapting behaviors based on lessons learned, and evolving with new insights contribute to personal growth and resilience in the face of challenges.

Submarines have a reflex for immediate course adjustment based on real-time data.

Life's currents may require immediate responses. Continuous monitoring cultivates a reflex for swift course adjustments, allowing individuals to navigate unforeseen circumstances effectively.

Submarines engage in a decision feedback loop, continuously assessing the outcomes of decisions.

Life decisions benefit from a feedback loop. Continuous monitoring of decision outcomes provides a basis for refining strategies, learning from mistakes, and making informed choices in the future.

Submarines perform holistic checks to ensure all systems contribute to well-being.

Life's journey demands holistic well-being checks. Continuous monitoring of physical, mental, and emotional aspects ensures a balanced and healthy approach to challenges and opportunities.

Submarines align with mission goals for continuous success.

Life requires alignment with personal goals. Continuous monitoring ensures that actions and decisions remain in harmony with overarching life objectives, promoting a sense of purpose and fulfillment.

Submarines continuously calibrate crew dynamics for optimal performance.

Life involves managing relationships. Continuous monitoring and calibration of interpersonal dynamics contribute to harmonious connections, effective communication, and collaborative endeavors.

Submarines adapt to changes in the underwater environment through continuous monitoring.

Life is marked by environmental changes. Continuous monitoring allows individuals to adapt to evolving circumstances, fostering resilience and the ability to thrive in diverse situations.

Chapter **36**

Ballast and Balance

Controlling a submarine's ballast is crucial for stability, as is maintaining emotional balance in our lives.
The vast, mysterious depths of the ocean conceal a marvel of engineering and precision: submarines. As these vessels navigate the underwater realms, a critical aspect of their operation lies in the control of ballast. Ballast, the material or substance used to provide stability and control buoyancy, ensures that the submarine maintains its desired depth and stability. Similarly, in the intricate tapestry of human existence, the metaphorical ballast is our emotional balance. Just as a submarine relies on the careful adjustment of ballast for stability in the unpredictable ocean currents, individuals must navigate the currents of life with a calibrated emotional equilibrium.

- **Fine-Tuning for Equilibrium:**

Engineers calibrate the submarine's ballast systems with precision, ensuring optimal buoyancy and stability.
Fine-tuning emotional responses involves a meticulous calibration of reactions, allowing individuals to respond to situations with emotional intelligence and avoid extremes.
Tilting in a submarine can disrupt its trajectory; hence, ballast adjustments prevent such deviations.
Emotional fine-tuning prevents tilting responses. By avoiding extreme emotional reactions, individuals maintain a steady emotional trajectory, navigating challenges with grace.
Uncontrolled ascent can be hazardous for a submarine. Ballast adjustments prevent sudden rises.
Emotional balance prevents uncontrolled emotional ascents, averting situations where emotions may escalate uncontrollably, leading to potential negative outcomes.
Uncontrolled descent can lead to perilous depths. Ballast adjustments ensure a controlled descent.
Fine-tuning emotional responses mitigates the risk of descending into despair. It allows individuals to navigate challenges without succumbing to overwhelming negative emotions.
Reactivity in ballast systems is adjusted to avoid sudden changes in the submarine's position.
Emotional fine-tuning involves adjusting reactivity levels, preventing abrupt emotional shifts that can impact mental well-being.
Striking the right balance in ballast ensures stability in various underwater conditions.
Maintaining emotional balance is about finding equilibrium. It involves balancing different emotions, perspectives, and responses to achieve stability in the face of life's challenges.
A well-tuned ballast system enhances a submarine's resilience in turbulent waters.
Fine-tuning emotional responses enhances personal resilience. It allows individuals to bounce back from setbacks, adapting to challenges without being overwhelmed.
Extreme ballast adjustments can lead to instability. Subtle, controlled changes are preferred.
Avoiding emotional extremes is crucial. Fine-tuning emotional responses involves making subtle adjustments to prevent emotional instability or excess.
Engineers calibrate ballast systems based on environmental factors.
Emotional intelligence is calibrated based on situational factors. Individuals adjust their emotional responses in different contexts, showcasing adaptability.
Overreacting in ballast adjustments can disrupt the submarine's equilibrium.
Emotional fine-tuning prevents overreactions, ensuring that responses align with the gravity of a situation.
External pressures, such as water density changes, necessitate adjustments.
External pressures in life demand emotional adjustments. Fine-tuning responses helps individuals navigate external challenges without compromising emotional well-being.
Harmony in ballast systems is essential for overall submarine stability.
Emotional fine-tuning creates emotional harmony, fostering a sense of balance and well-being in individuals.
Clear ballast adjustments contribute to better visibility and navigation.
Emotional balance promotes mental clarity, allowing individuals to think more clearly and make informed decisions.
Constant adjustments prevent the submarine crew from experiencing fatigue in managing ballast systems.
Continuous fine-tuning prevents emotional fatigue, ensuring that individuals can navigate life's challenges without feeling emotionally drained.
Agility in adjusting ballast allows submarines to navigate diverse underwater terrains.

Emotional fine-tuning cultivates emotional agility, enabling individuals to navigate the diverse landscapes of life with adaptability and resilience.

- **Buoyancy Control in Turbulent Waters:**

Turbulent waters can toss submarines uncontrollably without proper ballast control.

Life's challenges create emotional storms. Emotional ballast control helps individuals navigate through these storms, maintaining stability amid adversity.

Uncontrolled movement in turbulent waters can lead to tumultuous conditions for a submarine.

Lack of emotional control in challenging situations can lead to emotional tumult. Regulating emotional responses through ballast control helps avoid unnecessary turbulence.

Precise control keeps submarines grounded, even in turbulent seas.

Emotional ballast control enables individuals to stay grounded amidst life's chaos, fostering a sense of stability and composure.

Proper ballast adjustments prevent submarines from being overwhelmed by large waves.

Emotional control prevents individuals from being overwhelmed by the challenges life presents, ensuring they can navigate through difficulties without feeling inundated.

Submarines respond to changing currents by adjusting ballast for stability.

Life's currents of emotions can change. Emotional ballast control allows individuals to adapt to these changes, maintaining stability in the face of shifting emotional tides.

Ballast adjustments maintain equilibrium in turbulent waters.

Emotional balance is crucial for maintaining equilibrium amidst life's upheavals. Ballast control helps individuals adjust to changing circumstances without losing their emotional balance.

Improper ballast adjustments can lead to the risk of capsizing.

Lack of emotional control may lead to emotional capsizing, where individuals feel overwhelmed and unable to cope. Emotional ballast adjustments prevent such extremes.

Controlled adjustments allow submarines to make steady progress, even in turbulent conditions.

Emotional ballast control ensures steady progress through life's adversities, enabling individuals to move forward with resilience and determination.

Uncontrolled ballast adjustments can create whirlpools, affecting stability.

Lack of emotional control can lead to emotional whirlpools, where individuals feel trapped in negative emotions. Emotional ballast adjustments prevent getting caught in such emotional turbulence.

Submarines adapt to crosscurrents by adjusting ballast for stability.

Emotional ballast control enables individuals to adapt to emotional crosscurrents, allowing them to navigate through conflicting emotions with poise and adaptability.

Controlled ballast adjustments help submarines maintain their intended direction in turbulent waters.

Emotional ballast control helps individuals maintain their direction in the midst of emotional turbulence, preventing them from losing focus or purpose.

Precise ballast control enhances a submarine's maneuverability.

Emotional ballast adjustments facilitate emotional maneuverability, empowering individuals to navigate through life's challenges with agility and grace.

Adjustments in ballast contribute to the flexibility of submarine movements.

Emotional ballast control promotes emotional flexibility, allowing individuals to adapt their responses to different situations with ease.

Submarines navigate through swells by adjusting ballast for stability.

Emotional ballast adjustments enable individuals to navigate through emotional swells, maintaining stability and composure in the face of heightened emotions.

Controlled adjustments prevent submarines from drifting off course.

Emotional ballast control prevents individuals from emotional drift, ensuring that they stay on course in their personal and emotional journey despite life's challenges.

- **Adaptability to Changing Conditions:**

Submarines adeptly adjust ballast to navigate changing underwater conditions.

Life's dynamic nature demands adaptability. Maintaining emotional balance entails skillfully adjusting to the ever-shifting circumstances and challenges that unfold.

Ballast adjustments allow submarines to respond to the ebb and flow of ocean currents.

Adapting emotionally involves responding to the natural ebb and flow of life's circumstances, finding equilibrium amid the varying rhythms of personal experiences.

Submarines embrace change by adjusting ballast to new environmental dynamics.

Embracing emotional adaptability means adjusting to the winds of change in life, willingly acknowledging and navigating transitions with resilience.

Fluid ballast adjustments facilitate submarines in responding seamlessly to environmental shifts.

Emotionally adapting involves maintaining fluid responses to the shifts and changes in one's life, allowing for a more harmonious and agile approach to challenges.

Ballast adjustments prevent submarines from being tossed uncontrollably in turbulent waters.

Maintaining emotional adaptability prevents individuals from being overwhelmed in life's turbulence, ensuring a more stable and controlled response to challenges.

Submarines adjust ballast to ensure stability as they navigate through changing currents.

Adjusting emotional sails to the winds of change involves aligning emotional responses with the evolving currents of life, steering through transitions with grace and balance.

Ballast adjustments contribute to the harmony of submarine navigation amidst fluctuations.

Embracing emotional adaptability fosters inner harmony, allowing individuals to navigate through life's fluctuations with a sense of balance and poise.

Steady ballast adjustments keep submarines from swaying excessively in turbulent waters.

Emotional adaptability prevents individuals from swaying excessively in the face of life's challenges, helping them maintain a steady course despite external disruptions.

Ballast adjustments preserve equilibrium during challenging underwater conditions.

Emotionally adapting preserves personal equilibrium amidst the maelstrom of change, enabling individuals to navigate transitions with greater stability.

Flexibility in ballast adjustments is crucial for adapting to shifting underwater dynamics.

Flexibility is the key to emotional navigation, allowing individuals to adjust and flex their emotional responses in alignment with the changing circumstances of life.

Graceful ballast adjustments help submarines navigate through rapid changes in underwater terrain.

Emotional adaptability enables individuals to navigate through life's rapid changes with grace, responding thoughtfully to challenges and maintaining composure.

Adjustments maintain calmness in the submarine's response to stormy underwater conditions.

Emotional adaptability facilitates calm responses in the face of life's storms, helping individuals weather challenges with resilience and composure.

Submarines adjust ballast to control their depth in response to changing underwater realities.

Adapting emotionally involves adjusting the depth of emotional responses to align with changing realities, ensuring a more nuanced and appropriate engagement with life.

Chapter 37

Dive and Ascend

The cycles of diving deep and ascending in a submarine symbolize the cycles of introspection and action in life.

In the enigmatic depths of the ocean, submarines embark on a journey that mirrors the intricate dance of introspection and action in the human experience. The cycles of diving deep into the abyss and ascending towards the surface are not only a testament to the technical prowess of underwater exploration but also serve as a profound metaphor for the ebbs and flows of life.

- **Diving into the Abyss of Self-Reflection:**

Submarines courageously submerge into the profound depths of the ocean, where light diminishes, and solitude becomes the only companion.

This parallels the human experience of introspection where individuals willingly embrace the depths of their inner selves, venturing into the realms of their thoughts and emotions.

In the ocean's depths, submarines embrace darkness, relying on advanced technology for illumination.

Introspection involves confronting the darkness within – the unexplored corners of one's psyche.

Just as submarines use technology, individuals may use self-awareness tools to illuminate the shadows of their minds.

Submarines navigate in solitude, away from the external influences of the surface.

In introspection, solitude becomes a catalyst for self-discovery, allowing individuals to detach from external influences and delve into their inner world.

Submerging deep into the ocean signifies descending into uncharted territories.

Introspection involves descending into the unexplored depths of self-awareness, discovering facets of one's personality and motivations.

Water pressure increases with depth, testing the submarine's structural integrity.

Introspection may create internal pressure as individuals confront deep-seated emotions and unresolved aspects of their lives.

Submarines navigate through intricate underwater terrains.

Introspection requires navigating the intricate landscapes of one's mind, understanding the nuances of thoughts, emotions, and memories.

Reflections of artificial light reveal the mysterious underwater world.

Introspection brings forth self-reflection, shedding light on aspects of one's character and experiences previously hidden.

Submerging into the abyss requires courage to face the unknown.

Introspection demands courage to confront one's vulnerabilities, fears, and uncertainties, fostering personal growth.

Exploring the depths unveils hidden underwater realities.

Introspection unveils hidden aspects of the self, fostering a deeper understanding of personal motivations and behaviors.

Submarines navigate through underwater currents.

Introspection involves navigating through emotional currents, understanding the ebb and flow of feelings and reactions.

The profound silence in ocean depths resonates.

Introspection in solitude creates a resonant inner space, allowing individuals to hear the whispers of their thoughts and emotions.

The abyss serves as a canvas for reflection with the play of artificial light.

Introspection turns the inner abyss into a canvas, where self-reflection paints a clearer picture of one's identity and aspirations.

Submerging unmasks the secrets of the underwater world.

Introspection unmasks the secrets of the self, revealing patterns, motivations, and unresolved emotions.

Echoes resonate in the underwater silence.

In introspection, echoes of inner contemplation reverberate, providing insights and prompting self-discovery.

Submarines eventually ascend, returning to the surface.

Introspection concludes with an ascent to the surface, bringing newfound insights and self-awareness back to the external world.

- **Navigating the Underwater Realms of the Mind:**

Submarines navigate through the complex and intricate terrains of the underwater world.

Introspection involves navigating the intricate landscapes of one's mind, where thoughts, memories, and emotions intertwine in a complex interplay.

Submarines move through underwater currents that shape their course.

Thoughts act as currents in the mind, influencing one's mental course. Navigating these thought currents is central to the introspective journey.

Submerging comes with challenges like underwater pressure and darkness.

Introspection presents challenges such as confronting internal pressures, uncertainties, and the shadows of the mind.

Submarines explore the emotional depths of the underwater world.

Introspection delves into the emotional abyss within, uncovering buried feelings and understanding the emotional nuances of one's inner world.

The underwater world is characterized by profound silence.

Introspection unfolds in the silent realms of one's mind, creating space for deep contemplation and self-discovery.

Submarines adapt to changing underwater currents for effective navigation.

Navigating mental currents requires adaptability in introspection, adjusting one's approach to the ever-changing landscape of thoughts and emotions.

Submarines create mental maps to navigate underwater terrains.

Introspection involves mapping the mental topography, understanding the interconnectedness of thoughts, memories, and emotions.

Submarines explore beyond the surface of the ocean, where hidden wonders lie.

Introspection goes beyond surface-level thoughts, delving into the hidden recesses of the mind to uncover deeper insights.

Submarines maintain buoyancy to stay afloat; too much or too little leads to instability.

Introspection involves balancing emotional buoyancy, finding stability amidst the fluctuations of emotions without being overwhelmed or detached.

Submarines navigate through turbulent underwater currents.

Introspection may encounter turbulence in the form of internal conflicts, unresolved emotions, or challenging memories.

Echo soundings reveal the underwater landscape.

Introspection echoes with inner reflections, revealing the hidden aspects of the self and offering insights into personal growth.

Submarines may come across submerged artifacts and memories.

Introspection unveils submerged memories, allowing individuals to explore past experiences and understand their impact on the present.

The profound silence underwater serves as a canvas for exploration.

Introspection transforms the inner silence into a canvas where individuals can paint a clearer picture of their identity and aspirations.

Submarines showcase navigational prowess in underwater exploration.

Introspection requires navigational skills in the mind's ocean, guiding individuals through the complexities of self-awareness.

Submarines resurface with newfound insights.

Introspection concludes with resurfacing, bringing back insights and self-awareness from the deep exploration of one's inner realms.

- **Pressure of Inner Depths:**

As submarines descend into the ocean, water pressure intensifies, challenging the structural integrity of the vessel.

In the parallel of life, introspection delves into inner depths where emotional pressures may increase, challenging the individual's emotional and mental resilience.

Increasing water pressure causes turbulence around the submarine.

Introspection may induce internal turbulence as individuals grapple with emotional and psychological complexities beneath the surface of conscious awareness.

The submarine's structure must withstand the mounting pressure.

Similarly, during introspection, the individual's mental and emotional structure is tested, requiring resilience to navigate the internal pressure.

Submarines are designed to endure and remain resilient in the face of pressure.

Introspection builds emotional resilience, enabling individuals to withstand the pressure of self-discovery and personal reflection.

Submarines navigate through the increasing pressures of underwater depths.

Introspection involves navigating through the increasing emotional pressures that arise when exploring deeper layers of one's emotions and experiences.

Maintaining balance is crucial for the submarine's stability under pressure.

Introspection necessitates psychological equilibrium, ensuring stability amidst the internal pressures that may arise during deep self-reflection.

Under pressure, vulnerabilities in the submarine's structure become apparent.

Introspection may reveal vulnerabilities in one's emotional and mental structure, prompting a deeper understanding and fostering personal growth.

As submarines go deeper, the pressure increases, demanding heightened awareness.

Introspection deepens self-awareness, requiring a heightened understanding of one's emotions and thoughts as the internal pressure intensifies.

Submarines face challenges as they descend into greater depths.

Introspection involves facing inner challenges, confronting emotional complexities, and navigating the intricacies of one's internal landscape.

Submarines adapt to increasing pressure through design and technology.

Introspection prompts psychological adaptation, encouraging individuals to adapt their coping mechanisms and emotional regulation strategies to withstand internal pressures.

Submarines demonstrate strength under increasing pressure.

Introspection fosters emotional strength, empowering individuals to withstand and navigate the internal pressures that may arise during deep self-reflection.

Deeper dives reveal the ocean's hidden emotional depths.

Introspection reveals hidden emotional depths within the individual, bringing forth a deeper understanding of one's emotional landscape.

Submarines bear the increasing weight of water pressure.

Introspection involves bearing the weight of emotional revelations, accepting and processing the sometimes heavy emotions that arise.

Submarines demonstrate endurance under pressure.

Introspection cultivates psychological endurance, enabling individuals to endure the internal pressures associated with self-discovery.

Despite pressure, submarines ascend, having explored the depths.

Introspection leads to personal ascension, as individuals, despite the internal pressures, emerge with a deeper understanding of themselves and their emotional landscapes.

- **Balancing Darkness with Illumination:**

Submarines descend into the abyss, facing darkness.

Introspection involves navigating the inner abyss, confronting the shadows and unexplored aspects of one's psyche.

Submarines rely on artificial lights to pierce the darkness.

Introspection often requires the use of self-awareness, mindfulness, and external insights as artificial illumination to bring clarity to the inner darkness.

Submarines confront the shadows in the ocean depths.

Introspection involves confronting personal shadows, acknowledging and understanding the darker aspects of one's emotions and thoughts.

Artificial lights provide clarity in the submarine's surroundings.

Introspection brings clarity amidst the darkness of unresolved emotions, providing insight and understanding to one's inner world.

Artificial illumination reveals the complexity of the underwater environment.

Introspection illuminates the emotional complexity within, unraveling layers of feelings, memories, and experiences.

Chapter **38**

Environmental Awareness

Submarines must be aware of their surrounding environment, just like our need to be cognizant of our personal environment and its influences.

The puzzling world underneath the ocean's surface is domestic to submarines, wonders of designing that explore the profound with accuracy and reason. Within the quiet profundities, submarines are intensely mindful of their environment, depending on progressed advances to sense and translate the underwater environment. This mindfulness isn't only a matter of survival but a key basic, permitting submarines to fulfill their missions successfully. In a parallel vein, our lives, as well, unfurl inside interesting situations – not of water and streams, but of connections, societal elements, and individual settings. Much like submarines, our capacity to explore this complex embroidered artwork requests a significant mindfulness of our environment. Understanding the subtleties of our individual environment and recognizing the impacts that shape our encounters are crucial for charting a course through the complexities of life.

- **Sensory Perception:**

Submarines utilize cutting-edge sensors to detect elements in their underwater environment, emphasizing the importance of environmental awareness for their safety and functionality.

Emotional intelligence allows individuals to perceive and understand the emotions of themselves and others. This awareness contributes to a harmonious personal environment.

Empathy acts as a sensor in human interactions, enabling individuals to pick up on the emotions and needs of those around them. It fosters a connection with others and enhances the social environment.

Developing self-awareness serves as a personal sensor, allowing individuals to recognize their own emotions, triggers, and needs. This internal awareness contributes to a balanced and well-managed personal environment.

Subs read underwater conditions through non-verbal cues, and in life, interpreting non-verbal communication enhances our understanding of the subtleties in personal interactions.

Submarines must be aware of the impact of their surroundings on their operations. Similarly, individuals need to be mindful of how external factors influence their mental and emotional well-being.

Just as submarines navigate diverse underwater ecosystems, individuals in life benefit from cultural sensitivity, understanding and respecting the diversity within their personal and social environments.

They anticipate changes in underwater conditions to adjust their course. In life, being perceptive allows individuals to anticipate changes, fostering adaptability and resilience.

Submarines identify positive elements in their environment for safety. Likewise, recognizing positive aspects in life promotes a more optimistic and constructive personal environment.

They filter out potentially harmful elements in their surroundings. Developing strong boundaries in life helps individuals filter out negative influences, ensuring a healthier personal environment.

Mindfulness practices enhance sensory perception by bringing attention to the present moment. These practices contribute to a more focused and aware experience of one's personal environment.

Subs reflect on their data for better awareness. Reflective practices in life, such as journaling or meditation, provide insights into personal experiences, contributing to a deeper understanding of the environment.

Also, submarines respond to changes in their environment promptly. Similarly, individuals benefit from being responsive to shifts in their personal environment to maintain well-being.

They aim for a positive atmosphere onboard. In life, individuals can actively contribute to a positive personal environment through their attitudes, behaviors, and interactions.

Submarines use environmental data for decision-making. In life, being cognizant of the personal environment aids in strategic decision-making for both short-term and long-term well-being.

- **Environmental Adaptation:**

Submarines seamlessly adapt to the fluidity of underwater conditions, showcasing the need for environmental flexibility.

Life presents dynamic personal environments, ranging from relationships to career paths. Adaptability becomes crucial in navigating these changing landscapes.

Submarines contend with variations in temperature and pressure. Similarly, individuals face different pressures and emotional temperatures in various life situations, requiring adaptive responses.

They adjust to different water densities. Similarly, individuals navigate the varied densities of social structures, adjusting behaviors and communication styles accordingly.

Also, submarines adapt to underwater currents. In life, adapting to societal currents and trends ensures individuals stay relevant and connected to the evolving world.

Subs adapt to different depths and terrains. Similarly, professional environments demand adaptability to diverse challenges, roles, and work cultures.

Furthermore, submarines showcase adaptability to maintain stability. In personal relationships, flexibility helps in resolving conflicts, accommodating differences, and fostering stability.

Submarines operate globally, adapting to diverse environments. Individuals, too, benefit from cultural adaptation, understanding and respecting differences in a multicultural world.

They adjust to the confined space of underwater living. Likewise, adapting to the dynamics of family life involves finding harmony within shared spaces and responsibilities.

Also, submarines adapt to economic conditions. Individuals must be financially adaptable, adjusting budgets and financial plans in response to economic shifts.

Submarines adapt to different water compositions. Similarly, students need to adapt to varying educational environments, teaching styles, and learning approaches.

They adjust to maintain structural integrity. In life, adapting health and wellness practices ensures personal well-being and resilience against physical and mental challenges.

Subs adapt to technological advancements. Individuals need to embrace technological changes, staying current in the digital landscape for personal and professional growth.

Submarines adhere to environmental standards. Individuals can adapt by adopting eco-friendly practices, contributing to the sustainability of the broader environmental context.

They face unpredictable underwater conditions. Life's unpredictability requires individuals to be adaptable, navigating uncertainties with resilience and a positive mindset.

- **Sonar and Intuition:**

They employ sonar with precision to interpret underwater signals, highlighting the importance of accuracy in sensing the environment.

Similarly, intuition grants individuals a heightened perception, providing insights that may not be immediately apparent through rational analysis.

Submarines navigate underwater signals through sonar. In life, intuition aids in navigating subtle cues and energies, offering a deeper understanding of situations.

Sonar helps submarines interpret the undercurrents of the ocean. Intuition plays a parallel role in interpreting emotional undercurrents in human interactions, fostering emotional intelligence.

Subs adjust to changing underwater conditions through sonar. Intuition enables individuals to adapt to environmental changes, guiding them in making decisions aligned with their instincts.

Sonar enhances a submarine's sensitivity to its surroundings. Intuition similarly heightens sensitivity, allowing individuals to be attuned to the energies and dynamics of their personal and professional environments.

They detect immediate threats with sonar. Intuition acts as an internal radar, providing a sense of immediate detection of potential risks or opportunities in life.

Submarine sonar adapts to varying frequencies. Intuition, too, adapts to different frequencies of information, helping individuals discern and respond effectively to diverse situations.

Sonar aids submarines in understanding subtle underwater communication. Intuition facilitates the understanding of unspoken communication cues in interpersonal relationships.

Also, submarines use sonar to navigate through complex underwater environments. Intuition guides individuals through the complexities of life, helping them navigate challenges with a sense of direction.

Sonar deciphers non-verbal cues underwater. Intuition, similarly, deciphers non-verbal cues in human interactions, enhancing communication beyond spoken words.

Subs sonar prompts instinctual responses. Intuition acts as an instinctual response mechanism, guiding individuals in decision-making based on their inner sense of knowing.

Also, sonar allows submarines to swiftly adapt to changing conditions. Intuition aids individuals in adapting swiftly to shifts in personal and professional circumstances.

Submarine sonar enhances spatial awareness. Intuition contributes to enhanced spatial awareness in life, providing a broader perspective on one's position and relationships within a given context.

Utilizing sonar deepens a submarine's connection with its underwater environment. Similarly, relying on intuition deepens an individual's connection with their surroundings, fostering a richer understanding of the world.

- **Cultural Awareness:**

Subs operate in diverse oceanic regions, necessitating an understanding of various environments.

Furthermore, submarine crews must consider cultural factors even in ocean exploration. Awareness of local customs and international protocols is crucial.

Interactions among submarine crew members highlight the importance of cultural sensitivity. Respect for diverse backgrounds enhances teamwork and communication.

Submarine operations respect global marine ecosystems. Similarly, cultural awareness in life involves respecting and preserving the cultural diversity that contributes to the richness of society.

They learn from different oceanic regions. Cultural awareness allows individuals to learn from diverse communities, broadening their perspectives and knowledge.

Submarine operations involve interactions with underwater communities. Cultural awareness in life involves engaging with different cultural communities to build mutual understanding and cooperation.

Submarines adapt culturally when operating in unfamiliar regions. Similarly, individuals must adapt to cultural differences when navigating new environments.

Subs missions often involve international collaboration. Cultural awareness facilitates effective collaboration, ensuring smooth interactions among crew members from different countries.

They may learn from the cultural histories of oceanic regions. In life, understanding cultural histories contributes to a deeper appreciation of societal roots and influences.

Also, submarine activities may involve elements of cultural diplomacy. In life, practicing cultural diplomacy fosters positive relations and cooperation among individuals from diverse backgrounds.

Submarines acknowledge the diversity of oceanic cultures. Similarly, life benefits from celebrating and embracing cultural diversity, recognizing the unique contributions of various ethnicities, traditions, and customs.

Submarine crews navigate language considerations. In life, awareness of linguistic nuances contributes to effective cross-cultural communication and understanding.

Subs operations involve ethical considerations in diverse environments.

Cultural awareness in life includes navigating ethical considerations and moral values within different cultural contexts.

Social sensitivity is crucial within submarine crews. Life's cultural awareness emphasizes social sensitivity, fostering empathy and understanding in interpersonal relationships.

Submarines can build bridges across cultures. Similarly, cultural awareness in life helps build bridges, fostering connections and collaborations that transcend cultural boundaries.

Chapter **39**

Underwater Communication

Establishing communication methods in the submarine's silence reflects our need to communicate effectively in our internal silence.

In the submerged world beneath the ocean's surface, where silence reigns supreme, submarines become marvels of engineering and precision. In this quietude, effective communication is not just a matter of convenience but a vital necessity for the functionality and safety of the vessel. Similarly, in the intricate landscapes of our minds, there exists an internal silence – a realm of thoughts, emotions, and reflections that require adept communication. Just as submarines deploy sophisticated methods to break the underwater silence, understanding how to navigate our internal silence becomes imperative for personal growth, emotional intelligence, and holistic well-being.

- **Sonar Systems and Self-Awareness:**

Developing self-awareness is akin to deploying an internal sonar system. It involves emitting introspective signals to understand the depths of one's thoughts, emotions, and motivations.

Similar to sonar's precision in communication, self-awareness allows individuals to communicate with themselves with clarity, understanding the nuances of their internal world.

Life's emotional depths can be complex and challenging. Self-awareness acts as an internal sonar, guiding individuals through the intricate landscapes of their emotions.

In the internal silence, self-awareness aids in interpreting echoes of past experiences, allowing individuals to understand the reverberations of memories and their impact on the present.

Like sonar's continuous monitoring, self-awareness involves ongoing self-reflection, ensuring that individuals maintain a clear understanding of their thoughts and emotions over time.

Sonar systems adapt to changing underwater conditions. Similarly, self-awareness enables individuals to adapt to evolving internal circumstances, fostering resilience in the face of personal growth and change.

Developing self-awareness allows individuals to navigate the intricate mental terrain, exploring the subconscious and understanding the underlying factors influencing thoughts and behaviors.

Just as sonar clarifies the underwater environment, self-awareness clarifies the inner dynamics, revealing hidden beliefs, desires, and motivations.

Sonar helps submarines recognize patterns in the underwater landscape. Likewise, self-awareness facilitates the recognition of patterns in thoughts and behaviors, paving the way for personal development.

Internal sonar, in the form of self-awareness, enhances emotional intelligence, allowing individuals to navigate relationships and social dynamics with a deeper understanding of themselves.

- **Deciphering Underwater Signals and Emotional Cues:**

Submarines employ advanced sonar systems to decipher signals in the underwater environment, allowing for effective communication.

Similarly, in our internal silence, developing emotional intelligence acts as a personal sonar. It enables us to decipher subtle emotional signals, offering insights into our feelings and thoughts.

Submarines navigate through silent depths using sonar to avoid obstacles and communicate covertly.

In our internal silence, emotional awareness serves as a navigational tool, helping us navigate through the complexities of our emotions and thoughts.

Also, submarines rely on deciphering signals to communicate silently and efficiently underwater.

In our internal silence, the ability to interpret emotional cues facilitates effective self-communication. Understanding our emotions enables us to respond thoughtfully to our inner dialogue.

Submarines interpret underwater dynamics to communicate effectively in challenging conditions.

In our internal silence, understanding our inner dynamics is crucial. It involves recognizing the interplay of emotions, thoughts, and motivations that shape our internal world.

Submarines communicate beyond words through sonar signals, embracing a non-verbal form of communication.

In our internal silence, non-verbal cues within our emotional landscape become essential for self-communication, allowing us to grasp nuances that words may not fully express.

Submarines operate in silent spaces where effective communication is paramount.

In our internal silence, practicing mindful awareness fosters effective self-communication, encouraging a respectful and contemplative engagement with our thoughts and emotions.

Submarines use sonar to communicate during critical situations in the underwater environment.

In our internal silence, crisis moments prompt self-reflection. Understanding emotional cues during challenges aids in navigating personal crises.

Submarines adapt their communication strategies based on underwater conditions.

In our internal silence, adaptive self-communication involves adjusting our emotional responses and interpretations based on the ever-changing landscape of our thoughts and feelings.

- **Silent Communication in Crew Coordination:**

Submarine crews communicate silently using established protocols to maintain operational efficiency, especially in situations where verbal communication may be restricted.

Similarly, in life, silent communication within ourselves plays a role in personal efficiency. Non-verbal cues, intuition, and introspection contribute to effective decision-making and self-coordination.

Also, submarine crews utilize non-verbal signals and gestures to convey messages silently, fostering swift and covert communication.

In our personal realm, non-verbal signals within ourselves, such as body language and emotional expressions, communicate information that influences our choices and actions.

Submarine crews adapt their silent communication methods to various situations, showcasing flexibility in their coordination strategies.

Similarly, in life, adaptable self-communication involves adjusting our internal strategies based on the circumstances, ensuring effective personal coordination.

Subs crews often rely on intuition and a deep understanding of each other's roles for seamless silent coordination.

Life's challenges require intuitive self-coordination, where individuals trust their instincts and inner guidance to navigate situations without explicit verbal instructions.

Submarine crews prioritize precision in their silent communication to avoid misunderstandings and ensure accurate execution of tasks.

In personal realms, precision in silent communication involves clarity of thought, understanding one's emotions with accuracy, and making decisions aligned with internal cues.

Crews synchronize their actions based on silent communication, showcasing a harmonious coordination system.

In life, achieving inner harmony involves effective self-coordination, where different aspects of one's personality align to navigate challenges smoothly.

Silent communication contributes to the overall efficiency of submarine operations, ensuring tasks are carried out seamlessly.

Similarly, efficient self-coordination enhances personal effectiveness, allowing individuals to navigate life's complexities with agility and purpose.

Submarine crews build trust in silent communication, relying on each other's competence and understanding of the operational context.

In personal development, building self-trust in silent communication involves cultivating confidence in one's ability to interpret internal signals and make decisions aligned with personal values.

- **Clearing Underwater Noise for Clarity:**

Submarines employ technology to filter out underwater noise, ensuring clear communication in their operational environment.

In life, reducing mental noise involves practices such as mindfulness and meditation, contributing to clarity in self-reflection and decision-making.

Clear communication is crucial for submarines to convey messages accurately and prevent misinterpretation amid the challenges of underwater noise.

Similarly, achieving clarity in personal reflection and decision-making requires reducing mental noise to discern thoughts and emotions accurately.

Submarines utilize advanced technology for noise reduction, highlighting the significance of employing effective tools for clear communication.

Life parallels the use of mindfulness techniques and mental strategies to reduce internal noise, fostering a clear mental space for introspection.

Submarine crews coordinate effectively even in the presence of external noise, emphasizing the need for adaptability in communication methods.

Similarly, individuals must adapt their communication with themselves amid internal noise, adjusting their approaches to maintain clarity in self-reflection.

Submarines may intentionally operate in silence to avoid detection, showcasing the strategic use of quiet environments for effective communication.

In personal development, moments of intentional silence can be valuable for reducing internal noise, providing space for thoughtful self-reflection.

Submarines minimize distractions to enhance communication efficiency, recognizing the impact of external factors on message clarity.

In life, managing external distractions and cultivating mindfulness contributes to effective personal reflection by reducing interference.

Submarines navigate challenges posed by underwater noise, demonstrating adaptability and resilience in their communication strategies.

Individuals navigate internal challenges by addressing mental noise, fostering resilience in the face of distractions and uncertainties.

Submarines continuously improve communication methods to stay ahead of evolving noise challenges, reflecting a commitment to innovation.

Similarly, continuous personal growth involves refining strategies to manage internal noise, ensuring ongoing clarity in self-awareness and decision-making.

- **Utilizing Technology for Effective Transmission:**

Submarines employ cutting-edge technology, including communication systems, to ensure effective transmission of messages underwater.

Similarly, in personal development, leveraging tools like mindfulness practices, journaling, or therapy enhances the effectiveness of self-communication.

Submarines face unique challenges underwater, prompting the need for sophisticated communication technology to overcome obstacles like pressure and noise.

Life challenges may require specialized tools, and adopting practices like mindfulness or therapy provides individuals with effective means to navigate personal obstacles.

Submarines prioritize real-time communication, emphasizing the importance of instant information exchange in their operational context.

In life, adopting real-time self-communication practices ensures that individuals can promptly address their thoughts and emotions as they arise, promoting self-awareness.

Also, submarines prioritize secure communication to safeguard their messages from interception, highlighting the need for confidentiality in their operations.

Similarly, personal reflection often involves confidential thoughts and emotions, emphasizing the importance of creating a safe and secure mental space for self-communication.

Submarines use various communication modes to transmit messages effectively, recognizing the value of versatility in their methods.

Adopting versatile personal communication tools, such as combining mindfulness with journaling or therapy, allows individuals to address various aspects of their inner selves.

Submarines prioritize efficiency and speed in their communication systems, crucial for rapid decision-making and coordination.

Adopting efficient self-communication practices enables individuals to navigate their thoughts and emotions with agility, facilitating more effective personal decision-making.

Submarines evolve with technology, constantly upgrading communication systems for enhanced performance.

Similarly, individuals committed to personal growth continually refine and improve their communication tools to adapt to evolving self-awareness needs.

Submarines exhibit adaptability, adjusting communication systems to various conditions like depth, temperature, and underwater currents.

Likewise, individuals must adapt their self-communication approaches to changing life circumstances, ensuring resilience and effectiveness in personal growth.

Chapter **40**

Sensory Deprivation

The limited sensory input within a submarine can mirror periods of our life when we must rely on inner senses.

The confined and controlled environment of a submarine, submerged in the depths of the ocean, offers a unique analogy for certain phases in our lives when external sensory input is limited, and we must navigate through the uncharted territories relying solely on our inner senses. Much like a submarine's crew, who operate in a realm of restricted external stimuli, there are moments in our personal journeys where we confront solitude, isolation, or challenging circumstances that demand an acute reliance on our internal faculties. These periods, analogous to the sensory constraints within a submarine, prompt us to tap into our inner strengths, intuition, and resilience, unveiling the profound capabilities that lie within us.

- **Isolation in Submarine Depths:**

Submarines, navigating the profound depths of the ocean, encounter isolation due to the absence of external stimuli. The vastness and quietude of the underwater world create an environment where submariners are cocooned in solitude.

Analogously, life presents moments when external distractions diminish.

Whether during periods of introspection, personal growth, or unforeseen circumstances, individuals find themselves in a state of reduced external influence, akin to the isolation experienced within a submarine.

The isolation within a submarine prompts submariners to confront their thoughts and emotions. Similarly, in life, when external distractions wane, individuals are compelled to face their innermost feelings, introspecting on their beliefs, desires, and the intricacies of their emotional landscape.

Submarines retreat from the external noise of the ocean's surface, immersing themselves in a quieter, more contemplative environment. Life offers parallels when individuals intentionally retreat from external pressures, seeking solitude to find clarity, recharge, or navigate personal challenges.

The subdued environment within a submarine becomes an opportunity for introspection. Likewise, life's quieter moments become an opportune time for individuals to delve into self-reflection, gaining insights into their motivations, goals, and overall life trajectory.

Submarines, isolated from the external world, experience a reduction in distractions. In life, situations such as sabbaticals, retreats, or moments of seclusion provide a comparable reduction in external distractions, fostering an environment conducive to self-discovery.

Submariners, in their isolated environment, develop heightened awareness of their underwater surroundings. Similarly, when external distractions fade, individuals often experience heightened awareness of their internal world, gaining a clearer understanding of their emotions and thought processes.

Silence becomes a companion in the isolated depths of a submarine. In life's quieter moments, individuals learn to embrace silence as a supportive companion, finding solace and introspective clarity in the absence of external noise.

Submarines navigating through the isolation of oceanic depths parallel individuals navigating their inner seas. Both scenarios require a unique set of skills, courage, and adaptability to traverse the uncharted territories of the self.

The isolation in a submarine encourages emotional exploration among the crew. Similarly, individuals facing reduced external stimuli engage in emotional exploration, understanding and processing feelings that might be obscured during busier times.

Within the confines of a submarine, submariners discover internal reservoirs of strength, patience, and resilience. Analogously, life's isolated moments unveil untapped reservoirs within individuals—resilience, creativity, and an innate capacity to navigate challenges.

Isolation within a submarine can lead to moments of self-realization for crew members. Likewise, life's moments of reduced external influence often become catalysts for profound self-realization, prompting individuals to reassess priorities and values.

Submariners find a unique comfort in the solitude of their submerged vessel. Similarly, individuals navigating life's quieter phases often find a sense of comfort and peace in solitude, fostering a deeper connection with themselves.

Isolation within a submarine fosters an intimate connection with the inner world of thoughts and emotions. Life's analogous moments enable individuals to cultivate a more profound connection with their inner selves, fostering self-awareness and personal growth.

Submariners use moments of isolation to prepare for reemergence. Similarly, individuals use periods of reduced external stimuli to prepare for a reemergence into the external world, equipped with newfound insights, resilience, and a deeper understanding of self.

- **Internal Reflection in Solitude:**

In submarine depths, silence prompts submariners to contemplate mission objectives. Similarly, life's quiet phases encourage individuals to contemplate personal goals, values, and aspirations in the absence of external distractions.

Submarine crews, surrounded by the quiet vastness of the ocean, unveil their mission objectives.

Likewise, individuals in solitude unveil their inner aspirations, recognizing and aligning with their deeper life goals.

Submariners explore the underwater landscape mentally. Similarly, during internal reflection, individuals explore the intricate landscapes of their thoughts, emotions, and personal narratives.

In the quietude of submarine isolation, crews question mission values. Similarly, life's quieter phases allow individuals to question and clarify personal values, ensuring alignment with their authentic selves.

Submariners reevaluate mission priorities in silence. Analogously, individuals in moments of solitude reevaluate life priorities, reassessing what truly matters and where they want to direct their focus.

Submarine crews, in quiet moments, examine their trajectory. Likewise, individuals use internal reflection to examine the trajectory of their lives, ensuring it aligns with their evolving understanding of purpose and fulfillment.

Submariners may discover new aspects of their mission identity in silence. In life, internal reflection fosters the discovery of personal identity, unraveling layers and understanding oneself more deeply.

The quiet environment within a submarine allows crews to connect with mission motivations. Similarly, periods of solitude enable individuals to connect with their inner motivations, uncovering the driving forces behind their actions and decisions.

Submariners enhance self-awareness through introspection. Life's quieter phases become opportunities for individuals to enhance self-awareness, gaining insight into their strengths, weaknesses, and areas for growth.

In submarine isolation, emotional resilience is cultivated. Likewise, internal reflection fosters emotional resilience in individuals, helping them navigate the complexities of their emotions with a greater sense of understanding and control.

Submariners clarify mission values in the silence of the underwater world. Similarly, internal reflection aids individuals in clarifying personal values, ensuring that their actions align with what matters most to them.

The quiet moments in a submarine prompt crews to align with mission goals authentically. In life, internal reflection facilitates the alignment of actions and decisions with authentic personal goals and aspirations.

Submariners, in solitude, cultivate mindfulness for mission success. Analogously, individuals cultivate mindfulness during internal reflection, enhancing their ability to be present, focused, and attentive to their inner experiences.

Submariners may encounter challenges in mission reflection. Similarly, internal reflection brings individuals face-to-face with inner challenges, allowing them to address and overcome obstacles on the path to personal growth.

Submarine crews gain clarity for future steps in quiet moments. In life, internal reflection provides individuals with the clarity needed to plan and take deliberate steps toward a future aligned with their newfound insights and aspirations.

- **Dependence on Inner Senses:**

In submarine depths, where visibility is compromised, crews rely on intuition. Similarly, life's challenges necessitate reliance on inner senses, with intuition serving as a guide in decision-making.

Submariners draw from their experience in navigating when external visibility is limited. In life, individuals tap into their life experiences, using them as a valuable resource in making informed decisions.

Submarine crews utilize their inner expertise to navigate complex underwater terrains. Likewise, individuals in challenging life phases leverage their internal expertise, honed through learning and growth, to navigate intricate personal landscapes.

In the confined space of a submarine, crews develop emotional intelligence for effective teamwork. Similarly, life challenges foster the development of emotional intelligence, enabling individuals to navigate relationships and situations with heightened self-awareness.

Submariners trust their inner resilience in challenging underwater conditions. Life's difficulties prompt individuals to trust in their inner resilience, recognizing their capacity to bounce back and overcome adversities.

Submariners navigate ambiguous situations with instinctive judgment. Life's uncertainties require individuals to navigate ambiguity with a similar instinctive approach, relying on their inner senses to make decisions in the absence of clear visibility.

The reliance on inner senses in a submarine cultivates a reservoir of inner wisdom among the crew. In life, challenging situations contribute to the cultivation of inner wisdom, offering valuable insights for future decision-making.

Submariners adapt to changing underwater dynamics using their inner senses. Similarly, life's changing circumstances demand adaptability, and individuals rely on their inner senses to adjust their approach to new challenges.

Submarine crews, in limited visibility, enhance decision-making instincts. Life's uncertainties become opportunities for individuals to sharpen their decision-making instincts, trusting their inner senses to guide them in the right direction.

Submariners tune into subtle cues in the absence of clear visibility. Similarly, individuals in challenging life phases learn to tune into subtle cues within themselves and their environment, fostering a deeper understanding of nuanced situations.

In the silent depths of a submarine, crews recognize and leverage their inner strengths. Life challenges prompt individuals to recognize their inherent strengths, empowering them to face difficulties with resilience and determination.

Submariners connect with intuitive insights to navigate through obscured environments. In life, connecting with intuitive insights becomes essential for individuals to navigate through the obscured aspects of personal and professional challenges.

Submarine crews balance inner senses with external information for comprehensive decision-making. Likewise, individuals balance their internal wisdom with external perspectives, creating a holistic approach to navigating life's complexities.

In the confined space of a submarine, crews navigate interpersonal dynamics. Life's challenges, especially in relationships, require individuals to rely on their inner senses to navigate complex emotional terrains.

Submariners, dependent on inner senses, foster inner confidence in their abilities. Similarly, life challenges contribute to the fostering of inner confidence, empowering individuals to face uncertainties with a strong sense of self-assurance.

- **Navigating Emotional Depths:**

Submarines navigate through emotionally turbulent underwater conditions, facing challenges without external validation. Life parallels this by demanding individuals to navigate their emotional turbulence independently, fostering resilience in the face of internal struggles.

In the emotional depths of a submarine, crews learn the importance of self-validation. Similarly, during phases of limited external influence in life, individuals recognize the significance of validating their emotions internally, finding strength within themselves.

Submarine crews build emotional resilience as they navigate challenging emotional terrains underwater. Likewise, life's periods of limited external validation contribute to the development of emotional resilience, preparing individuals for navigating personal storms.

In submarine isolation, crews cope with emotional challenges independently. Life's isolated phases require individuals to cope with their emotions, learning to navigate loneliness and introspection without relying heavily on external validation.

Submariners understand internal struggles as they face emotional depths without external validation. In life, periods of limited external influence prompt individuals to delve into their internal struggles, fostering self-awareness and understanding.

Submarines navigating emotional depths contribute to personal growth among the crew. Similarly, life's challenges, especially during phases of limited external validation, become opportunities for personal growth, self-discovery, and self-improvement.

Submariners find strength in vulnerability as they confront emotional challenges. Life's moments of vulnerability, without external validation, become powerful opportunities for individuals to find inner strength and resilience.

Chapter **41**

Torpedoes and Conflict

Just as submarines engage in conflicts with torpedoes, we too face conflicts in life that test our resilience and strategy.

In the mysterious depths of the ocean, submarines engage in conflicts with torpedoes, navigating the vast expanse with strategic precision. Similarly, life plunges us into conflicts that test our resilience, strategy, and ability to navigate through challenges. The parallel between submarine warfare and life's conflicts lies in the profound lessons we can draw from the underwater battles—lessons of resilience, adaptability, and strategic thinking. Just as submarines face adversaries in the form of torpedoes, we encounter conflicts that demand a careful balance of strength and strategy.

- **Identifying Adversarial Forces:**

Submarines maintain constant vigilance to detect incoming torpedoes. Similarly, in life, being aware of our surroundings—both internal and external—helps identify potential adversarial forces early on.

Life's conflicts often manifest as personal challenges. Identifying these challenges, whether they are internal struggles or external pressures, enables individuals to address them strategically.

Submarines use advanced sonar systems to discern torpedoes. In life, the ability to discern external pressures, societal expectations, or influences from others is crucial for understanding the dynamics of conflicts.

Recognizing emotional cues and interpersonal dynamics is akin to submarines identifying torpedoes. Developing emotional intelligence enhances the ability to navigate conflicts by understanding the underlying forces at play.

Submarines anticipate potential threats in their path. Similarly, in life, anticipating potential conflicts allows for proactive measures, ensuring that adversarial forces are addressed before they escalate.

They, investigate the source of incoming torpedoes. In life, understanding the root causes of conflicts provides a foundation for strategic responses, addressing issues at their origin rather than merely dealing with surface-level manifestations.

Also, submarines analyze torpedo patterns for effective detection. Recognizing patterns in life's conflicts allows individuals to foresee challenges, adapt strategies, and implement preemptive measures.

Submarines acknowledge their operational limitations in identifying torpedoes. Similarly, recognizing personal limitations in navigating conflicts is crucial, prompting individuals to seek support, learn new skills, or leverage resources when needed.

Submarines consider environmental factors that may affect torpedo detection. In life, understanding the environmental factors—social, cultural, or situational—that contribute to conflicts enhances the ability to navigate complex challenges.

They rely on intuition for threat detection. Similarly, trusting one's intuition in life's conflicts provides an additional layer of insight, often guiding individuals toward a more nuanced understanding of adversarial forces.

Subs maintain open-mindedness in identifying potential threats. Life demands a similar openness to different perspectives, ensuring a comprehensive assessment of adversarial forces and potential solutions.

Submarines continuously learn to improve threat identification. In life, a commitment to continuous learning enhances the ability to recognize evolving adversarial forces and adapt strategies accordingly.

Also, submarines may receive information from other sources for threat identification. Similarly, seeking external perspectives and insights from trusted sources enhances the overall understanding of conflicts in life.

Submarines evaluate sonar signals against known benchmarks. In life, individuals can examine personal beliefs and values against the backdrop of conflicts, ensuring that responses align with core principles.

- **Resilience in the Face of Attacks:**

Submarines face the testing of their structural integrity when attacked by torpedoes. In life, conflicts act as tests of personal fortitude, challenging one's emotional and mental resilience.

Also, must adapt to the impact of torpedoes. Similarly, life's conflicts necessitate adaptability, requiring individuals to adjust to the repercussions of adversarial forces.

They learn from the impact of torpedoes to enhance future defenses. Life's conflicts offer valuable lessons, and resilience involves learning from experiences, gaining insights, and applying them to navigate future challenges.

Subs strengthen their structures to resist torpedo impact. In life, conflicts contribute to the building of internal strength, reinforcing one's emotional and mental resilience for future adversities.

Torpedo attacks demand psychological endurance from submarine crews. Similarly, life's conflicts require individuals to endure psychological challenges, fostering resilience in the face of adversity.

Submarines may undergo changes in response to torpedo attacks. Resilience in life involves embracing change, adapting to new circumstances, and finding strength in the face of unexpected challenges.

They strive to maintain operational efficiency despite attacks.

Resilience in life requires individuals to maintain personal efficiency, ensuring that conflicts do not disrupt overall well-being and functionality.

Also, submarines can experience post-impact growth in capabilities. Similarly, individuals can undergo post-conflict growth, developing new skills, perspectives, and strengths as a result of overcoming challenges.

They exhibit crisis management skills during torpedo attacks. Resilience in life involves cultivating effective crisis management skills, enabling individuals to navigate conflicts with composure and strategic thinking.

Submarines undergo recovery and repair after torpedo incidents. Likewise, in life, resilience entails the ability to recover from conflicts, engage in self-repair, and move forward with newfound strength.

Subs maintain emotional stability during attacks. Resilience in life involves emotional regulation, managing stress, anxiety, and other emotions effectively in the midst of conflicts.

Moreover, submarines may rely on support systems for recovery. Similarly, resilience in life often involves drawing on personal support systems, including friends, family, and communities, during challenging times.

Submarines respond strategically to torpedo attacks. Resilience requires individuals to develop strategic responses to conflicts, choosing actions that align with long-term well-being and personal growth.

They adopting a growth mindset may see challenges as opportunities. Resilience in life involves cultivating a growth mindset, viewing conflicts as opportunities for learning, development, and personal evolution.

- **Adapting to Dynamic Environments:**

Submarines adjust their response strategies based on torpedo movements. Similarly, in life, adapting response strategies to dynamic circumstances ensures effective navigation through conflicts.

Torpedo engagements demand flexibility in submarine decision-making. Life's conflicts often require individuals to be flexible in decision-making, considering alternative approaches and adjusting plans as needed.

They navigate through unpredictable torpedo movements. Life's conflicts, characterized by uncertainties, demand the ability to navigate through unpredictable challenges with resilience and composure.

Also, submarines remain composed under torpedo attacks. Similarly, in life's conflicts, maintaining composure under pressure enhances the ability to make clear-headed decisions and navigate challenges effectively.

Submarines swiftly adapt to changes in torpedo trajectories. Life requires individuals to adapt swiftly to changes in conflict dynamics, embracing a proactive approach to maintain control over the situation.

They learn from the evolution of torpedo engagements.

Similarly, in life, conflicts provide opportunities for learning and growth, with each evolving situation offering valuable insights and lessons.

Submarines strategically maneuver to avoid torpedoes. Life's conflicts necessitate strategic maneuvering, including avoiding unnecessary confrontations, seeking compromise, and choosing the battles worth fighting.

Torpedo engagements introduce uncertainties for submarines. Life's conflicts often bring uncertainty, and resilience becomes crucial in navigating through unknown and challenging situations.

They employ resourceful problem-solving during torpedo attacks. In life, conflicts demand resourcefulness in problem-solving, utilizing available skills, knowledge, and support to address challenges effectively.

Subs adopt a growth mindset to improve responses to torpedoes. Similarly, cultivating a growth mindset in life's conflicts encourages continuous improvement, learning, and adapting for better future outcomes.

Also, submarines view changes in torpedo dynamics as opportunities for improvement. Life's conflicts, when approached with a positive mindset, can be seen as opportunities for personal and interpersonal development.

Submarines display adaptability during crisis situations with torpedoes. Life's conflicts, especially during crises, require individuals to remain adaptable, adjusting strategies to mitigate negative impacts and foster resolution.

Submarines incorporate feedback from torpedo engagements for operational improvement. Likewise, in life, conflicts provide feedback for personal and relational growth, offering insights that can be used to improve future interactions.

They develop coping mechanisms for torpedo encounters. In life's conflicts, developing healthy coping mechanisms—emotionally, mentally, and socially—enhances resilience and facilitates effective navigation.

- **Precision in Decision-Making:**

Submarines meticulously analyze torpedo trajectories. In life's conflicts, attention to detail and thorough analysis of situational nuances contribute to precise decision-making.

They consider multiple factors in torpedo evasion. Similarly, in conflicts, considering various perspectives enhances decision-making, taking into account the diverse viewpoints and interests involved.

Submarines strategically evaluate evasion options during torpedo attacks. In life's conflicts, strategic evaluation of available options ensures a well-informed decision-making process.

They assess the risk of torpedo evasion maneuvers. Life's conflicts require individuals to assess the risk and potential rewards associated with different decision paths, guiding the choice of the most effective course of action.

Submarines align evasion decisions with mission goals. In conflicts, decisions should align with personal or collective goals, ensuring that the chosen path contributes to the resolution of the underlying issues.

They understand the consequences of each decision during torpedo engagements. Life demands a similar understanding of potential consequences, fostering responsible decision-making in the midst of conflicts.

Submarines integrate emotional intelligence in decision-making. In life's conflicts, considering emotional intelligence—both one's own and others'—ensures decisions are made with empathy and understanding.

Also, submarines anticipate future torpedo movements. Likewise, in conflicts, anticipation of potential developments helps in making decisions that consider the long-term implications and sustainability of resolutions.

Submarines consult experts for advice during torpedo engagements. In life's conflicts, seeking guidance from individuals with expertise or diverse perspectives contributes to well-informed decision-making.

Moreover, submarines maintain flexibility in evasion plans.

Life's conflicts often require adaptable decision-making, allowing for adjustments as the situation evolves.

They prioritize critical elements in torpedo evasion.

In conflicts, prioritizing essential aspects ensures that decisions focus on addressing the core issues contributing to the conflict.

Submarines avoid hasty decisions during torpedo attacks. Life's conflicts benefit from deliberate and thoughtful decision-making, avoiding impulsivity and considering the broader implications.

They draw on past experiences for decision-making. Similarly, in conflicts, leveraging lessons from previous situations enhances decision-making by applying proven strategies or avoiding previously ineffective approaches.

Submarines communicate for coordinated torpedo evasion. In life's conflicts, effective communication among involved parties fosters collective decision-making, ensuring that decisions are understood and supported by all stakeholders.

Chapter **42**

Concealment and Revelation

Submarines can hide beneath the waves; sometimes, we must conceal or reveal parts of ourselves depending on circumstances.

The vast expanse of the ocean conceals mysteries beneath its waves, and within this hidden realm, submarines navigate with a unique ability to both hide and reveal themselves. In a parallel sense, the human experience often demands a delicate dance between concealment and revelation. Just as submarines can submerge beneath the waves to remain unseen or emerge to show their presence, individuals grapple with the nuanced art of self-disclosure. Life, with its myriad circumstances, prompts us to consider when to conceal certain aspects of ourselves and when to reveal our true nature. This delicate balance, akin to the submarine's ability to navigate the depths, speaks to the complexities of human interactions and the multifaceted layers that make up our identities.

- **Strategic Concealment:**

Submarines strategically conceal themselves beneath the waves to gain a tactical advantage during covert operations.

Individuals may strategically choose to conceal certain aspects of their thoughts to gain an advantage in specific situations.

Concealing beneath the waves allows submarines to establish a boundary between themselves and potential threats.

Individuals may choose to conceal certain personal details to establish boundaries, protecting themselves from undue intrusion or maintaining a level of privacy that contributes to their well-being.

Submarines utilize concealment during operations to navigate through potentially hostile environments without being detected.

In professional settings, individuals strategically conceal personal emotions, opinions, or vulnerabilities to navigate workplace dynamics, fostering collaboration, and avoiding unnecessary conflicts.

They often employ silent running to avoid detection by passive sonar.

Individuals may strategically choose silence, withholding information or opinions, to navigate sensitive conversations or situations where discretion is paramount.

Concealing movements allows submarines to adapt to changing underwater dynamics.

Also, individuals strategically adapt to social dynamics, concealing certain aspects of themselves to fit into diverse social situations or to maintain harmony within a group.

Concealing positions may be part of building alliances with other naval forces.

Individuals might strategically conceal certain information or opinions to build alliances or strengthen relationships in personal or professional spheres.

Submarines share information selectively to maintain operational security.

Moreover, individuals strategically share information about themselves, choosing when and what to reveal, to maintain personal security and control the narrative about their lives.

Concealment adds an element of mystery to submarine operations.

Individuals might strategically conceal certain aspects to maintain a sense of mystery, adding intrigue to their personality and interactions.

Subs may conceal their location during crises to avoid becoming a target.

Also, individuals might strategically conceal their vulnerabilities or challenges during personal crises to avoid unnecessary attention or exploitation.

Concealment safeguards sensitive information related to submarine capabilities and operations.

Individuals strategically conceal sensitive personal information, safeguarding details that could be exploited or misused.

Concealment may vary based on cultural considerations during international operations.

Furthermore, individuals consider cultural norms and societal expectations, strategically concealing or revealing aspects of themselves to align with the cultural context.

Concealment contributes to the distinct identity of a submarine.

Individuals strategically conceal or reveal elements of their identity to shape their personal brand, whether personally or professionally.

Concealment is a tactical tool in naval negotiations.

Individuals strategically conceal certain information during negotiations, using it as a leverage tool to achieve favorable outcomes.

Concealing positions empowers submarines to control the flow of information.

Individuals may feel empowered by selectively concealing aspects of themselves, maintaining autonomy over what they choose to share.

Furthermore, submarines balance transparency with the need for strategic concealment in operations.

Individuals navigate a delicate balance between transparency and strategic concealment, recognizing when to reveal openly and when to strategically conceal to achieve personal and professional goals.

- **Selective Revelation:**

Submarines strategically surface to communicate or demonstrate strength, optimizing their visibility.

Individuals strategically reveal aspects of themselves, choosing opportune moments for self-expression or vulnerability to enhance personal connections.

Subs exercise control over when and how they become visible, aligning with mission objectives.

Also, Individuals control the visibility of personal aspects, deciding when and how much to reveal, aligning with their goals and interpersonal dynamics.

Submarines navigate hidden depths beneath the surface, concealing their presence until needed.

Individuals navigate hidden aspects of their identity, choosing to keep certain thoughts, emotions, or experiences private until they decide to share.

They strategically conceal themselves for tactical advantage during covert operations.

Moreover, individuals strategically conceal certain aspects of their identity, preserving personal boundaries or adapting to social environments.

Submarines surface to establish communication, fostering connection with other vessels.

Individuals reveal aspects of themselves to establish connections, sharing personal experiences or emotions to strengthen relationships.

Subs choose moments of transparency for strategic advantages during operations.

Also, individuals strategically choose transparency, sharing information about themselves when it serves a purpose in personal or professional contexts.

Submarines balance openness with concealment to maintain a tactical edge.

Individuals balance openness about their identity with strategic concealment, ensuring authenticity while navigating various social dynamics.

Submarines time their resurfacing for maximum impact, considering the operational context.

Furthermore, individuals time the revelation of personal information, considering the context and the potential impact on relationships or situations.

They strategically reveal themselves while preserving their structural integrity.

Individuals strategically reveal aspects of their identity while preserving their personal integrity, aligning with their values and beliefs.

Submarines adapt their visibility based on operational requirements and threats.

Individuals adapt the visibility of their identity based on evolving life circumstances, adjusting to personal and social dynamics.

Subs use concealment as a form of self-protection during certain situations.

Also, individuals may use strategic concealment as a form of self-protection, safeguarding vulnerable aspects of themselves when needed.

Submarines strategically reveal their strengths to assert dominance or deter potential threats.

Individuals strategically reveal their strengths in specific situations to assert themselves or influence positive outcomes.

They adapt their visibility based on the specific context of the mission.

Individuals adapt the visibility of their identity based on the context of relationships, professional environments, or personal goals.

Subs build trust by transparently revealing themselves during communication.

Moreover, individuals build trust in relationships by transparently revealing aspects of themselves, fostering connection and understanding.

They strategically reveal themselves to influence the perception of other vessels.

Individuals strategically reveal aspects of their identity to influence perceptions, managing how they are perceived in different social and professional settings.

- **Adapting to Environments:**

Submarines exhibit adaptability to various oceanic conditions, adjusting their concealment strategies based on environmental factors.

Also, individuals showcase a parallel adaptability in navigating diverse social environments, adjusting their levels of self-disclosure based on the nuances of each context.

Subs employ different concealment strategies, choosing optimal approaches for specific oceanic conditions.

Individuals tailor their self-disclosure strategies, adapting to social conditions by choosing what aspects of themselves to reveal in different situations.

They display sensitivity to environmental cues, adjusting concealment based on factors such as water clarity and depth.

Moreover, individuals demonstrate sensitivity to social cues, adjusting their self-disclosure based on factors like the nature of relationships, professional settings, or cultural norms.

Submarines optimize their concealment strategies to maintain a balance between visibility and strategic advantage.

Individuals balance self-disclosure, managing the delicate equilibrium between openness and strategic concealment to navigate social dynamics effectively.

Submarines employ fluid concealment tactics, adapting in real-time to changes in the underwater environment.

Furthermore, individuals dynamically adapt their self-disclosure strategies to the changing contexts of personal and professional life.

Subs navigate stealthily, adjusting their concealment to minimize detection and optimize operational efficiency.

Also, individuals navigate through life strategically, adjusting their self-disclosure to minimize vulnerability and optimize their interactions in various life situations.

Subs are aware of environmental variations, adapting concealment to maintain operational effectiveness.

Individuals are socially aware, adapting self-disclosure to maintain relational effectiveness by considering the ever-changing social landscape.

They conceal vulnerabilities to maintain operational security and integrity.

Moreover, individuals strategically disclose aspects of themselves, concealing vulnerabilities when necessary to uphold personal well-being and navigate challenges effectively.

Submarines exhibit flexibility in concealment approaches, adjusting to the dynamic nature of underwater conditions.

Individuals demonstrate flexibility in self-disclosure, adapting to the fluidity of life circumstances and interpersonal relationships.

They strive for effective concealment, optimizing their strategies for mission success.

Also, individuals aim for effective self-disclosure, optimizing their strategies to build meaningful connections, foster understanding, and achieve personal goals.

Chapter **43**

Limited Visibility and Insight

Operating with limited visibility in a submarine is akin to navigating life's uncertain moments with insight and foresight.

Navigating the depths of the ocean in a submarine is a formidable task, especially when confronted with limited visibility. The vast expanse underwater, often shrouded in darkness, poses challenges that demand a delicate balance of skill, intuition, and technology. In a parallel sense, our journey through life mirrors this submarine experience, as we encounter moments of uncertainty and ambiguity. Life's unpredictable currents can obscure our path, requiring us to operate with insight and foresight akin to a submarine navigating in conditions of limited visibility.

- **Dependence on Sonar Systems:**

Sonar serves as a crucial beacon guiding submarines through the dark, allowing them to "see" and understand their surroundings.

In life's uncertainties, our inner senses act as a guiding beacon, helping us navigate challenges by relying on intuition, gut feelings, and insights that may not be immediately visible.

Also, sonar helps submarines detect underwater obstacles that might be invisible to the naked eye.

Similarly, during uncertain times, our inner senses enable us to detect potential obstacles, challenges, or opportunities that may not be apparent through conventional means.

Submarines alter their course based on sonar feedback to avoid collisions or dangers.

Relying on inner senses allows us to adjust our life course, make decisions, and navigate challenges by being attuned to the subtle signals and feedback from our emotions and intuition.

Sonar systems allow submarines to perceive beyond the surface, providing a deeper understanding of the underwater environment.

Inner senses grant us the ability to perceive beyond surface-level appearances, offering insights into the underlying dynamics of situations and relationships during uncertain moments.

Sonar helps submarines create mental maps of their surroundings based on the echoes and feedback received.

Our inner senses contribute to the creation of mental maps in life, enabling us to understand and navigate our personal landscapes with a deeper awareness of the echoes of our experiences.

Also, sonar provides real-time data, enabling submarines to respond promptly to changes in their environment.

Inner senses grant us real-time awareness, allowing us to adapt swiftly to changing circumstances, make informed decisions, and respond effectively to the uncertainties unfolding in our lives.

Sonar communication is silent yet powerful, allowing submarines to interact without making noise.

Inner senses facilitate silent communication within ourselves, enabling introspection, self-reflection, and a deeper understanding of our emotions, thoughts, and aspirations.

Submariners trust sonar for navigation in challenging conditions, relying on its accuracy.

In uncertain moments, trusting our inner senses involves having confidence in our intuition and the insights gained from within, guiding us with a sense of accuracy and authenticity.

Sonar allows submarines to embrace the unseen and navigate through the depths that lack external visibility.

Inner senses empower us to embrace the unseen aspects of our lives, encouraging us to delve into the unknown with a sense of curiosity, resilience, and adaptability.

Moreover, sonar systems provide a comprehensive perspective in all directions, enabling submarines to have a 360-degree awareness.

Relying on inner senses offers a holistic perspective, allowing us to consider multiple dimensions of a situation and make well-rounded decisions during uncertain times.

Sonar echoes carry information about the past and present conditions of the underwater environment.

Inner senses bring echoes of past experiences, helping us learn from the lessons of the past and navigate current uncertainties with the wisdom gained from previous challenges.

Sonar aids in understanding emotional tones underwater.

Inner senses, particularly emotional intelligence, help us grasp the emotional tones of situations, fostering better understanding and response to the complexities of life's uncertainties.

Also, sonar aids in navigating through turbulent waters.

Inner senses assist in navigating through the turbulence of life, providing stability and resilience during uncertain and challenging periods.

Sonar operates silently, providing clarity in the absence of external noise.

Inner senses, in moments of silence and introspection, offer clarity by cutting through external noise, allowing us to make informed decisions.

Submarines strategically deploy sonar resources for optimal navigation.

Strategic use of inner senses involves consciously deploying intuition, insights, and emotional awareness for optimal decision-making and navigation through life's uncertainties.

- **Precision in Maneuvering:**

Precision in submarine maneuvering requires intricate calculations to ensure safe navigation in low-visibility conditions.

Similarly, life demands precise calculations—evaluating options, considering consequences, and making informed decisions, especially when faced with uncertainties.

Submarines navigate to avoid collisions in the dark depths. Precision is vital to safeguard against potential dangers.

Precision in life involves navigating relationships skillfully, making thoughtful choices to avoid collisions, conflicts, and potential harm to personal connections.

Adjusting the course of a submarine is critical for avoiding obstacles. Precision ensures a safe trajectory.

Precision in career decisions involves making calculated adjustments to one's professional trajectory, avoiding obstacles, and ensuring a path aligned with personal goals.

Maneuvering submarines requires financial investment in precision equipment. Financial decisions must align with strategic goals.

Precision in financial decisions is vital, involving strategic investments, budgeting, and aligning expenditures with long-term goals for stability and security.

Submariners make strategic choices in education for precision in navigation. Education aligns with operational needs.

Precision in education involves making strategic choices that align with personal and professional aspirations, ensuring a well-directed path toward one's goals.

Submarines adapt their maneuvers based on the environment. Parenting requires adapting strategies to different situations with precision.

Precision in parenting involves adapting approaches with care, considering the unique needs of children and adjusting strategies to nurture their growth effectively.

Maneuvering submarines requires attention to crew well-being. Precision is crucial to maintaining a healthy and functional crew.

Precision in personal wellness involves mindful choices for physical and mental health, ensuring a balanced and functional life.

Navigating through complex underwater environments requires precision to understand and negotiate social dynamics.

Also, precision in social interactions involves understanding and navigating the complexities of human relationships, requiring insight, empathy, and strategic communication.

Precision in navigation aligns with ethical considerations to avoid infringing on maritime laws.

Precision in life involves maintaining ethical integrity, making choices aligned with personal values to navigate challenges with moral clarity.

Maneuvering during crises demands precision to avert disaster. Crisis management skills are crucial for the crew's safety.

Precision in life's crises involves strategic decision-making, quick responses, and crisis management skills to navigate challenges effectively.

Moreover, precision in submarine maneuvers requires innovative problem-solving to address unexpected challenges.

Precision in life involves innovative problem-solving skills, thinking creatively to navigate unforeseen challenges and find effective solutions.

Submarines rely on precise communication for successful maneuvers. Precision in communication is crucial for crew coordination.

Precision in personal relationships involves clear and effective communication, ensuring understanding, trust, and coordination in navigating shared life experiences.

Navigating with precision involves balancing short-term objectives with long-term goals for overall mission success.

Also, precision in life demands balancing immediate needs with long-term aspirations, making choices that align with overarching life objectives.

Precision in maneuvering submarines extends to environmental considerations, avoiding damage to delicate ecosystems.

Furthermore, precision in life involves environmental stewardship, making choices that minimize personal ecological impact and contribute to sustainable living.

- **Maintaining Calm Amidst Uncertainty:**

In the submarine, crew members must cultivate emotional resilience to maintain composure during challenging situations with limited visibility.

Similarly, in life, developing emotional resilience empowers individuals to remain calm and composed amidst uncertainty, enabling them to navigate challenges effectively.

Submarine crews rely on teamwork to manage uncertainties with limited visibility.

In life, fostering a sense of teamwork and collaboration with others enhances the ability to navigate uncertainties collectively, drawing strength from shared perspectives and support.

Precise maneuvers in the submarine require strategic decision-making to avoid collisions.

Navigating life's uncertainties demands strategic decision-making, considering potential risks and benefits to make informed choices and avoid unnecessary obstacles.

Submarines need to adapt swiftly to changing underwater conditions for safe navigation.

Adapting to changing life conditions involves flexibility and resilience, allowing individuals to adjust their strategies and responses in the face of uncertainty.

Crew members rely on training to navigate with clarity in conditions of limited visibility.

Life training, including personal development and learning experiences, contributes to clarity in decision-making during uncertain moments.

Limited visibility requires submarines to stay focused on their objectives for safe navigation.

Staying focused on personal and professional objectives in uncertain times provides a sense of direction and purpose, guiding individuals through challenges.

Navigating with limited visibility requires patience to avoid rushed decisions.

Patience in life's uncertainties allows individuals to navigate with a steady hand, avoiding impulsive actions and embracing a more measured approach.

Submarines use available tools and technology for navigation during limited visibility.

In uncertain life moments, individuals can rely on their internal and external resources, such as skills, knowledge, and support systems, to navigate challenges.

Effective communication is crucial in maintaining composure during limited visibility.

Clear and calm communication is key in life's uncertainties, fostering understanding, collaboration, and shared efforts to overcome challenges.

Crew members anticipate challenges in limited visibility scenarios to proactively address potential risks.

Anticipating challenges in life allows individuals to prepare, plan, and proactively address uncertainties, minimizing the impact of unforeseen obstacles.

Crew members need a resilient mindset to navigate challenges in conditions of limited visibility.

Developing a resilient mindset equips individuals to face uncertainties with strength, adaptability, and a positive outlook.

Maneuvering with precision involves effective risk management to avoid accidents.

Precision in life's uncertainties requires individuals to assess and manage risks, making decisions that balance potential rewards with potential pitfalls.

Mistakes in navigation are opportunities for learning and improvement.

Embracing mistakes in life's uncertainties as learning opportunities allows individuals to grow, adapt, and refine their approach to challenges.

Competence in navigation builds confidence among crew members.

Competence in handling uncertainties in life builds self-confidence, providing individuals with the assurance that they can navigate challenges effectively.

Chapter **44**

Renewable Energy Sources

The push for submarines to use renewable energy parallels the shift towards sustainable personal energy practices.

In the quest for environmental sustainability, the maritime industry, particularly submarines, is undergoing a transformative shift. Traditionally reliant on conventional power sources, submarines are now embracing renewable energy technologies to propel themselves into a more eco-friendly future. This evolution in submarine propulsion draws a striking parallel to the global movement towards sustainable practices in our personal lives. As submarines explore the possibilities of harnessing renewable energy beneath the ocean's surface, individuals are navigating their own seas of change, adopting green and sustainable practices to reduce their ecological footprint.

- **Transition to Clean Energy Sources:**

The traditional reliance on fossil fuels for submarine propulsion is evolving, marked by a shift towards cleaner, more sustainable energy sources.

Mirroring this, individuals are witnessing a transformative shift in their energy consumption patterns, moving away from fossil fuels towards renewable alternatives.

Submarines are increasingly adopting electric propulsion systems, reducing reliance on traditional diesel engines.

Similarly, in personal transportation and energy consumption, the integration of electric vehicles and appliances minimizes dependence on conventional fuel sources.

Hydrogen fuel cells are gaining prominence in submarine technology, offering a cleaner and more efficient energy solution.

Individuals exploring hydrogen fuel cells for residential or vehicular use contribute to the broader adoption of this sustainable technology.

The transition aims to significantly reduce the carbon footprint of submarines, aligning with global environmental goals.

Individuals striving to reduce their carbon footprint consciously choose cleaner energy options, actively contributing to environmental conservation efforts.

Submarines set an example by adopting renewable energy sources for their power needs.

Households are increasingly adopting solar panels, wind turbines, or other renewable energy sources to power homes, exemplifying a commitment to sustainable living.

The shift represents a paradigm change in how submarines generate and utilize energy.

At a broader societal level, individuals recognize the need for a paradigm shift in energy consumption, moving towards sustainable alternatives.

Technological innovations are driving the adoption of cleaner energy sources in submarines.

On a personal level, individuals benefit from technological advancements that make sustainable practices more accessible and efficient.

The transition is not solely environmentally driven; it is economically viable in the long term.

Individuals are increasingly aware that clean energy options can be economically advantageous, with long-term savings and reduced dependence on fluctuating fuel prices.

Nations collaborate in developing and sharing sustainable submarine technologies.

On a global scale, individuals and communities collaborate to share knowledge and best practices in adopting sustainable lifestyles.

The transition underscores a sense of environmental responsibility within naval operations.

Individuals embracing cleaner energy sources demonstrate a personal commitment to environmental responsibility and ecological stewardship.

Crew members are educated about the benefits of clean energy, fostering a culture of awareness.

Public awareness campaigns and educational initiatives play a crucial role in encouraging individuals to make informed choices for sustainable living.

Governments may offer incentives and formulate policies to encourage the shift to cleaner energy in naval fleets.

Governments play a vital role in incentivizing individuals through policies that promote renewable energy adoption, such as tax credits and subsidies.

Submarines explore a diverse range of energy sources to enhance sustainability.

Individuals diversify their energy sources at home, combining solar, wind, or other renewable options for a more resilient and sustainable energy profile.

The transition involves strategic planning for a sustainable future in naval operations.

Individuals strategically plan their energy consumption, making choices that align with a sustainable and eco-friendly future.

The shift inspires future naval professionals to prioritize sustainability.

Individuals adopting clean energy practices serve as inspiration for future generations, promoting a collective mindset shift towards sustainable living.

- **Reducing Environmental Impact:**

The transition to renewable energy in submarines is driven by a commitment to reducing emissions, mitigating the environmental impact of traditional propulsion.

Individuals adopting sustainable practices prioritize activities and technologies that minimize carbon emissions, contributing to a cleaner atmosphere.

Traditional submarine propulsion relies on finite fossil fuel resources, prompting the shift to renewable alternatives.

Individuals recognize the limitations of finite resources on Earth and opt for renewable energy sources, acknowledging the importance of sustainability.

The move towards renewable energy in submarines helps preserve marine ecosystems by reducing the ecological impact of traditional propulsion methods.

Sustainable practices at the individual level contribute to the preservation of ecosystems, protecting biodiversity and natural habitats.

The transition aligns with the goal of submarines to minimize their ecological footprint in oceanic environments.

Individuals adopting eco-friendly habits work towards minimizing their ecological footprint, considering the impact of daily choices on the environment.

The reduction of emissions from renewable energy aligns with global efforts to mitigate climate change.

Individuals choosing sustainable energy sources actively contribute to climate change mitigation, recognizing the role of personal choices in the broader environmental picture.

Protecting marine environments through sustainable practices contributes to biodiversity conservation.

Sustainable living choices support biodiversity conservation efforts on land, safeguarding ecosystems and endangered species.

Transitioning to renewable energy is part of embracing circular economy practices within naval operations.

Individuals adopting circular economy practices prioritize reducing, reusing, and recycling, contributing to a more sustainable and less wasteful society.

The shift towards renewable energy promotes the development and adoption of green technologies in naval fleets.

Individuals endorsing green technologies in their homes or communities contribute to the growth of sustainable solutions in various sectors.

Innovation in renewable energy for submarines reflects a commitment to eco-friendly technological advancements.

Embracing eco-friendly innovations in personal lifestyles showcases a dedication to staying abreast of sustainable technologies for everyday use.

Naval personnel may engage in education and advocacy for sustainable practices within the maritime community.

Individuals who adopt sustainable practices often become advocates, influencing friends, family, and communities towards environmentally conscious living.

Transitioning to renewable energy is complemented by waste reduction strategies to minimize the environmental impact of naval activities.

Individuals focusing on waste reduction strategies, such as composting and reducing single-use plastics, contribute to a cleaner environment.

Sustainable energy practices aim to conserve natural resources by reducing their extraction and consumption.

Adopting sustainable practices in daily life contributes to the conservation of natural resources, fostering a balance between human needs and environmental preservation.

Naval operations may adopt sustainable procurement practices for renewable energy technologies.

Individuals engaging in sustainable procurement choices, such as buying from environmentally responsible companies, contribute to the demand for sustainable products and services.

131

The shift to renewable energy aligns with a broader sense of global environmental stewardship.

Individuals embracing sustainability consider themselves stewards of the planet, actively working towards the well-being of the global environment.

The transition aims to leave a positive environmental legacy for future generations.

Individuals adopting sustainable practices envision a long-term positive environmental legacy, creating a healthier world for generations to come.

- **Investment in Green Technologies:**

In submarines, there is a heightened focus on research and development to advance green technologies, ensuring efficient and eco-friendly propulsion systems.

The naval sector is exploring innovative ways to store renewable energy efficiently within submarines, a challenge mirrored in the advancements of personal energy storage solutions like home battery systems.

Submarines are transitioning to electric propulsion systems, eliminating reliance on traditional diesel engines. Similarly, individuals are embracing electric vehicles, aligning personal transportation with eco-friendly alternatives.

Submarines are incorporating hydrogen fuel cells as a clean energy source. This mirrors the growing trend of individuals exploring hydrogen-powered technologies, such as fuel cell vehicles or hydrogen-based energy solutions for homes.

The naval industry's commitment to reducing carbon emissions aligns with the personal choice of individuals to minimize their carbon footprint by opting for green technologies that have lower environmental impacts.

Navies globally are collaborating to enhance green technology adoption in submarines. Similarly, individuals worldwide are collectively contributing to sustainability by adopting eco-friendly practices and supporting green initiatives.

The surge in electric vehicles and other sustainable transportation options among individuals is indicative of a collective effort to reduce carbon emissions in the personal transportation sector.

Both submarines and modern homes are increasingly integrating smart technologies for efficient energy use. Smart home systems optimize energy consumption, contributing to sustainable practices.

Submarines are exploring energy-efficient lighting solutions, a parallel to individuals adopting LED and other energy-efficient lighting in homes, reducing electricity consumption.

Submarines are tapping into renewable energy sources such as solar and wind. Similarly, individuals are installing solar panels on homes and exploring wind energy solutions to harness sustainable power.

Both naval forces and individuals are investing in raising awareness and educating their respective communities about the benefits of green technologies and sustainable practices.

Governments are actively promoting green technologies in naval fleets, echoing the support for sustainable practices seen in various countries' policies and incentives for renewable energy adoption by individuals.

Submarines are incorporating eco-friendly materials in their construction. This parallels the conscious choice of individuals to use sustainable and recyclable materials in their homes and daily lives.

Some submarines are adopting hybrid propulsion systems. Similarly, individuals are exploring hybrid solutions for personal transportation, combining traditional and electric modes for greater sustainability.

Both naval strategies and personal choices reflect a shared long-term vision for sustainability, aiming to leave a positive environmental legacy for future generations.

Chapter 46

The Journey Homeward

Eventually, submarines return to port, as we too journey towards understanding and peace with ourselves.

The journey of a submarine, silently navigating the depths of the ocean, is a testament to both exploration and introspection. Submarines embark on missions, delving into the mysterious underwater realm, and eventually, they resurface, returning to the familiarity of port. This cyclical pattern of submergence and resurfacing draws intriguing parallels to the human journey. In life, we navigate the intricate depths of self-discovery, facing challenges and exploring the recesses of our emotions. Yet, like submarines returning to port, there comes a time when we journey back to a place of understanding and peace within ourselves. This introspective voyage is marked by growth, reflection, and the pursuit of inner harmony.

- **Exploration and Reflection:**

Submarines, equipped with advanced technology, embark on exploration missions that take them into the deep and uncharted waters of the ocean.

In our personal journeys, we utilize the tools of self-awareness and introspection to navigate the uncharted territories of our emotions, relationships, and personal growth.

Submarines encounter unknown and challenging underwater terrains, requiring constant adaptation and precise navigation.

Similarly, in life, we navigate the complexities of our inner world, adapting to the unknown aspects of our emotions, thoughts, and evolving relationships.

Submarines confront obstacles such as underwater cliffs and geological formations, necessitating strategic maneuvering to overcome these hurdles.

Life presents challenges that may manifest as personal or professional obstacles, demanding strategic thinking and adaptability to overcome and grow from these experiences.

Submarines develop resilience in the face of external pressures and adversities, ensuring their mission's success.

Similarly, our personal journey involves cultivating resilience, learning to withstand life's pressures and adversities to emerge stronger and more resilient.

Submarines resurface, symbolizing the completion of their mission and the transition to a different phase.

In our lives, there are moments of resurfacing—a return to a place of stability and reflection after navigating the dynamic challenges and experiences.

Submarines undergo specific phases during resurfacing to ensure a smooth transition from the depths to the surface.

Similarly, acknowledging and navigating transitional phases in our lives allows for a smoother integration of experiences and personal growth.

After a mission, submarines undergo debriefing sessions, analyzing the mission's outcomes and learning from successes and challenges.

In our personal journeys, moments of reflection and introspection serve as debriefing sessions, allowing us to integrate lessons learned and apply them to future endeavors.

Both submarines and individuals strive for continuous growth, using each exploration and resurfacing phase as an opportunity to evolve, learn, and deepen their understanding of the world and themselves.

- **Facing Challenges:**

Submarines navigate through the intricate underwater environment filled with obstacles such as underwater cliffs, geological formations, and varying currents.

In the human experience, challenges arise in various forms—personal, professional, or societal. These challenges demand resilience and problem-solving skills, becoming significant opportunities for personal growth.

Subs require precise navigation to overcome underwater obstacles, showcasing the importance of careful planning and execution.

Similarly, in our lives, challenges necessitate strategic problem-solving. Careful consideration and execution of plans help us navigate through obstacles effectively.

Subs display adaptability, adjusting their course and strategies to overcome unforeseen challenges underwater.

Life, too, demands adaptability. Learning from the adaptability of submarines, individuals adjust their approaches when facing unexpected challenges, fostering resilience and growth.

Also, submarines facing challenges contribute to their character development, honing the crew's skills and enhancing their ability to handle diverse situations.

Similarly, facing life challenges builds character. The lessons learned from overcoming difficulties shape our values, behaviors, and resilience in the face of future adversities.

Moreover, submarines showcase resilience when confronting challenges, ensuring that the crew and vessel can withstand the pressures of the underwater environment.

In our lives, resilience becomes a transformative quality. Confronting challenges head-on, individuals develop resilience, fostering the capacity to bounce back from setbacks and navigate uncertainties.

Subs exemplify teamwork when overcoming challenges, with crew members working collaboratively to address complex situations.

- **The Return to Port:**

Submarines resurface as a symbolic end to their underwater missions, marking the completion of exploration and a return to familiar territory.

In our personal journeys, there are moments of resurfacing—a return to a state of inner peace and understanding after navigating the intricate and sometimes challenging aspects of life.

For submarines, resurfacing signifies the culmination of an exploration phase, where they have delved into the depths and fulfilled their mission objectives.

Similarly, in our lives, moments of resurfacing represent the completion of specific phases—whether it be the achievement of personal goals, overcoming challenges, or gaining insights through experiences.

Submarines often undergo evaluation and maintenance upon resurfacing, reflecting on the challenges faced and lessons learned during the mission.

Likewise, in our personal journeys, moments of resurfacing invite self-reflection. Individuals evaluate their experiences, learnings, and personal growth during specific life phases.

Submarines may require adjustments or improvements post-mission. This mirrors the need for individuals to make adjustments in their lives based on reflections, ensuring personal growth and development.

Moments of resurfacing prompt individuals to make life adjustments—whether it's refining goals, adapting strategies, or embracing new perspectives based on past experiences.

Port serves as a safe harbor for submarines. Resurfacing allows them to return to safety and stability.

Similarly, resurfacing in life provides individuals a metaphorical harbor of inner peace. It's a return to a state of balance, tranquility, and understanding after navigating life's complexities.

Submarines returning to port reconnect with their base. In life, resurfacing often involves reconnecting with core values, priorities, and personal foundations.

Individuals, upon resurfacing from challenging life phases, reconnect with their core values, rediscover their passions, and strengthen their personal foundations.

Submarines often undergo debriefing sessions, integrating lessons learned and experiences gained during the mission.

Similarly, moments of resurfacing in life involve personal debriefing. Individuals integrate the lessons learned, reflecting on experiences, and using them as building blocks for future endeavors.

Submarines, after resurfacing, prepare for potential new missions. In life, moments of resurfacing become preparation periods for individuals to embark on new journeys with a wealth of experience.

Submarines adapt to changes post-resurfacing. Individuals, too, embrace change, demonstrating flexibility and openness to new possibilities.

Subs, upon returning to port, engage in debriefing sessions, a structured process to review and integrate the lessons learned from the completed mission.

Similarly, in life, moments of reflection and introspection serve as our debriefing sessions. We intentionally review our experiences, extracting valuable lessons that contribute to personal growth and understanding.

They debriefing aims to consolidate the knowledge gained during the mission. This process ensures that insights and experiences are not lost but become part of the submarine crew's collective knowledge.

In the human parallel, debriefing our life experiences allows us to accumulate wisdom. We consolidate the knowledge gained from various situations, transforming it into a resource for navigating future challenges.

Debriefing involves evaluating the performance of the submarine and its crew, identifying strengths, and recognizing areas for improvement.

In our lives, introspection serves as a personal assessment. We identify our strengths, acknowledging achievements, and recognize areas where personal development is needed.

Subs, based on debriefing insights, strategize improvements. This may involve refining procedures, enhancing technology, or adjusting crew roles for optimal performance.

In life, our personal assessments lead to strategic improvements. We devise plans for personal growth, setting goals, and adjusting our approaches to align with our evolving understanding of ourselves.

Debriefing encourages a learning culture within the submarine crew, fostering open communication and the sharing of experiences.

Similarly, in our personal lives, moments of reflection contribute to cultivating a learning community. We share insights, learn from others, and collectively contribute to personal and collective growth.

Submarines incorporate feedback from crew members into their learning process. This ensures that diverse perspectives contribute to the overall improvement of the team.

In our personal growth journey, we integrate feedback from others and, more importantly, from ourselves. Adapting to constructive criticism and insights accelerates our learning curve.

- **Holistic Understanding:**

During debriefing, submarines review their mission objectives and outcomes, gaining a comprehensive understanding of the broader goals they aimed to achieve.

Similarly, in life, moments of introspection help us revisit our personal aspirations and long-term goals, providing context to our actions and decisions.

Submarine debriefing may involve assessing the impact on the underwater environment, ensuring that the mission aligns with environmental sustainability goals.

In our personal narrative, introspection allows us to evaluate our ecological footprint—understanding how our lifestyle and choices impact the broader environment.

Subs recognize the interconnectedness of their actions and how each decision contributes to the overall success or challenges faced during the mission.

In life, introspection unveils the ripple effect of our actions. We understand how seemingly small decisions can have far-reaching consequences on our personal journey and the lives of those around us.

Submarine crews analyze whether their actions align with the values and principles guiding their mission, ensuring ethical conduct and responsible decision-making.

In introspective moments, we assess the alignment of our choices with our values. This ethical navigation guides our decision-making in a way that resonates with our core principles.

Submarine debriefing considers the impact on various stakeholders, acknowledging the role each plays in the success or challenges faced by the crew.

Similarly, introspection in life allows us to evaluate the impact of our actions on relationships and connections. Understanding how our choices affect those around us contributes to a more informed life narrative.

Subs use debriefing to identify lessons for future cooperation. They recognize the importance of teamwork and collaboration in achieving broader mission objectives.

In personal introspection, we reflect on our collaboration dynamics in relationships and professional settings. Recognizing lessons from past interactions informs our approach to future collaborations.

Submarines consider cultural factors during debriefing, understanding the broader implications of their presence in different oceanic regions.

In life, introspection involves acknowledging and respecting cultural nuances. We recognize how our actions may impact diverse cultural contexts, fostering a more inclusive life narrative.

Both in submarines and life, a holistic understanding gained through debriefing or introspection facilitates continuous growth and adaptation. It forms the foundation for informed decision-making and purposeful navigation in future endeavors.